THE WORLD ORDER AND REVOLUTION!

Essays from the Resistance

ANDRE VLTCHEK

CHRISTOPHER BLACK

PETER KOENIG

BADAK MERAH SEMESTA

2015

THE WORLD ORDER AND REVOLUTION!
Essays from the Resistance

Written by: Andre Vltchek, Christoper Black, Peter Koenig

Preface by: Andre Vltchek, Christoper Black, Peter Koenig

Edited by: Rossie Indira

Cover Design and Layout by: Rossie Indira, Andre Vltchek

Cover Photos by: Andre Vltchek

Andre Vltchek portrait photo by: Alejandro Wagner

Christopher Black portrait photo by: Toronto Star

Peter Koenig portrait photo by: anonymous

First edition, 2015

Published by PT. Badak Merah Semesta, Jakarta

http://badak-merah.weebly.com

email: badak.merah.press@gmail.com

ISBN: 978-602-70058-7-7

TABLE OF CONTENTS

Preface – BREAK THE CHAINS!

Andre Vltchek

Christopher Black

Peter Koenig

PREFACE

BREAK THE CHAINS!

Colonialism never really vanished. European and later North American imperialism, which took hundreds of millions of human lives on all continents, still continues, with its brutal onslaught against all proud and non-servile cultures and governments. Millions of men, women and children are dying as a result, every year.

While Western/Christian desire to control and to rule, is mainly to blame for this horrid situation, imprisonment, even destruction of 'disobedient' nations is often done through economic means, or through twisting of the international law, or through both.

International law is, after all, being dictated by the ruling group of nations, which either belongs or serves the Empire. Empire *is* the law. The same can be said about neoliberalism, which is economic expression of imperialism.

Neoliberalism, the plague and deadly killer of the 21st Century has invaded the western world and is increasingly also encroaching on the east. Neoliberalism, a boundless form of capitalism, is economic fascism. It's the white collar weapon with which the empire and its vassal states – mostly the European Union – wage financial war around the world, subjugate nations by imposed debt caused bankruptcy, impoverishing entire nations by privatizing public assets, like pensions funds, education, health services – causing unemployment, famine – and outright misery and death. Neoliberalism has killed millions of people around the world in the last 15 years.

The instigators of neoliberalism, Washington and its Western allies know no scruples. Their goal is full spectrum dominance of the world. The monster moves around the globe like a multi-tentacle octopus. Its three most deadly weapons are financial and economic strangulations of nations that need to be dominated with the objective of 'regime change', bombing a sovereign country into a state of sustained chaos, and – the voracious lie and propaganda machine that is false-flagging public opinion into consent for war, conflicts, fighting so-called 'terrorists'. Terrorists are all those who are defending their sovereign nations from being taken over and plundered by the west.

Neoliberalism works with a fake and fraudulent dollar-based monetary system which, de facto, has become the 'world's chief currency', when Nixon ordered in 1971 to abandon the gold standard, officially to pay the US Vietnam war debt. In reality, making the US dollar the major reserve currency, the currency in which international trade and compacts are denominated, and most importantly the currency in which all hydrocarbon trading has to be carried out – as dictated to OPEC in 1974 by the Carter Administration – such a US dollar would be much more valuable than gold that could be amassed by any nation, as it would make the dollar indispensable – the indispensable currency for the indispensable and exceptional nation.

This indispensable fact, allows the exceptional nation printing money at will to finance all three war tools, financial strangulations, armies and weapons and –

endless propaganda and indoctrination – to the point where the US real debt – the so-called unmet obligations, have reached in 2014 a level of close to 750% of US GDP – and rising – a debt that will never be amortized.

Why is neoliberalism so successful, expanding like brushfire around the globe? – Because neoliberalism addresses the three lowest human denominators – power, greed and ego (narcissism). Neoliberalism is boundless capitalism and market fundamentalism – *ad nauseatum*. It is the sledgehammer of submission, a weapon that subdues human consciousness.

In this context, the world situation often looks hopeless and, admittedly, the problems facing mankind are grave. But the situation is also pregnant with the possibility for change, transforming it, revolutionizing it. The capitalist / neoliberal system is the root cause of the present situation and it is the capitalist system that needs to be transformed, to complete its metamorphoses into its natural and necessary progression, socialism. But, this metamorphoses, cannot take place by itself. The capitalists expend immense effort and energy to maintain the system that profits them so much and beggars the vast majority of the world. A change can only happen with the determined struggle of the working people of the world in solidarity with each other, no matter what their nationality, their ethnicity, their gender, their age, or their fortune. And this they have done.

The working people of the world have fought for almost two centuries for their emancipation from the tyranny of capital, from the French Revolution to the European revolutions of 1848, from the Paris Commune to the great, Russian Revolution, that created the Soviet Union. They have fought from China to Laos, from Vietnam to Korea, to follow the Soviet example and have succeeded in defeating the competing empires that tried to crush them. They have fought from Latin America to Africa, from Asia to Europe and they have never given up. The wars of competition between the capitalist powers that have resulted in two devastating world wars and dozens of other wars between themselves or against socialist or resisting peoples and nations, in the past century, have now culminated in a Washington dominated empire, that appears as a giant on the horizon but up close is revealed as made of *papier maché* that can be blown away by stormy winds, that likes to appear omnipotent, but is instead tired and weak, and fearful of the quickly gathering storm.

One could often think that neoliberalism, that euphemism of the empire for the complete and ruthless exploitation of every living thing and every resource on the planet for private profit, has managed to spread its metastasis to every corner of the globe, and that soon it will kill everything in its way, even life itself. But that would be wrong. It is everywhere poisoning our planet and its people, but it is now everywhere encountering increased resistance, on all the continents of the world. It is despised by all, resisted by many and overcome by some.

The hatred for the Empire is deep and wide. Ask in the Arab world and in Latin America, in Russia and China, and in many countries of Africa. People will pronounce openly what was whispered for decades in South America, before the revolutions began: "They are rich because we are poor. And we are poor, because they are rich!"

But even in the Empire itself, not everyone is rich. Even the Empire does not belong to its people.

People on all continents are subject to the disgraceful process of brainwashing, conducted by the old and new colonial powers. One might often assume that nothing could successfully challenge, nothing could triumph over the propaganda that is being constantly broadcast by the Empire and its media, over their well-funded and complex corporate propaganda system. Imperialist powers have been perfecting their propaganda systems for centuries. But others have learned how to communicate ideas and move people to action. The Empire has lost its monopoly on defining the "truth". New media, all over the world, are now confronting the poisonous and grotesque dogmas coming from New York, London and Paris. New television and radio stations, newspapers and magazines, are challenging their overt lies, their depressing nihilism, their living, for the sake of buying, for the vanity and destruction of everything beautiful and harmonious in life; is the root of their antihuman ethos, and the root of their ideological onslaughts. Now information is flowing from Moscow and Beijing, from Caracas, Havana, and Teheran, and the world is listening.

*

The three authors of this book, are members of this new media. All three of us are fighting against neoliberalism and imperialism. Each of us engages in that struggle in his own way, the best way he knows how. We may be using different 'weapons', but our goals are the same: economic and social justice for those who do all the work in society, respect for the true freedom of the individual to experience and express their humanity, respect for the rights of others and dedication to learning of and writing about the true situation of the peoples of the world as they exist today and the future possible now and tomorrow.

An international lawyer, an economist, and a philosopher: we are joining our forces here, in order to fight for a better world. In this book, we have compiled our thoughts, our analyses, our dreams, as they have been expressed in our essays over time, and we humbly submit them to the people everywhere who are oppressed, as a sign of solidarity, as a handshake, to our brothers, our sisters our comrades, and as a warning as our oppressors, 'j'accuse!'

All three of us have seen the world as it is, and we have witnessed wrong in all its forms!

As an international lawyer, Christopher Black has had to confront the injustice of the laws and institutions of this criminal system. As an economist, Peter Koenig fights neoliberalism, which is, in summary, nothing else than economic fascism. As an observer and chronicler of history and world events, Andre Vltchek has witnessed some of the most atrocious moments in modern history, documented them, and exposed those responsible for the crimes against the people.

All three of us stood up to resist the destructive forces of imperialism and neoliberalism. All three of us refused to remain silent. All three of us became fighters. All three of us are hoping to spread seeds that may help awakening human consciousness.

We hope that you will join us.

Beirut, Toronto, Havana

31 March 2015

Andre Vltchek

Christopher Black

Peter Koenig

Andre Vltchek – Christopher Black – Peter Koenig

ANDRE VLTCHEK

1

Fascism Will be Fought

2015: DEFENDING HUMANITY BY REASON OR FORCE

by Andre Vltchek

One more step, one more explosion of insanity, and all that humanity fought for, what it labored for and has been aiming at for years, centuries and millennia, may disappear in a monstrous series of blasts. Our planet might break into pieces, or it may get poisoned and become uninhabitable, forever.

Hyperbolic? Not at all, given the track record of the Empire: war after war, invasion after invasion, with hundreds of destabilized countries, murdered leaders, and overthrown governments.

The storyline may be similar to that of the famous novella by Gabriel Garcia Marquez: "Chronicle of a Death Foretold". We can foresee what may soon happen, we are warning that carnage is likely to take place in a very near future and on a grand scale, but our warnings, while registering, are not propelling almost anyone to action. But this may soon change.

Those who are now pushing the world to an irreversible disaster are clearly identifiable: they are market fundamentalists, conservative Christian dogmatists who believe in the superiority of their doctrine and of the 'chosen nature' of the Western people and culture, as well as the millions of their lackeys and minor cohorts: thousands of CEO's and deranged 'military strategists'.

If they are allowed to choose: to destroy the world or to lose control over it, they would opt for destruction. And they would have no regrets in ending billions of human lives, because their 'logic' and 'morality' have foundations in some bizarre and hazy 'holy righteous' dogmas, and because, during the long and dark centuries, they managed to cultivate countless arguments, designed to justify their lunacy.

The only circumstance, under which they would let the rest of us survive and exist, would be, if we were to become their unconditional slaves; not just servants, but slaves.

They want to rule over us and simultaneously they demand to be feared, admired and adored. Yes, the control, the submission, has to be total. And all those servile, shameful feelings we are expected to demonstrate have to be absolute, 'pure' and unconditional.

You are guessing correctly: it all has its roots somewhere 'back there' – in the era of the 'Holy Inquisition'.

If we dare to resist, they are capable of nuking us, reducing all of us to dust, even if they and their families would also vanish in that fire.

It is because these people are true extremists and fanatics, because they want absolutely everything, because they are maniacs in possession not only of tremendous propaganda, surveillance and security apparatuses, but also of nukes.

***

After this regime and its rulers colonized and enslaved almost the entire planet Earth, there is very little decency left in the places that have fallen into their hands, as almost everything that used to be pure, everything natural and human, has been spat on, perverted, trivialized and commercialized.

People all over the world used to dream and desire things like solidarity, beauty, love, justice for all, equality and brotherhood, as well as permanent lack of fear.

Knowledge was supposed to have one and only purpose: to give people the intellectual tools to build better societies.

Now, children and adults go to schools to become obedient ants and half-wits, ready for the corporate drill. The more schooling and diplomas they receive the more stereotypical and conditioned their brains become.

In most of countries, medicine is nothing more than a well-remunerated business, while almost all pharmaceutical companies are busy plundering rainforests and registering their patents, instead of curing people.

Great science died, after being locked behind the doors of predominantly corporate laboratories or private universities and research centers. The best scientific brains are working for the military, or they are busy developing 'products' for markets, instead of advancing humanity.

The Arts, once the vanguard of human thought and progress, has been reduced to entertainment, into mainly indistinguishable mass of pop, as soulless and brainless, as the supermarkets or shopping malls. Instead of leading people to the barricades, instead of making them aim at something higher, artists have been reduced to the level of cheap entertainers.

Deliberately, form was put high above the substance. In all the major world cities ruled by the Empire, people in buses and trains now stare at the screens of their latest mobile phones, exchanging increasingly incomprehensible, idiotic and abbreviated infantile and self-centered messages. Hardly anyone reads books. Hardly anyone thinks. Hardly anyone has any feelings. Even love has become like that mass-produced pinkish pop cover of confetti.

Nobody seems to be happy. In the Empire itself, people are miserably atomized, lonely and lost. They are too scared to open their hearts to each other, to love, to give everything to others. In the colonies, horrendously retarded family and religious structures are put to work, to serve oppression, which in turn serves the Empire.

Ideals are being spat on, dragged through dirt by the omnipotent manufacturers of obedience and by their most powerful tools – the mass media, religious entrepreneurs, the private education system, and the pop entertainment machine. Only consumerism, commercialism, business achievements and loyalty to the regime are glorified. There is nothing that encourages people to dream of a much better world, or to struggle for a new, just and egalitarian society.

Any society or ideology that dares to put people first, is demonized, and ridiculed. It is ideologically attacked. If it refuses to succumb, it gets attacked militarily, it gets bombed, and eventually, it ends up being thoroughly destroyed.

*** *** ***

The Western Empire insists on controlling everything of any substance. It has even managed to radicalize non-Christian religions, most strikingly Islam: first through the British support of *Wahhabis*, then through Western creation of the Mujahedeen in Afghanistan, that subsequently gave birth to Al-Qaeda, and recently by NATO's creation of ISIS.

The Empire is only interested in controlling the world, not in its wellbeing or continued existence. It is actually showing a spectacular disinterest towards the survival of the human race and of our planet.

I have seen entire nations 'sinking', or becoming uninhabitable due to global warming: Kiribati, Tuvalu, and Marshall Islands. I have seen enormous islands like Sumatra or Borneo totally logged out, covered by black toxic rivers, thoroughly destroyed.

I have seen unimaginable horrors – cities that were fully abandoned to 'market forces' – Jakarta, Nairobi, Tegucigalpa...

I talked to people in New York City who were scared that they could get sick one day; not because of illness itself, but because they would not be able to pay their medical bills. I saw young people squashed under the deadly weight of student loans. I talked to armies of people who have 'no idea what to do with their lives' – all reason, all meaning for existence simply lost!

I have seen dozens of battlefields, cities and villages bombed to the ground. I saw millions of refugees. All this, so the Empire can maintain this monstrous self-serving and self-promoting system – a system which nobody really wants, and never really wanted.

And now, one more step, and it will trigger conflict with Russia, China, perhaps Iran...

***

The more I see, the more I think: We have to find a way how to disarm those maniacs who are ruling the world, as well finding a way how to disarm their servants and lackeys in the 'client-states'.

This is absolute madness! This is not where humanity should be, right now. They have kidnapped humanity, detained progress, murdered dreams and covered entire continents with a dark, sarcastic, depressing blanket of nihilism.

5

Instead of creating beautiful music and poetry, instead of building public parks and ecological cities, we are choking our urban centers with cars; we are murdering millions of people over access to natural resources. We live for over-production and over-consumption, while billions are rotting alive in a gutter. We are overthrowing decent political leaders and murdering journalists who refuse to lie. We are spying on each other, cheating on each other, and torturing each other, intimidating each other, murdering each other and hating each other.

Most of the people have been made to forget that human beings are essentially optimistic, sharing and loving creatures. Most people have been made to forget, or were never allowed to know, that building better societies is much more glorious and fun than living in some extreme individualistic nightmare. Living for humanity, not for profit, not for a 'me-me-me-goes first' dogma, is fulfilling and actually gives meaning to one's existence.

***

Our so-called 'leaders', political, religious and economic/ business, belong in a mental institution.

How to get them there, would require, doubtlessly, an extremely delicate maneuver.

I suggest: let us promise them; let us give them, all the imaginable golden parachutes they desire. Anything: just to get rid of them; push them away from power.

They should be behind bars, of course, facing charges ranging from fraud to genocide, but punishing them is not my priority, at least not right now.

The priority is for humanity to survive – to survive as a multitude of free people, not as slaves.

Those maniacs know that they can thrive only in a world, which they have created. They have no kindness, no creative power. Their system can only flourish because of deception, intimidation, and terror.

That is why they and their system will never go voluntarily, and peacefully.

Life is business, for them. They don't exist for humanity; they exist as slave-owners (slavery is a business for them, too, ever since the beginning) and as religious inquisitors; and they also exist for their deadly business games: for deals, for markets.

Let us find a way to buy back our world from them!

Let us find a way to buy grass and rivers, oceans and rainforests, ancient cities, creatures, trees and flowers.

Let us find a way to buy back the respect for human race. Let's buy it from them and then, let us never sell it again. Let us not sell it to anyone, no matter how beautifully he plays his flute!

Let us recover, even at a price, logic and reason: let love be love again; let pain be pain, let justice be exactly that – justice – and nothing else!

Any price will do, as long as they leave this planet alone.

For millennia, their Crusades, their colonialism, their plunder has turned our world into an enormous globe of fear, of torture, of smoke and of grotesque parody on morality.

And after all that madness and terror that has been committed, some people are still taking this regime, this Molotov Cocktail of fundamentalist Christianity, imperialism and capitalism, seriously!

Please, let us not take it seriously, anymore. It is just a terrible joke, a nightmare, and an insult to the very essence of humanity.

Let us laugh at it, let us throw up looking at it, or, as I suggested: let us negotiate an immediate deal, even if we become thoroughly broke for some time.

But, under no circumstances, should we take it

'seriously', anymore. And let us not continue living like this, any longer!

This regime has perverted all great aspirations of humanity. It has derailed progress and destroyed hope. It has choked kindness and solidarity. It has robbed the great majority of people, and then suggested that 'poverty should be eased through charity'. And it has murdered hundreds of millions of people, perhaps billions.

Let us insult it. Let us laugh at it. Let us throw money in its face.

If it refuses to leave: let us fight it!

***

Look at all that nihilism surrounding us!

The Empire has no beautiful songs – songs about building the nations; it has no poetry that could cover our backs with goose bumps. It has no leaders who could, with hardly any security; stand on a balcony facing a crowd, sharing with people their passion for building a great world for all of us.

It has no loyalty, and it offers no certainty. 'Love' it produces is 'interest and business oriented', it does not last, and it is cannot be counted on.

The Empire cannot even fight, anymore, because it is sickly and cowardly. It murders millions, yes; but it murders them by pushing buttons and by flying drones, and by using proxy regimes – its colonies.

It is because the ideals of the Empire are low, because its religious dogmas are depressing, because capitalism is shallow, because neo-colonialism is immoral!

***

If the Empire kills us, we would all die for nothing – only so the Empire and its maniacs could thrive!

Therefore, let us not die! Let us fight for life, against the fascism that is now choking our throats.

Let us unite and shout:

"We Want This Earth Back!"

"We Want Kindness, Decency And Love Back!"

But these shouts should not be slogans at some protest marches. Protest marches do not work.

We either fight, or we change nothing. These should be the demands on our banners, our battle cries!

Ask anywhere in Latin America and Africa, in Asia and Oceania, in the Middle East, even in the epicenters of the Empire – in Europe and North America: the people want to live in a world free of constant fear and irrational guilt. They want hospitals to cure the sick and to prevent others from getting ill, schools to really educate, and housing to give a roof and shelter to people, cities and villages to offer a great quality of life to their inhabitants. They want certainty.

People want life to have meaning again... and to be full of beauty, of hope and dreams! They want to watch the stars above, and to dream. Sometimes they can't even define it, anymore, but if you talk to them, this is what most of them really want.

"A journey of a thousand *li* begins with a single step", said great Chinese philosopher, Lao-tzu, some 25 centuries ago.

But in order to make that very first step, one has to stand up, to be erect.

And in order to stand up, one has to be alive; one has to be determined.

True, it is sometimes easier to kneel or to prostrate, than to stand, than to walk forward, than to struggle. Sometimes it is easier to betray, than to remain loyal to one's dream, to one's love, to the essential principles.

But one truly lives only when he or she is upright, when marching forward and aiming at a better world, when keeping promises and pledges.

The Empire broke many; it bought many, or scared them into submission. But others are standing up. Not everyone is for sale, neither is everyone ready to serve.

The first steps are being made, everywhere. Many thousand *li* distances will soon be covered.

Fascism will be fought. Humanity will be defended! By reason or by force, the regime would have to yield to the interests of humanity. It will not be allowed to make that final, the most destructive step!

January 2, 2015

*****

2

HAVANA, WHERE EVERYONE CAN DANCE

By Andre Vltchek

Havana, Cuba

It is crowded and loud. *La Froridita,* a famous old bar in *Havana Vieja* (Old Havana), is packed to the rafters. The patrons consist mostly of foreigners and some overseas Cubans. They are loud, trying to shout over the upbeat *son* music booming from an old stage where the confident lead singer of an all-girl band is threatening her boyfriend or husband, with a stunning re-arrangement of the old *bolero* 'Si Tu Te Vas' ('If you go away').

It is all very cool. This is the exact bar where Hemingway used to have his countless *Daiquiris*. Not those touristy and over-sugary ones that one gets anywhere in the world nowadays (even here, at *La Floridita*), but those very 'masculine' *Daiquiris*, bitter and unsweetened, made only from rum, squeezed grapefruits and crushed ice.

The waiters, all middle-aged men, work in unison, with perfectly coordinated movements, wearing "Havana Club" aprons.

Drinks here go for US$6, making them out of reach for most ordinary Cuban citizens. But this place is just a part of that huge hard-currency earning industry, which has countless outlets all over the island: beach resorts, clubs, restaurants, bars, and boutiques. Propaganda beamed from the North calls this arrangement 'cynical'. Some section of Cuban citizens, critics of the Communist system, as well as various revolutionary 'purists' also dislike the arrangement. But there is consensus among the rest of the population that this is the best way to maintain the free and excellent health system, education, housing and culture.

Clubs, theatres, galleries, are all powerful magnets for educated visitors from all over the world. Cuba has the reputation of being a cultural powerhouse. And unlike in any other nation in the world, Cuba's main attraction are its high-quality artists, and the main 'exports' are not manufacturing or agriculture; it is culture and the arts.

People from all over the world travel here to listen to some of the greatest music played anywhere on Earth, to visit countless research centers, art schools, to attend concerts and performances, or simply to stroll through the many magnificent cities, world heritage sites as declared by UNESCO, like those of Santiago de Cuba and Havana.

In Old Havana, the atmosphere is always electrifying. Unlike in Western Europe and United States where culture and the arts have become mostly decorative and 'form over substance', in Cuba, art is alive, it overflows onto the streets, and it is magnificently vibrant.

I lean over the bar and scream into the ear of old bar-keep whose name is Jose:

"They say this is like surrendering to capitalism. This bar; places like this bar..."

"Let them eat shit", he replies laconically, working his powerful mixer. "Look, do you see that door; the entrance door? It is open right? This place is air-conditioned but the door is open. All over the Old Havana, the doors and all those huge windows that grow from the floor are open. Do you know why? So everybody can hear the music. Windows here are like walls. And if they are open, it is as if there is nothing between the musicians and the street. Nothing at all! You just stand and listen, for free."

"And if they, the people, want to come inside?" I ask.

"So they come in," he replies. "They don't have to drink our booze here. It is their country. They can enter, and listen, of course. Do you see any bouncers here? Look, in this country we care about feeding people and curing the sick first... It is not easy with the embargo... We will make sure in the future that everyone can have a drink in places like this too. But for now, honestly, it is not a priority!"

At the end of the L-shaped bar, a bronze statue of Ernest Hemingway leans on a perfectly polished wooden surface. Several tourists take snapshots of the embracing great North American novelist, one of the best friends of revolutionary Cuba. Hemingway lived here. He donated money from his Nobel Prize for Literature, to this country.

Here, in this bar, Hemingway is not politicized too much. But it is clear what the Western establishment is ready to do to those who support Cuba and socialism:

> "The FBI tailed Hemingway, he was harassed and until now there are many unanswered questions regarding his death. Some suggest that his 1960 medical treatment was actually supervised by the government authorities and that he was given excessive doses of electric shocks that destroyed his memory and drove him to suicide."

This is of course not common knowledge embedded in the minds of North American and European visitors. They come here for the arts, for the unrepeatable atmosphere of lightness and good humor. They come here to listen to music and to dance. And to taste bits of 'forbidden fruits', and to break the US embargo here and there.

Very few can resist falling in love with the country, where entire streets and entire neighborhoods, are turned into concert halls and dance floors.

One of the iconic phrases symbolizing Latin American revolutions has always been: "Everybody Dances or Nobody Dances!"

In Cuba, music and dance are synonymous with life. Here, everybody dances, and that is how the revolution survives.

Yet things are not always 'light'. Cuba is under an embargo, *de-facto* under siege. It is often forced to literally fight for its survival. The East European bloc collapsed a quarter of a century ago. The Cuban economy was instantly pushed into a corner, it almost collapsed, as the 'newly capitalist' European countries almost immediately refused to honor trade agreements with its former ally, all too eager to join as quickly as possible, the club of global oppressors. And then, the brutal US trade embargo has been clearly geared, for decades, to destroy this proud Communist island-nation.

A short walk away from *La Floridita*, another iconic restaurant *La Bodegita de Medio* used to witness the indulgence and over-indulgence by Hemingway of yet another typically Cuban drink, *mojito*. And *La Bodegita* was just one of many places that were bombed by the Cuban exiles.

There were countless terrorist attacks against the island, coming from both the United States, and from the right-wing Cuban exiles settled abroad. Passenger airliners were blown from the sky in full flight, clouds were diverted to trigger draughts, crops were poisoned and tourist destinations were repeatedly bombed.

But Cuba stood proud and tall! It sometimes bled badly,

its people had to get used to tightening their belts, but the country managed to survive the worst hours, and began growing once again.

Even in its most difficult hours, Cuba continued to help poor countries by sending there their doctors and teachers. Even when it stood, for several years, almost alone, it never abandoned its internationalist path.

Its culture and the arts became the main pillars of the fight for its survival, and for the nation's identity.

During my latest visit, Mario Hubert Garrido, Director of *Prensa Latina Television* (Prensa Latina is the Cuban and International press agency founded by Ernesto Che-Guevara, after the revolution in 1956), explained the role culture plays in his country:

> "Cuban culture has always had deep roots in the Cuban nation. And it is what feeds the spirit of resistance so embedded in the psyche of our people, always, but especially during the most difficult times. Here, people are united, because of the blockade, and because of the aggression against our nation. Here, culture means, above all, solidarity."

We talk. I agree to write for *Prensa Latina*. Here, interiors are simple. There are photos of Vietnam on the walls, the iconic villages of Ha Long Bay. There is some artwork and paintings depicting Fidel jumping from a tank. There are exposed, naked light bulbs. A pre-historic radio receiver broadcasts a program about Jose Marti and his long journey; I can't comprehend from where to where, really.

I feel at home here, inside this old dilapidated villa, very close to the statue of my great Chilean hero, President Salvador Allende.

"Do Cubans really hate North Americans?" I ask. "Do Cuban artists?"

He smiles. His smile is gentle, despite the fact that he is the director of an important revolutionary television station.

"No," he replies after a while. "Here, despite the political situation, we still maintain many vivid cultural contacts between Cuba and the United States. You know: writers, film directors..."

He looks at me, and he almost winks.

"It has never stopped. It will never stop. It never will... Even right now, as we are speaking, there is a meeting of Cuban and North American academics taking place in Washington D.C."

"Culture is solidarity," I smile.

He nods. Before I go, we embrace.

At the historic "Hotel Inglaterra" a band of local *salseros* is playing in the open, right on the pavement: nothing special, honestly, but good and authentic stuff, nevertheless.

Inside, in the restaurant, the ceramics are magnificent, but the food is mediocre.

But I am actually content as I am sitting at an enormous wooden table with my best friend, the Chinese concert pianist Yuan Sheng. He flew in to Havana all the way from Beijing, in order to participate in a festival of some of the best pianists from all over the world. His former professor from the Manhattan School of Music, the legendary Solomon Gadles Mikowsky, has organized the festival himself originally from Cuba.

"I am tremendously impressed by the cultural life and art scene in Cuba", explains Yuan, excitedly. "I traveled to and performed in so many countries in North America, Europe, Africa and Asia... But what I see here is unprecedented. Music, ballet, arts... Even the art objects that people sell on the street... It all shows how heroic the national character of Cuban people is.

Cuba is also very open-minded and receptive of international culture; there is a constant interchange with the world. The plane, which I took here was bringing an entire delegation of Chinese artists and performers. And that is at the same time as I was coming to take part in yet another festival, which was featuring top international pianists. Coming here, I am helping to deepen the understanding between China and Cuba. And you know, in the last years, many educated Chinese people are fascinated with this island and its artists. When I was talking to my friends back in Beijing that I was going to Cuba, their eyes widened. They were envious; they kept telling me how lucky I was. They wanted to know, to understand Cuba."

Later that night we ended up drinking beer with the renowned North American concert pianist Simone Dinnerstein, talking about the music and artwork of her famous father, Simon Dinnerstein.

We are in a café, in one of those beautiful squares, at night. Nearby, some band is playing old Mexican *boleros*. Simone, Yuan and I switch our discussion to the piano festival, but then, suddenly we all fell silent.

There is an unmistakable, confident, perfect sound coming from nearby. It's the Buena Vista Social Club! The stars are brilliant. Historic buildings are brightly illuminated. Two great classic pianists, one North American and one Chinese, are trying to catch the sounds coming from the *Taberna*. It is not difficult: all the windows and doors are open!

One night, Yuan and I go to the National Ballet of Cuba, to see a performance of "Shakespeare and His Masques" under the choreography of the legendary Alicia Alonso.

There are literally thousands of people queuing in front of the entrance doors. The tickets cost almost nothing, just a symbolic token; everyone here can actually attend some world-class performances.

But that very particular evening, something goes wrong. The doors do not open 15 minutes before the performance, as they should; they do not open even when it is time to begin.

The crowd mumbles, but stays calm. The ushers look indifferent. I knock on one of the glass doors and ask what is happening? The "electric system has collapsed," I am told. "Does it happen often?" I ask. Not often, hardly ever.

The usher is at first rude, but then I 'win her heart' by smiling and explaining that I am a writer and my friend is famous Chinese pianist, and we would actually like to wait inside, walk through the semi-darkness of this legendary theatre, and just dream.

She likes that. She obviously likes dreaming in semi-darkness, too. So, she lets us in.

"It reminds me of China, when I was growing up," says Yuan.

To some extent it also reminds me of Prague some time ago. But what exactly is it that we feel?

People are absolutely real here. They are not 'trained' to be servile, even in the service 'industry'. They are gloomy if they are in a bad mood, or cheerful when something good happens to them. They are not afraid of losing their job.

Cuban people are honest, sometimes brutally honest. They laugh when they are happy and they cry when it hurts. They show affection to those they love, and scorn to those they hate. It is a pure and sincere society. And in many ways much freer than those societies that promote their own freedom, as the only model for the world.

Eventually, the enormous space of the Nation Theatre fills up with thousands of people. The performance begins. It is powerful, and as expected sharp as a razor blade, unmistakably brilliantly choreographed and with excellent dancers.

Love stories and stories of death, of betrayal and hope. It is Shakespeare at his best, converted into classical ballet, on this green tropical island obsessed with artistic and intellectual excellence.

But at the end, the audience does not cheer. The

applause is lukewarm. The long wait in front of the theatre was not forgiven. It is Cuba, after all, and in Cuba, one does not feel obliged to applaud, even when confronted by unmistakable greatness.

In the old lobby of the historic hotel San Felipe, in Old Havana, Solomon Mikowsky, continues to be impressed with Cuba, his native land:

> "Before, Cuba honored only great people, great artists like Jose Marti. But now, Cuba is honoring every single person, every single artist, who contributed to the creation of this great nation. Poets, musicians, actors, writers, alongside the great warriors... Now the history of Cuba has expanded to several hundreds of heroes who have made a true contribution... And by educating people, the government has made sure that so many citizens of Cuba are now thirsty for knowledge! Culturally, Cuba is to Latin America what Athens was to Europe. Cuban arts are not designed to 'please the audience'. They are designed to aim at excellence and creativity... they are geared to produce great poets in virtually every field of the arts."

Great bards and filmmakers, poets... That's Havana. Bookstores selling high quality, subsidized books...

I walk through the center of the city; I stop at an old and elegant bookstore. I decide to buy ten books of contemporary poetry. This store does not accept convertible currency (CUC).

"Please go next door and buy local pesos," I am told. I go to the bank. "What for?" the young clerk asks me.

"I need to buy books."

"How many?" Ten, I tell her. "Then change only 5 dollars and after you pay at the bookstore, you will get plenty of change for public buses, so you can ride for the rest of the week."

I talk to great artists, to journalists and students. For days I talk, and watch. I listen to music, day and night. I read.

"Obama, give me 5!" I see a poster on the wall. It is referring to the 5 Cuban patriots who have been held in high security prisons in the United States, for infiltrating the CIA, and for trying to prevent hostile, even terrorist actions, against Cuba. The posters are very artistic. But then, here, everything graphic could pass for art.

Then, one night, a young woman, a student, asks me about my impressions:

"What do you think about Cuban culture?"

We are in the old Basilica, where the piano festival is held. She is holding a small notepad in her hands.

"Do not think..." she smiles. "Answer quickly. Just few words..."

"Revolution... dignity... passion..." I shoot.

She nods.

I then turn the tables around:

"You? What is it for you?'

She thinks only for two or three seconds: "Everything... Life... Death... Love..."

Behind us, we hear Chopin's Etude. And behind the walls of the Basilica, as the sun goes down, one of the most beautiful cities on earth is beginning to explode in a perfect harmony of sounds and rhythms.

This is not necessarily how revolutions are made. But this is how they survive!

23 August 2013

*****

3

NAMIBIA – GERMANY'S AFRICAN HOLOCAUST

By Andre Vltchek

How outrageous, how heartbreaking, how truly grotesque! Windhoek City – the capital of Namibia – is, at one extreme full of flowers and Mediterranean-style villas, and at the other, it is nothing more than a tremendous slum without water or electricity.

And in between, there is the town center– with its Germanic orderly feel, boasting 'colonial architecture', including Protestant churches and commemorative plaques mourning those brave German men, women and children, those martyrs, who died during the uprisings and wars conducted by local indigenous people.

The most divisive and absurd of those memorials is the so-called "Equestrian Monument", more commonly known as "The Horse" or under its German original names,

Reiterdenkmal and Südwester Reiter (*Rider of South-West*). It is a statue inaugurated on 27 January 1912, which was the birthday of the German emperor Wilhelm II. The monument "honors the soldiers and civilians that died on the German side of the Herero and Namaqua 'War' of 1904–1907'".

That 'war' was not really a war; it was nothing more than genocide, a holocaust.

And Namibia was a prelude to what German Nazis later tried to implement on European soil.

A European expert working for the UN, my friend, speaks, like almost everyone here, passionately, but without daring to reveal her name:

> *"The first concentration camps on earth were built in this part of Africa... They were built by the British Empire in South Africa and by Germans here, in Namibia. Shark Island on the coast was the first concentration camp in Namibia, used to murder the Nama people, but now it is just a tourist destination – you would never guess that there were people exterminated there. Here in the center of Windhoek, there was another extermination camp; right on the spot where "The Horse" originally stood."*

"The Horse" was recently removed from its original location, and placed in the courtyard of the old wing of The National Museum, together with some of the most outrageous commemorative plaques, glorifying German actions in this part of the world. Nothing was destroyed, instead just taken away from prime locations.

Where "The Horse" stood, there now stands a proud anti-colonialist statue, that of a man and a woman with broken shackles, which declares, "Their Blood Waters Our Freedom".

***

A visit to those German genocidal relics is 'an absolute must' for countless Central European tourists that descend every day on Namibia. I followed several of these groups, listening to their conversations. Among these people, there appears to be no remorse, and almost no soul-searching: just snapshots, posing in front of the monuments and racist insignias, pub-style/beer jokes at places where entire cultures and nations were exterminated!

Central European, German-speaking tourists in Windhoek, appear to be lobotomized, and totally emotionless. And so are many of the descendants of those German 'genocidal pioneers'. Encountering them is like *déjà vu*; it brings back memories of the years when I was fighting against the German Nazi colony, '*Colonia Dignidad*' in Chile; or when I was investigating the atrocities and links, of the German Nazi community in Paraguay to several South American fascist regimes that had been implanted and maintained by the West.

And now the German community in Namibia is protesting the removal of "The Horse". It is indignant. And this community is still powerful, even omnipotent, here in Namibia.

Almost nobody calls the 'events' that took place here, by their rightful names, of holocaust or genocide. Everything in Namibia is 'sensitive'.

But even according to the BBC: "In 1985, a UN report classified the events as an attempt to exterminate the Herero and Nama peoples of South-West Africa, and therefore the earliest attempted genocide in the 20th Century."

On 21 October 2012, The Globe and Mail reported:

> *"In the bush and scrub of central Namibia, the descendants of the surviving Herero live in squalid shacks and tiny plots of land. Next door, the descendants of German settlers still own vast properties of 20,000 hectares or more. It's a contrast that infuriates many Herero, fuelling a new radicalism here.*
>
> *Every year the Herero hold solemn ceremonies to remember the first genocide of history's bloodiest century, when German troops drove them into the*

> desert to die, annihilating 80 per cent of their
> population through starvation, thirst, and slave labor
> in concentration camps. The Nama, a smaller ethnic
> group, lost half of their population from the same
> persecution.
>
> New research suggests that the German racial genocide
> in Namibia from 1904 to 1908 was a significant
> influence on the Nazis in the Second World War. Many
> of the key elements of Nazi ideology – from racial
> science and eugenics, to the theory of Lebensraum
> (creating "living space" through colonization) – were
> promoted by German military veterans and scientists
> who had begun their careers in South-West Africa, now
> Namibia, during the genocide..."

The Namibian government is still negotiating the
return (from Germany) of all skulls of the local people,
which were used in German laboratories and by German
scientists to prove the superiority of the white race.
German colonialists decapitated Herero and Nama people,
and at least 300 heads were transported to German
laboratories for 'scientific research'. Many were
'discovered' in the Medical History Museum of the Charite
hospital in Berlin, and at Freiburg University.

Leading German doctor, who was working on 'the pure
race doctrine' in Namibia (the doctrine later used by the
Nazis), was doctor Fisher. He 'educated' many German
physicians, including Doctor Mengele.

It is all to a very little surprise, considering that the first
German governor of the colony was the father of Hitler's
deputy Herman Goering.

Germany never officially apologized for its crimes
against humanity in what it used to call German South-
West Africa. It did not pay reparations.

Germany's holocaust in 'South-West Africa' is, among
other things, a proof that the common Western theory
about how German Nazism came to existence before the
WWII was totally wrong. According to that theory, after
the WWI, defeated and humiliated Germany got

radicalized and 'reacted' monstrously to its condition.

But in reality, before and during the Second World War, Germany simply decided to behave in Europe exactly as it was behaving in its colonies, for many decades.

***

There are Robert Mugabe and Fidel Castro Streets in the center of Windhoek. And there is that tremendous National Museum, commemorating the national-liberation struggle and the role of the heroic Cuban and North Korean troops in their fight against Western-supported apartheid.

Bizarrely, German pre-Nazi/WWII monuments and insignias literally rub their shoulders alongside those great liberation struggle tributes.

Divisions are shocking: ideological, racial, social.

In Namibia, there is segregation on an enormous scale, everywhere.

While neighboring South Africa is moving rapidly away from racial segregation, introducing countless social policies, including free medical care, education and social housing, Namibia remains one of the most segregated countries on earth, with great private services for the rich, and almost nothing for the poor majority.

"Apartheid was even worse here than in South Africa", I am told by my friend from the United Nations. "And until now... You go to Katutura, and you see who is living there, they are all local people there, all black. Katutura literally means 'We have no place to stay'. 50% of the people in this city defecate in the open. Sanitation is totally disastrous. Then you go to Swakop city, on the shore, and it is like seeing Germany recreated in Africa. You also see, there, shops with Nazi keepsakes. Some Nazis, who escaped Europe, came to Windhoek, to Swakop and other towns. In Swakop, men march periodically, in replicas of Nazi uniforms."

***

Katutura is where the black people were moved to, during apartheid.

My friend, a 'colored' Namibian, who fought for the independence of his own country and of Angola, drove me to that outrageous slum which seems to host a substantial amount of the capital's population, with mostly no access to basic sanitation or electricity.

He has also chosen to remain anonymous, as he has explained, in order to protect his lovely family. To speak up here, unlike in South Africa, which may, these days, be one of the freest and most outspoken places on earth, can be extremely dangerous. But he clarifies further:

> "In Namibia, it is very rare for people who used to suffer, to speak about it publicly. In South Africa, everyone speaks. In Angola, everyone speaks... But not here."

Then he continues:

> "What we can see in Namibia is that many German people are still in control of big business. They are ruling the country. They have hunting farms and other huge estates and enterprises. Germans bring money to Namibia, but it stays with them, and it consolidates their power – it does not reach the majority. You cannot even imagine, how much local people working on their farms, are suffering. It is still like slavery. But it is all hushed up here."

***

"Sprechen Sie Deutch?" A black Namibian man intercepts me, as I am walking down the Fidel Castro Street.

"I do, but I would rather not, here", I explain.

"But why not?" He grins at me. "You know... It is not only them... Germans... I grew up; I was educated, in East Germany during our fight for independence. And my friend that you see over there – he was flown to Czechoslovakia and he went to school there. Communist countries did so

26

much for us, for the Africans: Cuba, North Korea, Soviet Union, Czechoslovakia and East Germany. We are so grateful!"

"Yes", I say. "But it is over, isn't it? Czechoslovakia, East Germany... They joined the imperialists, the rulers. They exchanged ideals for iPads."

"Yes", he said. "But one day... who knows... things could be different, again."

Yes, definitely, I think. But most likely not in Europe...

***

At the new and lavish National Museum in Windhoek, I salute the Namibian and foreign fighters against apartheid – those who struggled and died for freedom, and the independence of Africa.

Then, I descended to the "Goethe Institute", the German cultural center, a colonial building surrounded by barbed wire.

There, a local starlet is loudly rehearsing for something called 'a night under the stars', or something of that sentimental, over-sugary pop nature. These are basically evenings designed to bring together the pampered international crowd and those 'feel-good-about-life' local elites.

I ask the starlet, whether this institute is trying to address the most painful issues of the past and present, all connected to Germany, of course.

She is black but she speaks and behaves like a German. She gives me a huge and pre-fabricated smile:

> "At Goethe we don't want that... We are trying to get away from all this (meaning colonial and segregation issues). We are just trying to get Germans and Namibians together, you know..."

I later peek at those Namibians who are being brought together with the Germans. No Katutura here, naturally...

And for some reason, what came to my mind is a conversation I had, on the phone, many years ago, with one of the editors of the German magazine, Der Stern, after I offered him my findings and photos from Nazi *Colonia Dignidad* in Chile. He said: "Oh, Colonia Dignidad! Hahaha! Never again, ja?"

***

One evening I eat at Angolan/Portuguese restaurant in Windhoek, *O Portuga*; an institution known for its great food and mixed crowd. What an evening, what a place!

After dinner, I dive into German 'Andy's Bar', a nearby place that was described to me as "An institution, which not even a black or a colored person from the embassies or the UN would dare to enter".

The Beer is flat, but the conversation of the local crowd is extremely 'sharp'. Patrons are freely giving black Namibians names of local farm animals. Their spite is open and sincere. I listen, I understand. Eventually I leave.

I catch a taxi, driven by a corpulent black man. The radio is blasting and I hear the socialist, anti-imperialist lyrics of 'Ndilimani', a brilliant local political band.

It is now well past midnight, and despite the warnings from all those 'well-meaning Germans' that I met in Windhoek, I feel much safer in this taxi than in Andy's Bar and in so many other similar institutions.

"Is this country really governed by Marxist SWAPO?" I wonder aloud.

"No way", the driver points back, towards the bar. "'They' never left. 'They' are still controlling the country. The revolution is not over."

I tell him that I am beginning to understand what drove Robert Mugabe mad and angry, in Zimbabwe. The driver nods. I push my seat back, and make it recline.

"It is all fucked up", I say.

The driver thinks for a while, but then replies, using almost the same words as the man who spoke to me on Fidel Castro Street: "Yes, brother, yes! But one day... who knows... things could be different, again."

September 19, 2014

***

Andre Vltchek – Christopher Black – Peter Koenig

4

From Oppressed to Free

IN SOUTH AFRICA, AFRICA IS RISING!

By Andre Vltchek

Soweto is not just a suburb of Johannesburg located right near the mining belt; it is an enormous urban sprawl, with over 1.2 million inhabitants. It is more populous than Boston or Amsterdam.

It used to be a place synonymous with misery, with sadness, with the depravity of apartheid.

This is the township where Nelson Mandela lived with his first family and then with his second wife, Winnie. This is where he was forced underground in 1961, before being arrested one year later and sentenced to life in prison by the pro-Western apartheid regime.

And this is where, in 1976, a student uprising against apartheid erupted, and up to 700 young people lost their lives, among them the 12-year-old-boy Hector Pieterson, whose death became a symbol of regime's savagery.

Soweto, which gets its name from 'South Western Townships', with its tin roofs, unpaved roads and excessive crime rate had been, for many years and decades, an emblem of poverty and hopelessness.

But since the end of apartheid, South Africa has become a totally new nation – progressive, socialist and increasingly compassionate. Two decades after the new rainbow flag was raised, Soweto looks cosmopolitan, upbeat and forward-looking.

Most of the roads are now paved; a commuter train system transports tens of thousands of people between Soweto and the center of Johannesburg. There are elegant, South American-style bus lanes, as well as a super modern motorway ('Soweto Highway', which branches from the N1) with dedicated lanes for public transportation.

Soweto counts an architecturally stunning stadium, with enormous playgrounds for children, new green areas, and countless lanes of high quality social housing. Not far from 'Mandela House', which has been converted into a museum, there are countless hip restaurants, cafes and art galleries.

There are also two modern medical facilities: the Baragwanath hospital, and the new Jabulani, 300-bed hospital that was handed over to the Gauteng health department in 2012.

New schools are opening their doors.

As was written by Bongani Nkosi in 2011:

> *"The community of Soweto now has access to a state-of-the-art higher learning facility, following the multi-million rand upgrade of the University of Johannesburg's (UJ) campus in the township.*
>
> *Formerly known as Vista University, the UJ campus is now of the same stature as universities in South Africa's more affluent towns. It sports a more exciting look than*

Vista, which was built by the apartheid government to prolong racial segregation in tertiary education.

The university was transformed at a cost of R450-million (US$62-million), a sum allocated by the government in 2005. Science and Technology minister Naledi Pandor commented that the design "inspires creative thinking"."

This is Africa; this is a proud and determined African nation rising, taking off.

It is not perfect; this is no paradise. But those of us who are well acquainted with hell; with those African countries that were forced to become client-states of the West, all over East, West and Central Africa, where the poor are literally made to eat shit, where the sick are dying in agony, where there is no justice for the under-privileged majority... for those of us who know, South Africa is a tremendous force of enormous hope and true pride! This is BRICS, or more precisely, BRCS.

A few weeks after being told by slum-dwellers in New Delhi (the capital of 'democratic' India) that they would never dare go near 'that enormous building near us' (they were referring to the luxury mall), because the guards would beat them up, I saw several old women in Soweto pushing huge shopping carts out of the elegant, marble-glass-and-fountains, Maponya Mall.

Yes, in Soweto they now have malls and the huge Virgin Active Health Club.

I asked one of the ladies, whether she can really afford shopping here.

"It is cheaper here," she explained. "Small shops are bit more expensive. And... it is very clean and nice here".

Does she have any problems with the guards?

She does not understand my question. We smile at each other, and then she leaves.

But by now, there is a small group of people that has formed around me. Men and women are curious; they want to know why I find it so surprising that they are shopping here. I explain that in many capitalist countries like India, Indonesia or Kenya, people like this gentle old lady would never have been allowed to enter, or would never be able to afford to shop in a place like this.

There is laughter coming from the group, but it is friendly, encouraging laughter. People have finally realized that I am a foreigner, and that I came here to understand and to write about their country.

"This mall was built for us," explained an elderly man. "And in South Africa, we can go wherever we want and nobody would dare to stop us. We fought for this, and we won."

I suddenly realize that at one of the entrances to the mall, there is a statue of a young boy, being carried...

"Who is it?" I ask, although I know the answer to my own question almost as soon as it leaves my lips.

"Hector Pieterson," I am told. "He is the boy who died in 1976, fighting against apartheid."

Outside, after I enter a hired car, my Burundian driver explains as we begin driving towards Pretoria:

"South Africans have no fear. They can talk about anything here; they are very brave. They can praise or insult, they can criticize President Zuma or the police, military... no problem. It is a very free country. Before I only knew Burundi, Rwanda, Tanzania and Kenya – I could never imagine what it is to be free, to have no fear. A country where you can say what you think, go where you want to go, do what you want to do... In South Africa you see the guards, but they would never stop you... Poor people, black people: they can go to any of the expensive shops, even to the privately-owned platinum mines, and no one would stop them. Nothing would happen. Here, you can photograph anything, discuss anything... I never thought that such country could exist."

***

34

I test that freedom on many occasions, during this latest visit of mine to South Africa. I test it at the platinum mines, near the military installations during clashes between protesters and the police. South Africa passes all the tests gracefully and confidently.

One day I go to the Constitutional Court of South Africa, in Johannesburg. It is not in session, but there are judges and clerks present there.

In front of the building, a young woman is shouting insults directed at the government of South Africa. She is very vocal and very vulgar, and her 'audience' consists of several confused and titillated foreign visitors (they perhaps feel that they are 'witnessing a piece of history in the making').

I knock at the door. The door opens. "I would like to enter the Court," I say.

A security personnel officer looks at me, embarrassed. "Could you come back in a few minutes? We are bit... concerned that the lady outside will try to enter and will try to shout inside, disrupting work..."

"But I have nothing to do with her..."

"Oh, OK then..." They let me in. I only have to put my phone and cameras through an X-Ray machine. Security procedures are lighter here than when entering a Kenyan supermarket. Then, soon, I am in. No questions are asked.

"A Luta Continua" is written on the wall. A revolutionary slogan, that means "The Struggle Goes On!"

I enter the courtroom. Nobody cares what I am doing or where I am going. I photograph and again, nobody cares.

I don't know why the lenses of my glasses suddenly become foggy.

I talk to a judge... I am not supposed to be talking to a judge, on the record...

We manage to get around the restrictions: I don't ask

his name, and he talks.

I ask about President Zuma, about that endless, toxic propaganda howls against him, coming from abroad.

"He was acquitted," says judge. "The entire world, even the West, keeps repeating that South Africa has the best, or at least one of the best and freest, judiciary systems on earth. But when a decision is made, as in the case of President Zuma, and it is not to their liking, they are suddenly questioning the integrity of our entire judiciary system."

'President Zuma taking shower after unprotected sex', or 'President Zuma allegedly involved in corruption'. Over and over again, the same old tune.

One never hears: 'The President of Indonesia used to be an army general responsible for atrocities in East Timor during the occupation, and then in charge of the on-going genocide in Papua... he is also unwilling to stop the plundering of the natural resources of the country...' We never hear that 'Both the presidents of Rwanda and Uganda are responsible for much of those 10 million deaths in the Democratic Republic of Congo; people butchered on behalf of Western governments and multi-national companies'. That is because all of them – SBY, Kagame and Museveni – have been dutifully serving the interests of the Empire.

While presidents Zuma, Mugabe and Afwerki, are committing the highest crime in the eyes of the Empire – they are trying to serve the interests of their people.

***

More obvious is the progress in socialist or socially-oriented countries/societies that are trying to improve lives of their people – such as South Africa, China, Brazil, Eritrea or Venezuela – the louder and more vitriolic become the insults by the Western mainstream/corporate propaganda media.

Realizing that 'socialist' is once again seen as something

positive, at least by billions of people all over the world, the Western propaganda is now using a very effective weapon of deception – it portrays countries like South Africa and China as 'not socialist enough', or even as 'more capitalist than those countries in the West'. Unfortunately, it is an extremely effective tool of trickery.

On the other hand, brutally capitalist or feudal countries like India or Indonesia are hailed as 'democratic' and tolerant, even if these countries are openly devouring their own miserably poor majorities.

In Indonesia or in India, governments and the private sector can get away with just about anything – from genocides (in Papua and Kashmir) to corruption on an epic scale – as long as they are loyal to market-fundamentalist doctrines, and as long as they are willing to sacrifice their own citizens for the interests of the Empire.

Countries like South Africa or China are constantly under the microscope. They can get away with absolutely nothing.

***

South Africa is not unlike Brazil, its fellow BRICS country, as it used to be a decade or so ago. It is a rich nation with excellent infrastructure, but with deep social problems. It is a great multi-racial and multi-cultural society with enormous potential.

It is a beacon of hope, not only for the African continent, but also for the entire world.

South Africa matters! If it succeeds as a country, with a progressive political and social system, then it will deliver to its long-suffering people what they fully deserve: true freedom and prosperity. It would also offer another great alternative model for humanity. If it fails, much of the African continent will lose trust in daring and fighting for a better world. That is why South Africa should never be allowed to fall!

Chris Lwanga, Political Assistant to leading opposition

politician, James Akena MP who is a son of the late progressive President of Uganda, Milton Obote, expressed his opinion about South Africa, for this report:

> *"Potentially South Africa is the true engine and hope of Africa. This is in terms of resources both developed and un-developed. That potential couldn't be fully tapped because the ANC went into talks for ending apartheid minus a global ally standing on her side. The formation of the BRICS states is good news for ANC/South Africa and Africa! It shall enhance the role of South Africa. It is supposed to play to realistic levels. Africa feels proud of the younger rainbow nation and treats South Africa as her newly-born child that is destined to defend and promote Africa in a hostile global world. A newborn child after the dismantling of apartheid and attainment of majority rule since 1994! Majority rule can be viewed as that of a child's growth and development, one that must be nurtured! The emergence of the BRICS grouping is a move in the right direction that South Africa, Africa and the rest of the progressive world must support. And if South Africa matures into a socially responsible state, that would be a development the imperial and colonial forces don't want to happen, hence an early attack on South Africa, its policies and membership of BRICS."*

Yes, hence an early attack! The usual strategy of the Western propaganda system: to vulgarize all genuine attempts to improve the lives of people in Latin America, China, Russia and Africa; to inject nihilism and to spit on enthusiasm.

In Kenya, Edris Omondi, who is a lawyer and Editor-in-Chief of Frontline International Magazine, is clearly inspired by South Africa and its prominent Marxist, Joe Slovo:

> *"I draw inspiration from Joe Slovo the then General Secretary of the South Africa Communist Party, that a party such as the ANC should consider the complex social fabric, ranked from communists, non-communists, workers, capitalists and middle class in designing its policy. He said: "It's a forum of the people,*

the whole people, whereas the party goes beyond just the struggle against racism and believes that in the end the only rational form with which humanity should order its life is through a system in which one person can't live off the labor of another, a system of socialism. And we don't postpone the advocacy of that until after the ANC flag flies over Pretoria. We regard it as our independent task as a party to begin to explain, to get acceptance for the doctrine of socialism and its ultimate implementation in South Africa." These words of Joe Slovo are the ultimate critical truth to salvage tribal politics in Kenya and any part of Africa and every political party work should embrace the same in their manifesto for ultimate party and national success."

South Africa is increasingly inspiring the continent's 'Left', which has been for decades derailed, beaten, manipulated, even murdered, mainly by the outside forces of former and present (European and North American) colonialist powers.

My friend, Mwandawiro Mghanga, opposition leader and Chairperson of the Social Democratic Party of Kenya (Marxist), a poet and former prisoner of conscience under the pro-Western dictatorship of Moi, explained to me, on several occasions:

"We are in contact with the leftist movements of Africa... we are actually connected to the South Africa Communist party... ANC is truly progressive nationalist political party. It consists of the COSATU and the South African Communist Party. They call it the Tripartite Alliance – ANC, COSATU and the Communist Party. The ANC is the great hope for Africa. It is serious and it is a progressive socialist party."

I mentioned to Mwandawiro Mghanga, that South Africa in general and President Zuma in particular are steadily demonized in the West. He replied, passionately:

"They are! Very much so... but the only thing they, the West, can do is to bark to deal with it, because it's the only party that is controlling the government; it was elected by the people, it's in power, and they are very much alert about being constantly undermined. I have

been reading and also receiving direct information from South Africa... You know we are partners to the likes of COSATU. Communists dominate it; even President Jacob Zuma is coming from there."

Wherever I went, the eyes of Africans were pointing towards South Africa – be it in Ivory Coast, Uganda and Kenya, in Namibia and in Lesotho.

I witnessed the deployment of the South African police force, in Maseru, Lesotho, after the aborted coup there. Again, what came to my mind were Brazil and its acts of regional solidarity towards countries like Venezuela and Bolivia.

Even in Namibia, a country that had been occupied and battered by South Africa during the apartheid regime, most of the people see their big neighbor now as a country in transition, a nation that is taking off, and becoming a thoroughly sovereign and free homeland for all of its citizens.

"They do things well there," a man who fought for both the independence of Namibia and Angola tells me in Windhoek, the capital of Namibia. "It seems that the welfare of their people is the most important thing for the government."

In front of the Constitutional Court of South Africa, the promise of the future, Preamble to The Constitution, is engraved in stone:

> *"We, the people of South Africa*
>
> *Recognise the injustices of our past;*
>
> *Honour those who suffered for justice and*
>
> *freedom in our land;*
>
> *Respect those who have worked to build*
>
> *and develop our country, and*
>
> *Believe that South Africa belongs to*
>
> *all those who live in it, united in its diversity..."*

***

South Africa is not a 'perfect country', because there are no perfect countries in this world.

But it is one of those very few places on earth, which manages to cover my body with goose bumps whenever I arrive, and encircle me with great sadness, whenever I have to leave.

It is a country that is capable of evoking great and pure emotions – a country worth fighting for.

My South African friend who works for the United Nations and therefore is not allowed to speak on the record, expressed his outrage over the treatment his country is receiving abroad:

> *"The West ran out of its propaganda ammunition against Zuma. They tried to smear him by all means: calling him a polygamist, ridiculing his sexual practices. But despite everything, he is still there and under his leadership, his country, our country, South Africa, is clearly improving."*

I mention that it is so obvious that huge progress has been made, all over the country.

"But of course there is!" Proclaims my friend, who is actually white, but to whom being African and South African in particular, means much more than the color of his skin. I don't even know whether he voted for Zuma, it is irrelevant. What is essential to him is that his country should be judged and portrayed fairly:

> *"There is enormous progress, and people voted for Zuma again... Zuma came from the grassroots of the ANC. Some may say that ANC itself is not necessarily a left-wing party, anymore... But its youth-wing and its women league, its alliance with COSATU and the Communist Party – because of them its politics are left wing.*
>
> *What irritates me the most is that Western media is using totally different measures and language, when it comes to South Africa. They don't care what is*

happening in the political space of South Africa. They are just throwing stereotypes at Africans. I always feel like saying: 'you propagate for democracy, but when it happens in countries like South Africa, you cannot accept it'. They refuse to understand that as in any other country on earth, there are social classes in South Africa. They do not judge us with the same measures as they judge themselves.

Some South African media outlets are also treating South Africa unfairly. It is because foreign interests own several of those outlets, and local elites and their interests own many. And the 'elites' have lost!"

***

Not to see how South Africa has progressed on the social front requires huge discipline.

I witnessed cheering children from poor neighborhoods taking a ride on that new legendary Gauteng Train, which now counts on three lines, connecting at the speed of 160km/h, the cities of Pretoria, Johannesburg and O.R. Tambo International Airport. What I saw was part of a school excursion, something one sees in the countries like Venezuela.

I saw people painting their fences and beautifying their streets, on so-called Mandela Day.

I traveled to Alexandra that in the past used to be one of the most terrible townships in the country, and atop it the posh suburb of Sandton is located nearby. Now, everything here is in transformation, with several new areas dedicated to state-subsidized social housing, like Bothabela Village.

In the middle of Alexandra, I asked Richard Baloist about life in the township, and he answered without any hesitation: "Things are much better now. We are free now... and we are supporting this government... There is sanitation here, electricity and water..."

Ms. Irene passes by and when she overhears our conversation, she decides to join in. She is against Zuma and his government: "There is no change," she utters.

I begin asking her practical questions and she replies, honestly:

> "*Yes, they dropped school fees... yes they supply children with school uniforms, notepads, books... We have clinics here, and yes they are free, and so is medicine for the poor. We have 'medical cards', and the quality of medical care is OK... All mothers in South Africa get around $30 dollars a month per each child, and giving birth here is free, for both South Africans and foreigners.*"

I ask Ms. Irene why she is against Zuma, and she replies: "I simply am... But most of the people here are voting for him."

In almost every town of South Africa, there are public libraries, sport facilities, and playgrounds. In every township there are clean shopping centers and medical posts. And slums are undergoing great transformation, mutating into livable neighborhoods, from what had been something that could easily be described as hell on earth.

On the outskirts of Alexandra, there is still the appalling Mokuku slum, located right next to the river. But immediately across the bridge, there are entire neighborhoods of high-quality social housing and green areas.

I speak to a security guard of the Bothabela compound, which is part of a Johannesburg Social Housing Compound. He explains:

> "Here, people are paying what they can afford, and they get all necessary services. As you can see, construction of social houses is everywhere – here or in Soweto, everywhere... Many people who live here are working, but there are also unemployed people living here, as well as single mothers. People are really happy to live here."

Is crime an issue?

"In social housing, there is almost no crime. Crime is now generally much lower than 20 or 10 years ago. Even crime in the center of Johannesburg has gone down, dramatically."

A man wearing a Zuma T-shirt approaches us, grinning happily.

I shout at him: "Are you supporting President Zuma?"

He looks at me as if I'd have fallen from the Moon: "But of course I support him!"

And he smiles and poses.

I feel like I am in Venezuela.

***

South Africa is becoming a true Rainbow Nation, a real tolerant and multi-racial, multi-cultural society.

It is not fully there yet, of course. The horrors of apartheid, its 'boxing of people', dividing them, has created a legacy which will take many years to fully dismantle.

As I am about to board my train from Cape Town station, bound for Simon's Town, I hear some loud screams and I see two black women and a man being pushed by police off the station. There is actually no police violence; the officers are black and white, men and women. People being pushed off are shouting a few insults, trying to throw plastic boxes at the law enforcers.

I asked what happened. Police pointed at a convenience store owned by a man of Indian descent.

I go there.

"What happened?" I wonder.

"I can tell a thief before he or she begins stealing from me," he begins shouting. "They came here for nothing good!"

I am beginning to understand that he called police simply on suspicion that something could be stolen from his store. There was no theft, no action.

A white man who entered the store begins shouting: "I already left this shithole country twice. I should have never returned!"

The violence of those outbursts truly shocks me. Especially considering that nothing really happened.

Buying my ticket to Simon's Town, I get into a conversation with a local 'colored' (as people of mixed blood are called in Africa) girl. Soon she detects from my accent that I am not from South Africa.

"You know," she tries to explain, "Things like this happen, but this not a norm, anymore. There has been great progress. People of different races now get along really well... most of them."

"I know," I say. "I have travelled all over South Africa..."

"And how do you find it?"

"I love it," I reply, honestly.

"Really? That makes me... so happy."

"I really do. I feel at home here, just as I feel at home in Venezuela, Cuba, China and Russia."

She gives me a big smile. Then she pokes me on the shoulder: "Welcome to South Africa!"

***

On commuter trains in South Africa... here, along these lines it shows, it is so evident, how South Africa is struggling, how it is trying to fly high and to become a wealthy nation for all... But it cannot fly too high yet, although it will, soon, no doubt. There are still too many weights it has to shake off, too many ropes and bandages that it has to cut off. It is trying so hard, its muscles are working to the extreme, its brain is working, and its heart is pounding.

Cape Town stations, still painted with graffiti, still scary and tough... still barbed-wire... still the desperate look in the eyes of cornered teenagers.

Better, yes, much better, but still...

Steenberg... Almost there, to that cozy middle class neighborhood, but not yet there... too many fences and the pavement is too broken. Nearby are standing new and modern, elegant houses. Then suddenly a lake appears, and the lakeside, so similar to neighborhoods in Australia or New Zealand... rugby fields and suburban 'bliss'. We laugh at suburbia in the United States or in Canada, but here it is not funny; it is millions of people rising up from poverty and for the first time, given a chance to live! Not really rich, but definitely 'First World'. The population here is mixed, totally mixed. Finally! Oh South Africa! What a fight, what a struggle, what heart, what courage!

Then the train hits the coast, and suddenly it is moving along some of the most beautiful scenery on earth. It is bit like Chile, my faraway imaginary homeland.

Kalk Bay... Beaches and beaches all along the track... all the way to Simon's Town... and beyond that, there is no train, only a road, just the marvelous wilderness until the very end, the very tip of Africa – the Cape of Good Hope.

On the opposite seat, a father, a white man, is playing with his two sons. One son is white and one is black. Perhaps they are from two different marriages. He is spoiling them both, corrupting them with candies and his love. He looks at both children with equal pride. Soon, one forgets that the children belong to two different races.

This is the new South Africa. This is Africa rising!

***

And here it is – that damned Lonmin Marikana mine; the mine strikes of 2012... the massacre that took 44 lives in total, and made South Africa 'notorious', just two years ago.

I don't want to go into the political details of the tragedy, as they are too murky.

But I have to testify that this terrible drama was once again twisted and exploited by the foreign media and those who wanted to discredit South Africa.

The mine, let us not forget is owned by a giant British mining company, not by the ANC, not by the South African Government, not by President Zuma. The fact that some ANC cadres have stakes in that mine is not proof of anything: the mine is one of the biggest in South Africa, employing tens of thousands of people. Many, many people have investments in it.

Then, it should be remembered that the AMCU (union organization) is the one that ordered the strike. And AMCU is a breakaway faction from NUM (that is COSATU-affiliated, therefore to a large extent, Marxist). AMCU proudly claims that it is "apolitical and noncommunist".

Many believe that if the strike was organized by NUM, there would have been no bloodshed.

The Communist Party of South Africa strongly criticized AMCU for the way it was conducting the strike. It even called for the leaders of AMCU to be arrested.

Furthermore, the British owners of the mine kept the working conditions of the miners (at least until the 2012 strike and the massacre) at an appalling level, and they refused to accept the conditions of the strikers and to negotiate, which led to the escalation of tensions.

The South African Trade and Industry Minister, Rob Davies, testified that "the conditions in the mines was "appalling" and said the owners who "make millions" had questions to answer about how they treat their workers."

I drove to Rustenburg and to Lonmin Marikana in order to speak to the miners.

I wanted to hear directly from them what really took place in 2012.

To my great surprise, this was the only place in South Africa, where fear was clearly detectable.

While the entire world 'knows what happened', or more precisely was made to consume a well-massaged digest of the events that took place two years ago, at Marikana itself, an investigator who dares to ask direct and 'uncomfortable' questions is greeted with blank faces and sometimes with a chilling silence.

Mr. Leonard is a 55 years old miner and he has worked here for 15 years:

> *"The company warned us not to touch or damage anything. The company was of course involved in the killing. I don't know about the government. I was there when it happened. It was horrendous. All we wanted was to be paid a bit better and to have our conditions improved. The company refused. We were paid then, some US$500 (5,000 Rand) a month, for an 8h45min working day, and for 6 days a week labor. People here are getting sick from overwork. The working conditions are really poor. Now we are paid 7,000 Rand, an increase, but not a really dramatic one. We know it is a foreign – British – company. And it is only interested in profit and production, not the people. In 5 years from now, after I retire, I will most likely have nothing."*

I speak to a lady-miner. She refuses to provide her name. But she is pessimistic:

> *"Our working conditions have not improved. I have worked here for 3 years and it is now the same as before. I don't understand anything: our country is improving, working conditions are improving everywhere... but not here."*

And then it comes: two miners, one after another speak to me, anonymously:

> *"We think that it was the company that paid the police and security forces to kill the workers, not the government. We actually think that the government in the end pushed for and secured many changes here, on our behalf. We are afraid to speak openly... Because the killings are still going on... if we talk, we could disappear..."*

This is not the South Africa that I know and admire. This is not that brave and fearless country. This is a country that is still under the colonial boot. Here it is capitalism, exposing its sharp and ugly teeth, corrupting and murdering in the process.

After Marikana, I drove further, to the luxury and private resort, Sun City, a complex of casinos, resorts and hotels. There, for the first time in this country, I was stopped, right in front of 'The Palace of the Lost City', a six-star hotel

I asked the guard who is usually accommodated there.

He looked uncomfortable. "Some stars," he answered. "And..."

"Some executives from mining companies, foreigners?" I asked.

"Them too," he replied.

The nightly rate in this hotel goes for between 1,100 dollars and 10,000, I was told.

The increase in the monthly wages of the miners was, on average, 200 dollars.

Situations and scenarios like this exist, of course, even in Latin America. It is clear that the private sector, particularly multi-nationals, want to tie-down, to enslave progressive governments, and to make them dependent. We all know, and it was so well described by Naomi Klein and others, what blackmail and tricks were used by the multi-nationals and Western powers against the young and inexperienced South African State, and its leaders, right after the country broke off the shackles of apartheid.

And once someone stumbles, Western and local right-wing propaganda go into top gear, claiming that the entire South African Left is 'corrupt, money-hungry and essentially the same as the previous regime'.

For one week in my hotel in Pretoria I sat next to a judge who has been investigating the Marikana case. I knew who he was and I knew how respected he is in his country. I also knew how exhausted he must have been. I was also aware that even if he'd want to, he would not be able to speak on record, while he was involved in the case.

But at the end of my stay I approached him, and we spoke for one hour.

He spoke about his country with love and with passion.

At the end I gave him my full report on Marikana; I told him what I had heard and saw. I also pointed out that there is fear. Those who have something negative to say about the ANC or the government are not afraid – they freely put their names on the record. But those who believe that the company orchestrated the killings are petrified.

The Judge listened to me. Then he said: "But there is no investigation related to the government or ANC. There was no case brought against them in relation to the Marikana killing..."

***

I could talk for much longer about South Africa.

About entering the "Joburg Theatre", without being stopped, and about just sitting in darkness admiring the rehearsal of a Brazilian play.

I could write about the bands playing on the historic Waterfront of Cape Town. About the great overhaul of public transportation, about new hospitals and schools, about so many things...

I could say many more great things about the country, and also pass some critical observations, like the one concerning the new immigration law from 2013, which could be considered as biased. And I could comment on some discrimination of foreigners, particularly Zimbabweans, who come here with great education, ready to take low-wage jobs, but encounter hostility, even violence.

I could talk about land, and how arduous the land reforms really are.

But no country is perfect, and immigrants face much worse violence in Italy, France, Australia and the United States, than in South Africa.

I could talk about BRICS. Here, unlike India, almost everybody knows what BRICS is. While in India BRICS is an abstract concept, more masonry than political, South Africa is fully with this proud and progressive project, and often on its vanguard.

My friend in Pretoria, Ibrahim, regularly watches RT.

"I love that station," he says. "It is so objective; a real breath of fresh air!"

He follows and supports BRICS and their stand against the West. He says that many South African people feel this way.

At the Pretoria Art Museum, a huge event is taking place. There are several openings. *Vernissages* are for invited guests only. But when I mention that I make films for Venezuelan Telesur TV and write for RT, all barriers disappear and I am warmly welcomed to "come and see how we are doing." Someone pats me on the back. The color of skin matters nothing. This is, after all, the rainbow nation. What I do matters.

In South Africa, everything is in motion; everything is changing. It is a peaceful but nevertheless determined and socialist revolution.

Once, one of the most oppressed nations on Earth is becoming one of the freest. One of the saddest countries is now one of the most vibrant, optimistic and onward looking. One of the most segregated places just twenty years ago, South Africa is now receiving its strength and brilliance from all the races and cultures of the world that proudly call it home.

October 3, 2014

5

PRO-DEMOCRACY PROTESTS IN HK: BUT WHAT IS DEMOCRACY FOR THEM?

By Andre Vltchek

For decades Hong Kong has been a turbo-capitalist, extremely consumerist, and aggressive society. Its people are facing some of the most unrealistic prices on earth, particularly for housing...

What is it? It is not orange or green, and definitely not red! It has an umbrella as its symbol. 'That humble umbrella', as many people in Hong Kong are often saying.

But is it really benign?

We are talking, of course, about the 'democracy protests' in Hong Kong, also known as 'the Umbrella Movement'; the latest addition of the 'popular uprisings' promoted by the West!

At the North Point in Hong Kong, near Kowloon Ferry, a middle-aged man is waving a banner that reads "Support Our Police". On the photo, the tents and umbrellas of the 'pro-democracy' 'Occupy Central' protest movement (also known as the 'Umbrella Movement') are depicted in sepia, a depressing color.

"Are you against the protesters?" I ask the man.

"I am not for or against them", he replies. "But it is known that they have some 1 million supporters here. While all of Hong Kong has over 7 million inhabitants. We think that it is time to clear the roads and allow this city to resume its normal life."

"On the 28. September", I continue, "Police fired 87 canisters of tear gas at the protest site, and now this fact is being used in the West and here as some proof of police brutality and of Beijing's undemocratic rule. Protesters even commemorated this event few days ago, as if that would turn them to martyrs..."

"They are spoiled", a man smiled. "They mostly come from very rich families in one of the richest cities on earth. They don't know much about the world. I can tell you that the students in Beijing know actually much more about the world... 87 canisters of tear gas are nothing, compared to what happened in Cairo or in Bangkok. And in New York, police was dragging and beating protesters, even female protesters, during the endgame of the Occupy Wall Street drama."

Earlier I spoke to my friend, a top Western academic who is now teaching in Hong Kong. As always, he readily supplied me with his analyses, but this time, he asked me not to use his name. Not because of fear of what Beijing could do, but simply because it could complicate his position in Hong Kong. I asked him whether the 'opposition movement' is actually homegrown, or supported from abroad, and he replied:

> *"To answer the question as to foreign interference in Occupy Central, we would have to answer yes. As a global city par excellence Hong Kong is more than exposed to international currents and ideas and, historically, that has also been the case. Doubtless as well certain of the pan-Democrat camp have shaken hands with international 'do-gooders', a reference to various US or western-based 'democracy endowments' or foundations active across the globe. Taiwan may have a leg in. A British Parliamentary Foreign Affairs Committee seeks to wade in. But "foreign interference" is seen here as Beijing's call echoed by C.Y. Leung and with the letter holding back from naming the culprits."*

The protesters have an alarmingly skewed view of "democracy". Western propaganda has penetrated deeply. Spitefully, they regard Venezuela, Bolivia and Ecuador as "dictatorships."

Protesters may have some legitimate grievances. They want direct elections of the chief executive, and there is, in theory, nothing wrong with such a demand. They want to tackle corruption, and to curb the role of local tycoons. That is fine, too.

The problem is, that the movement is degenerating into a Beijing bashing mission, happily supported by both Western and local (pro-business and pro-Western) mass media.

Several students that I spoke to, at Admiralty and Mong Kok sites, did not even bother to hide their hatred towards the Communist system, and towards the government in Beijing. All of them were denying crimes that are being committed by Western nations, all over the world, or they were simply not aware of them. 'Democracy' to them means clearly one and only thing – the system or call it regime, that is being defined, promoted and exported by the West.

"China is surely on the right side of the history", I tried, at Admiralty, when I met protesters on the 31th October. "Together with Russia and Latin America it is standing against the brutal Western interventions worldwide and against Western propaganda."

I was given looks of bewilderment, outrage and wrath.

I asked students what do they think about Venezuela, Bolivia, or Ecuador?

"Dictatorships", they replied, readily and with spite.

I asked them about Bangkok and those 'pro-democracy movements and demonstrations' conducted against the democratically elected government; demonstrations that led to the coup performed by the elites and the army on behalf of the West.

I asked about 'pro-democracy' demonstrations against democratically elected President Morsi in Egypt, and about yet another military and pro-Western coup that brought army back to power. In Egypt, several thousand people died in the process. The West and Israel rejoiced, discreetly.

But the Hong Kong students 'fighting' for democracy knew absolutely nothing about Thailand or derailment of the Arab Spring.

They also could not make any coherent statements about Syria or Iraq.

I asked about Russia and Ukraine. With those topics they were familiar, perfectly. I immediately received quotes as if they were picked directly from the Western mass media: "Russia is antagonizing the world... It occupied Crimea and is sending troops to Ukraine, after shooting down Malaysian airliner..."

Back to Hong Kong and China, two girls, protesters, at Admiralty, clarified their point:

> *"We want true democracy; we want rights to nominate and to elect our leaders. Local leader now is a puppet. We hate communism. We don't want dictatorship like in China."*

I asked what do they really want? They kept repeating

"democracy".

"What about those hundreds of millions that China raised from misery? What about China's determined stand against Western imperialism? What about its anti-corruption drive? What about BRICS? What about its attempt to rejuvenate socialism through free medical care, education, subsidized culture, transportation and mixed/planned economy?"

Is there anything good, anything at all, that China, the biggest and the most successful socialist country on earth, is doing?

Brian, a student at Mong Kok, explained:

> *"We want to express our views and elect our own leader. It is now dictatorship in China. They chose the committee to elect our leader. We want to have our own true democracy. Our model is Western democracy."*

I asked at both protest sites about brutality of British colonialism. I received no reply. Then I noticed quotes by Winston Churchill, a self-proclaimed racist and a man who never bothered to hide his spite for non-white, non-Western people. But here, Churchill was considered to be one of the champions of democracy; his quotes glued to countless walls.

Then I noticed 'John Lennon Wall, with the cliché-quotes like': *"You may say I'm a dreamer, but I'm not the only one"*.

The Hong Kong protest movement reeks of upper middle class bourgeois consciousness, including its cloying cheap sentimentality and unexamined worshipping of Western "heroes", like Churchill.

What exactly were they dreaming about, I was not told. All I saw were only those omnipresent banalities about 'democracy' and 'freedom'.

There were Union Jacks all over the place, too, and I even spotted two English bulldogs; extremely cute creatures, I have to admit, but explaining nothing about the aspirations of the protesters.

While hardly anyone speaks English here, anymore, all cultural, ideological and propaganda symbols at the demonstrations and the 'occupy' sites, were somehow related to the West.

And then, on the 29 September, in the evening, near Admiralty, I spotted a group of Westerners, shouting and getting ready for 'something big'.

I approached one of them; his name was John and he came from Australia:

> *"I have lived in Hong Kong for quite some time. Tonight we organized a run from here to Aberdeen, Pok Fu Lam, and back here, to support the Umbrella Movement. Several foreigners that are participating in this have lived in HK for some time, too."*

I wondered whether this could illustrate the lack of freedom and Beijing heavy-handedness?

I tried to imagine what would happen under the same circumstances, in the client states of Washington, London and Paris, in the countries that are promoted by the West as 'vibrant democracies'.

What would happen to me, if I would decide to organize or join a marathon in Nairobi, Kenya, protesting against Kenyan occupation of Somalia or against bullying of the Swahili/Muslim coast? What would they do to me, if, as a foreigner, I would trigger a run in the center of Jakarta, demanding more freedom for Papua!

Thinking that I am losing my marbles and with it, objectivity, I texted a diplomat based in Nairobi. "Wouldn't they deport me?" I was asking. "Wouldn't they see it as interference in the internal affairs of the country?"

"They would deport you" the answer arrived almost instantly. "But before that, you would rot for quite some time in a very unsavory detention [spot]".

I thought so...

In the meantime, protests are causing chaos; dramatically increasing commuting time and damaging businesses.

Even the great number of Hong Kong professionals now wants protestors off the streets.

The *South China Morning Post*, reported on October 29, 2014:

> *"Protesters criticized by Bar for flouting court orders, as doctors sign petition to end sit-ins."*

But some people actually see demands as genuine and legitimate.My friend, Mr. Basil Fernando, head of the Asian Human Rights Commission (AHRC), wrote to me:

> *"As for Hong Kong protests, they are very genuine local protests over serious local concerns. People of Hong Kong in their recent history acquired many rights, which people in other Asian countries have only in name, but not in real life. Reason is independent and functioning public institutions. The beginning of them can be traced to the Independent Commission Against Corruption (ICAC), which started in 1974. It was a success and as a result, Hong Kong is quite a bribery and corruption free society. Having lived 25 years [in there] I can confirm that.*
>
> *People have genuine fear of losing these and that is why they want a greater say, to elect the Chief executive. This is a genuine local movement with limited political objectives."*

But one week later, when Basil and I met, face-to-face, in Hong Kong, he admitted:

> *"Many students in Hong Kong are uninformed, and some are spoiled. They never had to undergo any hardship in life. This is one of the richest places on earth. Some kids are scared of China. Ok, we can say that some of them are reactionaries... But it is understandable; there are those whose families fled Mainland China, in the past... The parents and grandparents were feeding their kids with all negative things about the PRC."*

Few minutes later I am having lunch at Cafe de Coral, a local chain. A young man walks in, wearing a T-shirt, which proclaims: "Real Time NAVY. US Military Base."

In Hong Kong, it means nothing. It is not even a political statement, just a T-shirt.

As long as the city remains rich, anything goes. And it has been rich for many years and decades; under British rule, and as part of China.

The question is, if they don't care about politics, why do protesters block important arteries of the city, and for more than a month demand direct elections and 'democracy', whatever democracy means to them?

Or could there be something hiding underneath all this, and also, 'in between the lines'.

"We have also our own poor people" I am told by Brian, one of the protesters at Mong Kok.

The truth is that Hong Kong is not a social bastion like the neighboring Macau, former Portuguese colony. And, tellingly, while visiting Macau just a few days earlier, I was explained by several people that what is happening in Hong Kong, could never happen there, because in Macau, people feel 'very close to Beijing', have closer ties with PRC, and feel more satisfied with their lives'.

Hong Kong, for decades, is a turbo-capitalist, extremely consumerist, and aggressive society. Its people are facing some of the most unrealistic prices on earth, particularly for housing. It is not at all the land of milk and honey; it never was – under British colonial rule, or now.

There is also great frustration over losing that 'uniqueness' and the cutting edge. Several Mainland Chinese urban centers are now becoming more attractive, with greater cultural life, bigger parks, more daring architecture, and more extensive public transportation. Quick trip to Shenzhen or Guangzhou, Beijing or Shanghai, and it becomes clear where the future and vibrancy and optimism really are.

It is likely the recent protests are ventilating the general frustration of many Hong Kong residents, not only with Beijing, but also, or mainly, with Hong Kong itself.

Lacking ideology and political awareness, and for decades being bombarded with Western anti-Communist and anti-socialist propaganda, protesters simply blame Beijing for everything, even for what they should be blaming its own extreme capitalist system.

There are some exceptions. At the protest sites, there are several small groups demanding social justice. Not many of them, but there are some Marxists and Trotskyists, even urban anarchists.

My academic colleague remarked:

> *"Their agenda is professed democracy and direct elections of the chief executive, but the social demands highlighted by Occupy Central cannot be ignored, namely extreme income gaps, property prices out of reach for the young, and generally an uncertain future..."*

But overall, frustration here is walking hand in hand with apathy. There is nothing revolutionary about this city or the movements it produces.

I used to drink, heartily, with Mr. Leung Kwok-hung (known as 'Long Hair'), who has a reputation for being the only prominent left-wing politician here. Long Hair is a member of the Legislative Council of Hong Kong. But being 'left-wing' did not prevent him from being admired and constantly interviewed by the right-wing press in the East European countries, as 'Long Hair' did not only criticize the West, he was also persistently trashing the People's Republic of China. I never really figured out where exactly does he stand and at some point he and I lost contact.

A 'progressive' professor of a prominent university in Hong Kong once confessed to me, in the wilderness of a noisy drinking establishment, and well after midnight, that her greatest achievement in life was to have had some lesbian sexual experiences, and admitting to herself that she was bisexual. That came just a few hours after I showed at her school my documentary film about Indonesian massacres of 1965, in which 1-3 million people lost their lives.

"Let's have dinner tomorrow night", I was told, a few days ago, by another lady academic. "But under one condition – this time no politics." I cancelled.

Perhaps unwillingly, or maybe some of them willfully, protesters are playing to the hands of the West, which is presently busy antagonizing, demonizing and bulldozing its way over all countries, governments and movements that are resisting its quest for global dominance.

For years, Western propaganda has tried to convince the world that China is actually 'not communist', not even socialist. A highly successful communist nation would be the worst nightmare to the Empire; it would torpedo Western dogma about the ideological victory over non-capitalist and non-imperialist forms of government.

So far, the propaganda has been extremely successful. If people were asked in Berlin, London or Paris, many would make ludicrous statements that 'China is more capitalist than many openly capitalist countries.'

By provoking China, directly and through its client states like Japan, Philippines and South Korea, the West hopes that the big dragon will eventually lose its patience, will snap, and consequently gain a reputation as a highly aggressive creature. That could, in turn, 'justify' another arms race, perhaps even a direct conflict with China.

The more socialist China becomes, the more the West panics. And China is becoming increasingly socialist: by maintaining the central planning system, by holding in state hands its key industries, by commanding the private sector what to produce, or by declaring that if the people would not be given free medical care and free education, the country would lose its right to call itself communist. The more public parks are built, the more high-speed trains and urban subway lines, as well as theaters and cultural centers, the more terrified the West becomes.

Now the revanchist students in Hong Kong admit that China (PRC) actually is a communist nation, but from their lips comes something extremely negative. And they declare openly how much they hate communism.

It all goes really well in the West, because China, together with Russia, Venezuela and Iran, are on the top 'hit list'.

Protests in Hong Kong surely came in at an extremely opportune time, for the Empire.

Although China is acting with tremendous restraint (much greater than the US, France or UK have shown towards their own protesters), it has become a target of yet another smear campaign in the Western mass media outlets.

Even if the Hong Kong protesters had only one goal, which is direct elections of their top executive, this is not the way to accomplish it.

Bringing out dirty laundry, when China, together with other BRICS countries is facing intimidations and direct provocations, is not going to evoke much sympathy in Beijing, or arouse desire to compromise. These are tough and dangerous times, and everyone is edgy.

The mistake of the protesters is that some of them are attacking directly the entire Chinese system, instead of concentrating on local and practical demands. Or maybe, if the goal is to actually destabilize China, then it is a well-planned move, not an error. But it will and should backfire.

In a way, Hong Kong's 'Umbrella Movement' is doing to China what the 'Euro Maidan' did to Russia, or what the right-wing protesters in Caracas did to *'El Processo'*.

Willingly or unwillingly, the Hong Kong protest movement joined the network of the color and other 'revolutions' designated to destabilize opponents of

Western imperialism: those in Syria and Ukraine, in Cuba and Venezuela, in Thailand, Egypt and all over Africa.

When asked, many Hong Kong protesters say that 'they are not aware of that'. One could state that it would do no harm if they could get at least some political education, before erecting the barricades and 'unwillingly' joining the global battles—on the wrong side of history.

***

On the last nigh before leaving Hong Kong, I visited the Mong Kok protest site.

It was tense, but not because police would be bothering to intervene and clean the streets, but because many protesters had been drinking. Stench of alcohol was felt at the 'frontline', near the barricade that was separating protesters from police.

"Any developments?" I asked one of the cops.

"Nothing", he replied. "We are not supposed to do anything."

"How do you feel about all this?" I asked him, frankly.

"I am not supposed to say anything", he replied. "Or to do anything."

But there was one squabble after another among the protesters; not a lovely site, a bit like on Maidan in Kiev.

An old man was yelling at the protest leaders, who felt embarrassed, trying to first push the old man away, then to ridicule him, publicly.

"What is he saying? I asked.

"Nothing!" screams one of the leaders, who did not look much as a democrat. He said his name was Benny. "Don't worry! You can just leave. We will take care of this ourselves."

"Take care of what?" I wondered.

"The old man said that he is going to call the People's

Liberation Army on us", someone whispered into my ear. "Then he suggested that he is going to fight the organizers, kung fu style."

It said 'occupied' on several tents. That was supposed to be quite funny, or witty, or something... Few meters away was a store advertising Rolex watches, next to it a massage parlor.

'A Rolex revolution', I thought.

The mood on those protest sites was truly sordid; nothing grand, nothing optimistic, nothing really 'revolutionary'.

For many long decades, Hong Kong has been busy becoming obnoxiously wealthy by serving faithfully British and other Western colonial and neocolonial interests. It readily betrayed, again and again, its Chinese and Asian identity, siding with the political, military and economic imperialism of Europe and the United States.

It showed no mercy towards the nations destroyed all over Asia Pacific. As long as money flowed, Hong Kong was in business. Money, money, money! Its wealth was often built on the suffering of others. The city was servicing anyone who ruled here, and paid, no matter how appalling were his pains for the rest of Asia.

Of course many of its citizens hate socialism, and especially socialist China, as it is fighting against Western imperialism, alongside Russia, Latin America, South Africa and other nations undergoing true social transformations.

Seeing great Chinese cities grow, all over the mainland, citizens of Hong Kong, or at least some of them, realize that one does not have to rob or to side with the brigands, to become wealthy.

Even those who are fully indoctrinated are subconsciously realizing that something went very wrong with their 'territory'.

As the waterway between Hong Kong and Kowloon is

shrinking due to unbridled development, as new and new malls where almost nobody can afford to shop are growing; as the real-estate is now out of reach for the great majority of the population, Hong Kong now has only two choices: to rethink its own political and economic system, or to sell itself even further, serve the mammon and then bark at the moon or at Beijing!

October 31, 2014

6

The Anti-Socialist Western Left

DO WESTERN LEFTISTS HATE SOCIALIST COUNTRIES?

By Andre Vltchek

The multitudes in Europe and North America did not really pay attention, did not notice, but in so many parts of the world, the Left was elected or it fought and won revolutions that propelled it to power. This is a totally different world than it was some twenty years ago; we are living in increasingly optimistic times, full of wonderful alternatives.

For the first time in centuries it seems possible to dream about a world that will not be defined by Western imperialism and colonialism!

In so many places, people are once again in charge of their countries, standing tall, building their cities and villages, erecting towers and bridges, putting to work mighty turbines, giving light to the poor, healing the sick and educating those who were kept in darkness, for decades and centuries, as a result of Western colonialism and savage capitalism.

Entire modern and ecological neighborhoods are growing up all over China; entire cities are being built, with enormous parks and public exercise grounds, with childcare centers and all the modern sanitation facilities, as well as wide sidewalks and incredibly cheap and super modern public transportation.

In Latin America, former slums are being converted into cultural centers, connected to the rest of the other urban areas by super modern cable cars.

Cuba, despite its extremely low (national) income (if measured in dollar terms), joined the exclusive group of countries with a 'very high development index', as calculated by the UNDP. That group also consists of other Latin American countries with socialist-leaning governments – Chile and Argentina.

Many things that would be unimaginable just a decade or two ago, are now considered normal. The Chilean President, Michelle Bachelet, has been elected for a second time. During the Western-backed Pinochet's dictatorship, she was held prisoner and brutally tortured. Her father, a military man loyal to Allende, was murdered. She was eventually exiled and became a doctor in East Germany. Ms. Bachelet now governs from the same palace – La Moneda – that was bombed to ashes during the fascist onslaught. Her country with only 18 million inhabitants, is an intellectual powerhouse, as are Argentina, Brazil and Uruguay. Chile is not 'purely' socialist, but it is implementing sweeping socialist reforms. Now it is so rich that tens of thousands of jobless Europeans are seeking work in its cities and countryside.

In Brazil, a lady, a former guerrilla leader, is lifting tens of millions out of poverty, while turning her country into one of the most important and loved nations on earth. It is one of the pillars of BRICS. Its intellectuals, filmmakers, and writers, are stirring emotions and giving birth to dreams about a much better world.

It is all thoroughly breathtaking, if one really pays attention, if one is there, if one goes out of his or her way to follow the events!

In South Africa, formerly hopeless slums are now full of life and hope, and initiatives, many connected by modern bus lanes and trains. They have stadiums, malls and fitness centers, modern hospitals and schools. By many measures, socialist South Africa is a super first world country, but still with terrible social problems. But each and every problem it has is discussed, openly and honestly, and thousands of impressive initiatives are moving this awesome country forward! As I wrote in my recent report from there, in South Africa, the African continent is rising!

Eritrea, Iran, and North Korea, are standing defiantly against Western embargos and intimidation. Their people work hard in order to maintain their freedom to move forward their own way, without taking diktats from the same nations that used to plunder and humiliate them.

And Russia, the mighty Russia that was once on its knees, during that monstrous government of the pro-Western puppet Boris Yeltsin, is now back in its saddle, standing on the side of many progressive nations, all over the world. It has forgiven a tremendous, multi-billion dollar debt to Cuba, it is forging powerful alliances with Venezuela, Brazil, and other left-wing nations, and above all, it is finally creating a grand alliance with China.

The world has never been so close to a real breakthrough – to true freedom.

***

But much of the Western Left refuses to acknowledge

that this is a great opportunity for mankind. It is because it feels left behind, humiliated by the tremendous defeat on its own turf.

It is because, despite all the rhetoric and political correctness, many of its members are actually chauvinists, and even racist. And many thinkers in China, Russia, Africa and Latin America, are actually aware of it.

The perception of the Western Left is that a revolution – a true and pure revolution – has to always come from Europe or North America. It is the West that has to liberate poor Asians, Latin Americans and Africans.

The Chinese revolution is 'impure'. Who cares that hundreds of millions, the majority of the country, are now eating healthy and nutritious food, live in good housing with high quality services, travel on modern modes of transportation, and getting a very good education? Who cares? It is 'not real communism', according to most of the Western left-wing gurus, or it is not even socialism, according to some!

Only the Western thinkers can define such things as 'socialism' or 'communism', not Asians, and 'Chinese socialism' means nothing to them; it is just a pose, a charade.

Several years ago, in Venezuela, I traveled with a very prominent Western intellectual who had been reporting, very well I have to admit, on the events that have been taking place in the Bolivarian Republic. One evening, after several pints of beer, we began talking about China.

"I hate China", she said. "I don't trust Chinese people."

I told her that I had travelled all over PRC and that I am extremely impressed and convinced that China is actually a very successful socialist, even Communist, country. She began arguing with me, passionately. I asked her whether she had ever visited China.

She replied, loudly and clearly: "I would never go there! I hate the place and I hate the people."

Her statement impressed me: at least she was brutally honest and it was all in the open. Racism against Chinese people is hardly ever pronounced in Western 'progressive' circles. It is there, inside all that biased set of 'analyses'. But it is never admitted. All is covered up by the 'objective criticism'.

It begins with "can you imagine what would happen to our planet if every Chinese were to have his or her own car and television set, like us in the West?" and ends with "The Chinese are as brutal as we are and they have the same imperialist tendencies".

While China's transformation into a middle-class socialist society is clearly a miracle (but more than a miracle, it is actually proof of the superiority of central planning, and of the general excellence of the system), perhaps the single greatest success on our planet in the last 100 years, the Western Left mumbles something about what has happened is actually not pure, that it is not really Communist, and that in many ways it is all extremely sinister.

It is because, from their point of view, only what is designed and implemented in the West can be trusted. They would never say so, but it is by now so obvious! That scorn is directed at the great non-Western societies of China, South Africa or Venezuela! That black sarcasm. That overall lack of support for countries that are truly trying to take care of their people!

To most Western intellectuals, one billion human lives that have become comfortable and full of dignity, means nothing! It is because to them, Chinese people mean nothing, as individuals or as a group.

Instead of talking with pride and encouragement about the enormous parks and green areas of Chinese cities, all that is repeated ad infinitum is Beijing's pollution, or the destruction of some 'hutons' – those filthy and unsanitary hives where dozens of families used to shit into one hole. That, to Western eyes, was good – stereotypical and typical of 'ancient' China, full of poor people. On the other hand, those proud, modern, high-quality housing towers with all their modern facilities, that are now the norm in all corners of the country, are 'annoying', even disturbing. And the fact that Chinese people want and have phones, good clothes, even cars, is seen as a proof of 'consumerism' and is used as an argument that China is not socialist, anymore! Because for many Western leftists, while they themselves have nothing against having villas by the sea, those living in the non-Western world have to be pure and poor, functioning like some sort of guinea pigs, if they want to be called Marxist.

No comrades! It is total bullshit! And by now it is clear who really cares for the people.

The goal of socialism or un-dogmatic communism is simple and clear – a better life for the people. Better cities and villages, less fear, more culture, education, dignity and yes, more fun!

And that is clearly what China is achieving, as well as South Africa, Venezuela and other socialist countries!

***

In the past few years, it has become evident that the West is ready to destroy everything that is standing in its path to the total dominance of the planet.

But suddenly, four powerful countries have refused to tolerate such banditry, and have become determined not to allow the global dictatorship to succeed. These countries are China, Venezuela, Cuba and Russia. There are more states joining, gradually, but this is the core.

The West has attempted to destroy Venezuela, openly and shamelessly, on several occasions, through orchestrated coups and by financing and supporting the 'opposition'; some believe, even by assassinating the President of the nation.

The smear campaign that was directed against Caracas became epic! I have made several documentary films for

Telesur, and I will never forget the words of one of the editors there, during the height of the anti-revolutionary riots sponsored by the West: "We are all working under the barrels of guns!"

It was a war then, and it still is, now. It is a war against fascism, and for humanity. Those who have not noticed should pay better attention.

And in a war, one has to choose sides.

The Western rulers also see China and Russia as the arch-enemies. Day and night, these two giant and mighty countries face vicious propaganda, smear and hate campaigns, provocations, and indirect attacks.

In Asia, the Empire's goal is to isolate China, to provoke and to challenge it. The West is literally sticking a hot iron rod into the dragon's mouth. This is common knowledge in the academia in both Philippines and Japan, two client-states of the West in the region. But it is a very little known unknown fact among the Western public.

So where is the mobilization by Western left-wing intellectuals, in support of China, which is clearly being threatened by the United States and its allies?

There is no such mobilization! Instead, some of the left-wing intellectuals are actually repeating, like parrots, most of the lies invented by the mass media outlets in both Europe and North America! All that nonsense about China having imperialist ambitions, in Asia and Africa!

If they would only bother to speak to the African people, they would hear that China is admired and seen as the hope, by the African majority. They will hear that "Chinese people are the first foreigners who treat Africans as human beings, even as equals", as I was repeatedly told at infrastructure construction sites all over East Africa.

But the propaganda invented in the colonial centers like London, Paris or Berlin, is actually consumed and trusted, even disseminated further by many from the ranks of the Western Left! The West plundered, raped and destroyed tens of millions of African people. It hunted them down like animals, and turned them into slaves. It has perpetrated countless genocides, from those in which 10 millions died during the reign of the Belgian King Leopold II, to the German holocaust against the native Namibian people, or the present 8 million murderous drive to secure the supply of coltan and uranium, in DR Congo, using their Ugandan and Rwandan allies, and their deranged armies. Somalia is destabilized, Mali; tens of countries are screaming and bathed in blood. But 'China has the same ambitions'!

And the Western Left is silent or complacent. A great majority of its members do not even bother or dare to travel to places where China is doing a great good.

When the US and Japanese air force flies over what China claims is its territory, when new military bases are built surrounding PRC, the Western Left does nothing, absolutely nothing, to support Beijing!

But when Russia was confronted, smeared and provoked, over Ukraine and Novorussia, there was actually almost immediate mobilization. It is good, very good, that there was one. But why did the Western Left suddenly opt for supporting the Russian government, which is actually not even socialist (although, by inertia from the Soviet days, it is still doing some great things for the nations oppressed by Western imperialism)? Why Russia and not others? Why Russia but not dozens of really socialist countries that are in great need of support?

Could it be that it is because Russia is a predominantly Western and 'white' country, while China, Venezuela, Bolivia, Cuba, South Africa or Eritrea, are not?

There should be serious and honest soul-searching, answering these questions. And soon!

***

These days it appears that most Western left-wing intellectuals are not even seeking power, anymore. They are comfortable with their feeling defeated and powerlessness. They appear to enjoy hopelessness and gloom. They constantly describe the faults and crimes of the Empire, but are unwilling to really confront it, in any determined way. They do not build barricades and they hardly fight intellectually.

It actually gets much worse than that: there is an easily detectable and open hostility from the Western Left towards most of the left-wing and anti-imperialist governments, all over the world, be it Cuba, Venezuela, Bolivia, China, North Korea, South Africa or Eritrea.

Those trusted and supported are only underdogs – those who already lost. That is the company in which many Western progressive intellectuals feel good and cozy.

The strength of those who fought, proudly, against the neo-colonialism and corporatism, and who are now actually governing their countries (or at least some of them are), is being ridiculed, at times even demonized. Nothing is good enough and nothing is 'sacred' for the Left in Paris, Berlin or London: definitely not Cuba and Eritrea, South Africa or China.

Again, that 'religious' search for the ideal movements, parties and societies!

It is like trashing the French resistance or Serbian partisans, during WWII, for not being fully 'democratic' or considerate. Of course they were not! Because there was no time to try being perfect: they were not faultless, they were not ideologically refined; they were single-mindedly fighting a war against great evil.

The Western Left is playing safe, even when it comes to world history. Some are (have for decades now) even comparing the Soviet Union to Nazi Germany, that greatest of brainwashing propaganda scoops invented by the chief propagandists of the Empire! They are actually talking about that very Soviet Union, which helped dozens of enslaved nations to attain their independence from Western imperialism, that very Soviet Union which actually, almost single-handedly, defeated Nazi Germany at the price of more than 25 million of its people; that Soviet Union which helped to build and to educate newly independent countries on all continents. Such comparisons are not only historically ludicrous; they are insulting and outrageous! If the Western Left needs to compare something to German Nazism, it should be the European constitutional monarchies and the Western 'democracies' themselves, as well as Western colonialism – all these institutions and political/ideological concepts have been destroying hundreds of millions of lives on all continents, for centuries, and until now!

***

Chinese intellectuals are indignant. I spoke to some, in 2013, when Tsinghua University in Beijing held a seminar on my work.

All that I am writing here is actually well known in China, South America and Africa!

The arrogance and self-righteousness of the Western Left is infuriating and the result is that there is very little of a working relation now, between the European/ North American left-wing movements and the PRC. Predictably, again, the Europeans will say, "Because China is not left wing enough". Rubbish! Ask Fidel Castro whether China is socialist. Ask the government of Venezuela, or South Africa.

The main problem actually is, that the Western Left is not internationalist enough, or not internationalist at all! And to me, and to so many other comrades worldwide, internationalism is the essence of true socialism.

What is the European Left fighting for? It fights primarily for the privileges of its own people, not for the privileges of the other people of the world. It cares nothing about who actually pays for that free medical care or free education, or for the subsidies that the European farmers get.

During the colonial era, hundreds of millions of destroyed and enslaved people in the colonies paid for all those palaces, theatres, railroads and parks of Europe. Not much has actually changed, even to date. Ruined West African farmers are dying so those French farmers get their subsidies, and drive BMW's and other luxury cars for producing or not producing, depending on the year. Hundreds of millions of destitute, overworked people in the neo-colonies, with no medical insurance at all, pay for those old people in Europe so that they can have free clinics/hospitals/social clubs.

And the Western 'Left' is fighting for more privileges for the European people. China is nothing to them. China or Vietnam... Just some annoying Asian nations that are 'taking 'their' jobs away'! Chinese or Vietnamese people are just the multitudes and are un-people.

While China is reintroducing free medical care, it pays for it by the labor of its own people. And so do of course Cuba, Venezuela, Chile, Argentina and South Africa.

***

The Western Left is narcissistic, undisciplined and arrogant, self-righteous and morally defunct. That is why it lost. That is why it has no spark. That is why it does not inspire people.

And the less people it inspires the more bitter it gets, more vitriolic.

It attacks the Soviet Union (post mortem), it attacks China, and it is buying into yet another Western propaganda scoop, that the Khmer Rouge were Communist genocidal forces, not a band of deranged rural desperados that came to power after the US murderous carpet-bombing of the Cambodian countryside. It attacks Cuba and Venezuela for being 'undemocratic', and with unforgiveable and sickening consistency, it attacks South Africa.

And even when China fights malaria in Africa, and

builds schools and hospitals, when it defends tiny nations in Oceania from total destruction, due to the rise of the ocean level by building sea walls and by planting mangroves (I saw all this with my own eyes, as I have lived in both Oceania and Africa), it is still wrong, because the entire world has to be shit, just because the West and its policies are! This nihilism is sickening, it is defeatist and it is having a vile effect even on the people in the West itself.

One has to conclude, with shock, that most of what remains of the Western Left is actually anti-leftist!

As a result, the people of Latin America, of Asia and Africa, feel much better in each other's company than with the progressive wing of their former colonizers, and they are increasingly seeking and finding inspiration in each other.

***

Russia has joined, too, in her own way. The more the merrier!

Almost 2 billion people are now living in or building their own socialist homelands. Each country is different in terms of culture and political models. Not one single country belonging to this group is perfect, but all of them are attempting to build a much better future for their citizens, and they are fighting against Western imperialism and fascism – for centuries now, really the only serious threat to the survival of our human race!

The world is now full of hope and optimism. The cranes are helping build and turbines are humming, new television stations and publications are inspiring billions to reject and fight the old colonialist propaganda.

It will be a good world in the foreseeable future. Maybe after some battles, but in the end, it will be.

Instead of preaching, the Western leftists should admit that they have failed, together with that aggressive Western culture, once described by the great Swiss psychiatrist Carl Jung as pathology – a culture that has been enslaving the entire world for centuries.

Then, they should go and learn from the countries where the people have won, countries that are fighting for the survival of mankind!

November 14, 2014

*****

Andre Vltchek – Christopher Black – Peter Koenig

7

ISIS, Destroyed Iraq, and the Kurdish State

'IRAQI KURDISTAN' – WESTERN FIFTH COLUMN IN THE MIDDLE EAST

By Andre Vltchek

This report is dedicated to Serena Shim. Because both of us, had been covering an almost identical story. Because she is dead and I am still alive. Because she was brave. Because even as she was being threatened, and scared, she did not stop her dedicated quest for the truth, and as long as people like her live, work, struggle and die for our humanity, all is not lost, yet!

***

The weather is gloomy; it is drizzling and heavy fog is covering the entire countryside. After leaving Erbil, the capital of the Kurdish Autonomous Region of Iraq, large and small military as well as police checkpoints appear;

like ghosts, on both sides and in the middle of an old, dilapidated motorway, which was built during Saddam Hussein's years.

There are huge Kurdish flags waving above the checkpoints. Small ones are attached to the bumpers of cars.

"We cannot slow down, unless the guards order us to stop", explains my driver, as we pass by the mountains of sandbags and the aggressive black muzzles of machine guns. "They have orders to shoot without warning."

We don't stop, but I photograph whenever it is possible, even through the windshield.

We are driving on the road that leads straight to Mosul, the city that was taken by ISIS, or as it is known here, in Arabic, Da'ish, in June 2014.

My driver is scared. The entire region is tense and this time even the city of Erbil (also known as Arbil) has not been spared. On the 19th of November, a car bomb exploded in front of the Governor's office, killing at least 6 people, and injuring dozens. Almost immediately, ISIS took responsibility, declaring their aim to spread insecurity in the Kurdish, which is pro-Western, enclave of northern Iraq.

As our car literally flies over the bumps and potholes, on the right-hand side of the road, stand huge oil-drilling installations and refineries that are barely visible, belonging to KAR, the Kurdish oil company. The flames of the refineries burn confidently, and there are countless tanker trucks with Turkish license plates, parked or driving all along the main and secondary roads.

We soon pass Kalak Town, also known as Khabat. This used to be a major checkpoint; this is where refugees from Mosul used to stream through into the Kurdish region, by the thousands daily, after the ISIS surprise offensive. There used to be posts of several UN agencies here, as well as staff from all sorts of NGO's, spies from countless countries, and armed forces wearing different uniforms.

Now – there is just the road and some desperate makeshift fruit stalls. The road has been destroyed, broken, much the same as almost the entire country of Iraq has: battered, bleeding, and hopeless.

Soon after, there is a huge checkpoint, which ends with a wall made of concrete blocks. Now that is the end of the motorway. All around are antennas and watchtowers, SUVs and military vehicles.

"We cannot go any further", says my driver. "ISIS is just a few kilometers away from here. Nobody can go any further."

But I have everything arranged. A few minutes of talking, a few hot cups of tea, and from the post I go in further, in a Toyota Land Cruiser, driven personally by a Kurdish battalion commander of the Zeravani militarized police force (part of the Peshmerga armed forces), Colonel Shaukat.

We drive towards the massive concrete wall, and as we get very close, I realize that there is a small tunnel wide enough for military vehicles. We pass through it, and then the countryside opens up, becomes open and wide, and we speed towards the city of Mosul.

The road is totally empty and eerie. There are a few machine guns scattered leisurely around the cabin of the 4WD. There is one under my feet; I actually have to rest my shoe on it. Mechanically, I make sure that it is secured.

A few kilometers from the post, and there is a huge sand wall, then, a little bit further along, another one. The walls cut across 4 lanes of the motorway, leaving only one narrow passage.

"These used to be border lines between us and ISIS", explains the colonel. "You can see how we are gradually pushing them further and further back, towards Mosul."

War mementos dot the highway:

"This car blew up; exploded by a suicide bomber", the colonel continues. "ISIS also detonated the tanker truck over there, as we were forcing them towards Mosul and the hills."

And suddenly, the road ends. There is a river and a totally wrecked bridge.

"Khazer River!" the colonel gets emotional. "They –ISIS – were all over this area. They blew up the bridge... They destroyed my checkpoint, see over there?"

It all looks desperate around here, totally ruined. But there is a new military bridge, a metal one, just one lane wide. A few fighters approach us.

"We pushed ISIS from here" I am told again.

"How far is Mosul?" I ask.

"7 kilometers", they say. "At most 10."

I don't think so. I have a navigation system in my phone, and it appears that we are at least 15 kilometers from the doomed city.

"And where is the nearest position of ISIS, now?"

The Kurdish military men take me to the provisory military bridge, and wave their hands towards the hills, SSW from our present position.

"They are there, on those hills. And they are still shelling us, day and night?"

"Mortars?" I wonder.

"Not those. Mortars would not make it that far. They are shooting artillery rounds – 155 calibers. They get that stuff from Iran."

"Are you sure it comes from Iran?" I wonder.

"We are told..." I don't ask by whom.

Next to the bridge there is Sharkan Village, totally empty, and de-populated.

The colonel comes back to me: "I will drive you through the villages", he says. "We will make a detour. The US bombed ISIS into the ground, here, on the 9th of September. Then we attacked, and recaptured this territory. We lost some people... We lost Captain Rashid... We lost a soldier whom I knew – his name was Ahmad. ISIS also killed many Peshmerga troops. Several soldiers died because everything around here was mined."

We drive straight to that mess: Sharkan Village, then Hassan Shami.

"This is the village of the former Minister of Defense", the colonel tells me. "This used to be his house."

Almost everything has been flattened, but the mosque stands. The bombs penetrated countless houses and there is debris all over the place.

"How many civilians died?" I ask instinctively.

"Not one", I am told. "I swear! We provided great intelligence, so the US forces knew what to bomb."

I wonder... House after house: all destroyed.

Soldiers of the Kurdish army keep emerging from the fog, as we drive through this desolated land. There are many different uniforms being worn here, but everyone salutes the colonel. Some even come up and kiss him.

No one lives in the villages, anymore. The villages were 'liberated', but destroyed. People were killed, or they escaped. Or maybe something else happened to the survivors: I do not ask because I know that I would not be told.

"Do you also plan to liberate Mosul?" I ask.

"We are not going to take Mosul", says the colonel at one of the stops and consequent military gatherings. Others nod in agreement. "We have nothing to do with that city... We just want to recapture what is ours."

As we drive back to the Khazer base, I am told that the

ISIS contingent, fighting around here, is truly 'international'. Recently, the Kurdish forces killed 3 Chechen fighters, 4 Afghanis, 2 Germans and 2 or 3 Lebanese.

I suddenly realize that the colonel speaks perfect English, something very unusual in this part of the world. And he only identifies himself with a single name.

"Colonel Shaukat", I ask. "Where did you learn to speak English so well?"

He gives me a big and bright smile: "In the United States and in the UK. I spent 2 years in the UK and 14 years in the US, where I was trained. I was also trained in Austria..."

"Where exactly were you trained in the US?"

"In North Carolina", he replies.

At the base, we sit on some rugs: with about ten Kurdish officers and me. Again, we drink tea. I pass my name cards, but the colonel only gives me his phone number: "No time for the internet, but come back, anytime! We like real war correspondents, here."

I interview two doctors in Mosul, a long-distance call, as we drive back to Erbil; the mobile phones are still working:

> "ISIS do not kill anymore", I am told. "Those who had to die are already dead. Now you smoke, and they cut off your finger. You work during the time for prayer, and they punish you. They have killed Shia Muslims, Kurds, and Christians... They had their list of the people to murder... Now Mosul is screaming from pain: we are out of medicine, milk formula, pampers for children, food..."

***

In the evening I have a cup of tea with an old scientist, a nuclear physicist, called Ishmael Khalil, originally from Tikrit University, now a refugee. We are in the ancient tearoom in the center of Erbil. He speaks:

> "All that I had was destroyed... Americans are the main reason for this insanity – for the total destruction of Iraq. Not just me, ask any child, and you will hear the same thing... We all used to belong to a great and proud nation. Now everything is fragmented, and ruined. We have nothing – all of us have become beggars and refugees in our own land."

Machko Chai Khana is a true institution: an old, traditional tea-room carved into the walls of the ancient Citadel of Erbil. This is where many local thinkers and writers gather; where they sip tea and play cards.

Now local intellectuals rub shoulders with refugees arriving from all over Iraq, and from as far away as Syria.

"I used to teach and to create, I used to contribute to building my country. Then Iraq was invaded and destroyed. I can do nothing, now... I have nothing... Now I only sleep and eat. And that is exactly what the West wants – they want to destroy our minds!"

As he speaks, Professor Khalil browses through his smart phone, showing me photos of his university, of his office and his former students.

"I escaped five months ago, after my university was devastated by ISIS. And we all know who is behind them: the allies of the West: Saudi Arabia, Qatar and others... I often dream about my country, as it used to be, during Saddam Hussein. The infrastructure was excellent and people were wealthy. There was plenty of electricity, water... There was education and culture for all..."

***

Now the Autonomous Kurdish Region of Iraq (with Erbil as its capital) is trying to promote itself as relatively stable and increasingly prosperous, 'unlike the rest of Iraq'. It has some of the greatest oil reserves in the world, and therefore attracts huge investments from the West. While the rest of Iraq is bathing in blood, decomposing economically and socially, this part of the country is 'not allowed to collapse', due to the strategic importance it has to the United States and Europe.

There are foreigners everywhere. As I find myself detained at a checkpoint, for an hour, just before the city of Kirkuk, allegedly for routine questioning and 'for my own safety', I see a convoy of several white government Toyota Land Cruisers speeding towards Erbil, with a Western man wearing sunglasses, sitting behind an enormous machine gun mounted on the back of the leading vehicle.

In a luxury hotel, the Rotana, I share an elevator with a British bloke walking barefoot, his filthy boots carried by a butler.

"I ruined my boots in the desert!" The Westerner confesses, smiling at his servant. "I teach people how to shoot, you know? Do you like shooting?"

"Oh yes, sir!" The man carrying the pair of dirty boots replies. He is most likely from Syria, a refugee. He is very eager to please. "I love shooting so much, sir!"

Foreigners are in control of oil production, they are 'dealing with the military issues', they run hotels, and they even work here as masseuses, waiters and domestic servants. Westerners are in charge of business, and there are Turks, Lebanese, Egyptians, Syrians, Indonesians, and people from the sub-continent, doing all sorts of managerial, skilled as well as menial jobs.

Turkey is investing heavily, and it has been building everything here, from shiny glass and steel office towers, to the brand new international airport on the outskirts of Erbil. It is Iraqi Kurdistan's most important trading partner, followed by Israel and the United States.

Turkey, a staunch ally of the West and of Israel, is also deeply involved 'politically'. Some of my academician friends in Istanbul actually claim that it is running almost the entire Iraqi Kurdistan.

Despite all that positive propaganda and hype that is being spread about Iraqi Kurdistan by the Western mass media, the place feels chaotic, even depressing. As any country or region of the world, which is under the total control of Western business and geopolitical interests, Iraqi Kurdistan is mainly geared towards the exploitation of natural resources and the neglect of its own people. While the income disparities are growing, there is very little done to improve the living standards of the impoverished, uneducated and deeply frustrated majority.

As a top manager (he is from an Arab country, and is afraid to reveal his identity on the record) of one of Erbil's luxury hotels explained:

> "We were young and ready for any adventure; we wanted to experience the world. And we were told: 'grab the opportunity and come to Erbil! It is soon going to be another Dubai! But look at it now, after all these years: the people are very poor, and there is no infrastructure. Basically, there is no drainage and the electricity is constantly collapsing: we have blackouts for long hours every day, and all the hotels have to use their own generators. Can you imagine, a country with so much oil, but with constant blackouts? They want to be independent from Iraq, but they have ended up in the deadly embrace of the foreigners: Westerners, Turks and Israelis are running their country. It is perfect for the rich, for the elites. Only the rich and corrupt are benefiting from the way this country is structured. There is not a single solid factory here... I am just wondering what they going to eat after they run out of oil."

I drive to the Erbil Refinery, belonging to KAR (a local oil conglomerate), located in Khabat district, at Kawrkosek town (also known as Kawergosk), just 40 km west of Erbil city. The army, police and paramilitary are everywhere, protecting the installations. There are Turkish tanker trucks parked all along the road. But as I drive just a few minutes further, up to a hill, the misery screams out loudly in my face.

I speak to Mr. Harki, whose house faces the refinery. He is indignant, like most of the common citizens:

> "All this is for the rich... All this is for the corporations

and nothing for the people. This oil company has taken our land. It said that we would get compensation: money, fuel, jobs... But until now, we have got nothing! I am very angry. Now my family is sick: we have respiratory problems, the air is just terrible."

A few kilometers further, away from the motorway, the entire area is contaminated with garbage and filthy scrap yards. All types of fences, some even high-voltage ones, partition the land, just as in the rest of 'Iraqi Kurdistan'.

In the town of Kawergosk, I see several Muslim women picking up some roots, right off the road, obviously in order to fill the stomachs of their families.

Not far from them, I spot a public elementary school. It is dilapidated, and extremely basic.

This Muslim community is obviously neglected, despite the nearby oil basins and refineries. No wonder: the pro-Western regime in Erbil is openly anti-Arab and pro-Western. President Barzani repeatedly speaks about the Eurasian character of his enclave, disputing that it has anything to do with an undesirable Middle-Eastern Arab character.

A school principal, erect, beautiful and proud, wears a headscarf. I dash into her office, and then slow down and apologize. I have only one question for her: 'Do any of the proceeds from those oilfields and refineries outside, end up here, in her school, in the education sector'?

Her reply is as short and precise, as my question: "No, nothing! Our people and our schools get absolutely nothing!"

But the number of Kurdish millionaires is growing, as is the number of luxury limousines and SUVs, as are the flashy malls for the elites, as are the armies of arrogant security guards, local and imported.

Like in so many 'client' states of the West, in Iraqi Kurdistan it is uncertain whether all those men flashing their machine guns are actually protecting the country from terrorists, or whether they are guarding the elites from the impoverished masses.

***

Not far from the oilfields, there is a massive refugee camp; this one is for the Syrian exiles.

After negotiating entry, I manage to ask the director of the camp – Mr. Khawur Aref – how many refugees are sheltered here?

"14,000", he replies. "And after it reaches 15,000, this place will become unmanageable."

I wanted to know whether all the refugees housed here actually come from Syria?

"They are all from the northern part of Syria; from Kurdish Syria. Almost all of them are Kurds; we have very few Arabs."

I am discouraged from interviewing people, but I manage to speak to several refugees anyway, including Mr. Ali and his family, who came from the Syrian city of Sham.

I want to know whether all new arrivals get interrogated? They do. Are they asked questions, about whether they are for or against the President Bashar al-Assad? Yes they are: everybody is asked these questions, and more... And if a person – a truly desperate, needy and hungry person – answers that he supports the government of Bashar al-Assad, and came here because his country was being destroyed by the West, then what would happen? His family would never be allowed to stay in the Iraqi Kurdistan.

***

Inside the magnificent Citadel, one of the longest inhabited places on Earth, and now a World Heritage Site, so designated by UNESCO, Mr. Sarhang, a curator at the impressive 'Kurdish Textile Museum', is as discontented with his country, as are almost all people in and around the city of Erbil:

"We are supposed to be safe, but just a few days ago, on the 19th of November, a bomb blast killed 6 people, just a few minutes walk from here. ISIS claimed responsibility. Now as you can see, nobody dares to walk around here, and the museum is empty. But that is not the only problem that we are facing. Look at the outskirts of Erbil: they are building brand new posh apartments for the local elites and for foreigners. A flat goes for around US$500,000! Who can pay that? Money that is made here is siphoned out, by foreigners and by our corrupt officials and businessmen. There is almost no public transportation here, and extremely bad infrastructure..."

Back in Machko Chai Khana, Professor Ishmaeal Khalil raises his voice, as the owner of tearoom blasts old tunes by the great Egyptian singer, Am Khalthom:

"Kurdish people are playing it both ways: they say one thing to the West, another to the Iraqi government. France, Germany, US – they are clearly betting on an 'independent' Kurdistan. The West wants to break Iraq, once and for all. They have already created a deep divide between the Shia and Sunnis, and they will go much further. Saudi Arabia, Qatar, Jordan, Egypt, Turkey – those are all close allies of the US and they are involved in the project. You speak against the plan – and you get killed."

He suddenly stops talking and looks around. Then he changes the subject:

"Today, again, there is no electricity in Erbil."

I recall some of the last words of the Kurdish Colonel Shaukat, uttered near the frontline with ISIS: "Our allies are the US, the UK, France, and other Western countries."

As if to confirm his words, some 40 kilometers away, at the gates of Erbil International Airport, there are jets that have just come directly from Frankfurt, Vienna, Ankara, Istanbul and many other 'friendly cities': Lufthansa, Austrian Airlines, Turkish Airlines, also some unidentifiable 747s.

***

There is an increased nervousness in and around the city of Kirkuk, which sits on tremendous oil deposits, and which has been for several months now, governed by both the Kurds and the Iraqi government in Baghdad.

"Some anti-Western forces are operating there, right now", I am told.

It appears that almost no one likes the government in Baghdad, and no one, except some Kurds in Iraqi Kurdistan likes Westerners.

It is no secret that ISIS was welcomed in Mosul and other places, by desperate citizens. But many, or most of the educated Iraqi citizens, see them as some sort of routine nightmare – an offshoot of the US and European client-movements, created and armed in order to destroy President's al-Assad's Syria.

All of this is an extremely dangerous game. Millions have already died over the last few decades, in all parts of the Middle East; victims of the barbaric Western geopolitical games, victims of the West's allies: in Iraq, Iran, Syria, Lebanon, Palestine, and all over the Arab world.

People like Serena Shim, a Lebanese-American journalist who had been covering these horrendous events for Press TV, get intimidated. If they don't stop working and telling the truth, they get liquidated, murdered – exactly as happened to her.

In the meantime, corrupt businessmen and local officials, but mainly foreigners, are stripping Iraqi Kurdistan naked, systematically.

And there is very little left in the rest of Iraq.

As has become extremely common, thieves and murderers are now calling themselves 'liberators' and good Samaritans.

Iraq is bleeding, but almost nothing of the truth has been allowed to penetrate the rest of the world, about the awful fate of this country once known as the cradle of our civilization.

November 26, 2014

*****

8

Eritrea

AFRICAN IDEOLOGICAL EBOLA FOR IMPERIALISTS

By Andre Vltchek

Qohaito is a mysterious, ancient, pre-Aksumite settlement in the Eritrean highlands, with several impressive monolithic columns rising towards the sky. It is said that right there, under the surface, exists another entire lost city. As you walk, the earth shakes, and somewhere deep below; you can hear the echo of your footsteps.

Just a few minutes drive from the columns, the plateau suddenly ends. There is a cliff and a breathtaking view into the deep valley. This place is called Ishka. And this is where thousands of Eritrean freedom fighters and civilians used to hide from the brutal Ethiopian occupation forces.

I set up my cameras right near the cliff, asks my local cameraman to roll, and then put the first question to a local mountaineer, Mr. Ibrahim Omar: "How was life here, for you, before and after the independence?"

"There were two separate lives", he explained. "The first one, before independence – that was harsh, brutal. And then came the other life, a totally different one, after we won. This is when our basic human rights got recognized and respected. The schools, health posts and roads were built. Everything was suddenly transformed."

I ask Mr. Omar for an example and he readily replies:

> "Before, a pregnant woman would have to ride on a camel, for long hours, to reach some medical post, in order to give birth. Many women would die during the journey. Now medical posts are readily available in this area..."

He thinks for a few seconds, then adds: "And this is what I call life."

As we drive back to the capital city – Asmara – we can see new roads, some paved, some not yet, cutting through the rugged, mountainous terrain. And parallel to them, new electric wires are stretching out towards the horizon.

In the car, I am thinking about what Mr. Omar defined as 'human rights'. Here, it is in direct contrast to what the expression stands for in the West. In the United States and in Europe, 'human rights' were created as an ideological tool, a weapon in the Cold War period. In Eritrea, it has a very simple meaning: feeding the people, giving them free education and medical care, building new roads, supplying them with electric power.

***

To understand Eritrea is not easy. But outside Asmara, everything is exposed; nothing can be hidden. Both poverty and the heroic attempts to eradicate it are right here, in my face. Farmers are working hard; many roads and electric grids are under construction.

But Western propaganda against Eritrea is so mighty, that often even I catch myself recalling its slogans, instead of concentrating on observing the reality with my own eyes. And I am professional: I have dedicated my life to uncovering Western indoctrination campaigns!

I film and photograph, in order to capture the truth, through my lenses.

After just a few days, a very clear portrait emerges: Eritrea; the African Cuba – country that stands on its own feet.

Eritrea – a proud and determined nation, which fought for a long 30 years for its independence, and in the process, losing hundreds of thousands of its sons and daughters during the struggle.

Eritrea – a country with its own egalitarian development model, working relentlessly for the welfare of its people.

Eritrea – a nation unwilling to sacrifice its citizens for the whims of the Empire and its corporations.

All this is in direct contrast to the propaganda that is emanating from London and New York, smearing the country, and trying to portray it as an outlaw state which supports terrorist groups in East Africa, oppresses its citizens, and violates all basic 'human rights'.

On this journey, on my search for the truth through the country which the West describes as perhaps the most hermit place on earth, I am accompanied by only three people – Ms. Milena Bereket, (Director of "African Strategies", an independent research and outreach think tank based in Asmara), by a local cameraman Azmera, and by a driver.

African Strategies is hosting me in Eritrea, but practically it is responding and accommodating my requests, arranging interviews and transportation to the places that I want to visit. We are planning together, working shoulder to shoulder. African Strategies is an independent research think-tank, established online in 2011, initially created to respond – virtually – to the growing demands of the Diaspora and continent-based Eritreans, as well as other Africans for fact-based and localized information regarding the Horn of Africa region, and more specifically Eritrea.

In a relatively short time, I have managed to visit three regions (zones) of the country, and I would have been allowed to visit all six of them, were I to have more time. As it is, in eight days in the country, I hardly sleep, but I encounter people from the mountain villages and from the port city of Massawa, I lead a roundtable discussion with several prominent young intellectuals, and I discuss politics and the development model of Eritrea with officials from the Ministry of Education and Health, as well as with former liberation fighters, and Eritrean diplomats.

All of my encounters are spontaneous. Eritrean people are well informed and educated. Our political discussions are open and often passionate. I cannot believe my own eyes, or more precisely: I cannot believe the lies that are being told about this country.

***

In the Hotel Asmara Palace (former Inter-Continental) I met a distinguished Ethiopian author and researcher Dr. Mohamed Hassan, a former Ethiopian diplomat in Washington, Beijing and Brussels, as well as an MP representing the militant Belgian Labor Party. He now spends a substantial amount of time in Eritrea, which is extremely close to his heart and to his ideological beliefs.

Without wasting much time on formalities, we began working together, almost immediately, filming and recording the discussion.

Dr. Hassan offered his well-defined thesis, right from the start:

> *"I am from the horn of Africa, and I saw the of Eritrea's point of view, even in the time of their struggle, which was not just the national independence struggle for*

Eritrea, but for the whole Horn of Africa in general. It is true that Eritrean people's strife for freedom had been denied and the Eritrean people had to embark on a very long journey to reach their independence... it took them 30 years to defeat the enemy, which consisted also of my country – Ethiopia – that was supported by many powerful forces... At one point it was the United States and all other Western countries... then Israelis supported special troops fighting against Eritrea... In 1991 the struggle ended, and we thought that we would build, all of us together, the new Horn of Africa, on the basis of equality, as brothers and sisters, with no differences between us and no hierarchy... 1991, I thought, was the best moment that our region ever had. Eritrea defeated the neighboring regime, and it was supporting revolutionaries in Ethiopia; people like us... There were great changes taking place in Ethiopia, then. We hoped that our economies would get integrated, and that we would establish new people to people relations..."

But it was not meant to be. There were huge changes in the world, as Mr. Hassan recalled. The Soviet Union disappeared and the balance of power had tipped to one side.

Mr. Hassan continued:

"Suddenly, in the United States, an officer, one of the very important officers in the Pentagon, wrote for a military journal called "Parameters", his memoranda and his understanding of what should be done to Africa. It described the US interests in Africa, and it divided Africa into 4 regions... One region was to become the Southern part of Africa, all that huge area from South Africa to Congo; the region full of minerals; that region that was 'very important for the US military and the US companies... Second region was Horn Of Africa, which was supposed to be integrated with East Africa and 'greater Middle East', which G.W. Bush was later trying to create. Western military bases located in the Horn of Africa were supposed to be ready to intervene in the Middle East and in other African countries..."

The 3rd zone was to become West Africa; rich in oil that

is extracted in order to satisfy demand in the North America. 4th zone was to cover North Africa, from Egypt to Mauritania.

All 4 zones had to be, of course, fully controlled by the West.

"Immediately after this document was published, Mr. Anthony Lake, who was then a national security advisor under Clinton Administration, published his new theory called 'Anchor States'. He also divided the African continent into 4 bases; defining 4 'anchor states'. One: South Africa, 'responsible for southern Africa, two: Ethiopia, 'responsible' for the Horn of Africa, three: Egypt for northern Africa, and four: Nigeria 'in charge of' western Africa. Very soon, Nigeria intervened in Sierra Leone and Liberia, and Ethiopia accepted its role as well, becoming the base for Western aggressiveness in the region."

Eritrea never sold out. It did not accept the imperialist's games in the region. It stood patently in the way of the Western domination of the region, because of its principles of national independence, non-interference, no military bases in the Horn of Africa, and its desire to build the new Horn of Africa... All this was considered by the big powers as 'negative', according to Dr. Hassan. This is why Eritrea was identified as pariah state.

***

How brutal, how consistent could the punishment be – retribution for attaining independence and for taking care of the people, for social justice?

Embargos against Cuba are a very good example of how far the Empire is willing to go. Or 'making the economy scream', under the socialist government of President Allende in Chile, who was obviously having an extremely 'bad influence', according to Mr. Kissinger and the corporate bosses, on the entire Latin America and even on the far away Mediterranean countries. Or maybe direct military attacks, as those that were performed against Indonesia during the reign of the independent-minded

President Sukarno.

Both Indonesia (in 1965) and Chile (in 1973) were bathed in blood, in the Western-orchestrated coups. Chile recovered recently, Indonesia never did. Cuba stood firm, at a tremendous price and with incomparable determination and courage.

And so Eritrea has been as well– standing and fighting against constant subversions, attacks, propaganda, embargos and provocations.

That is why it is often called the "African Cuba". Or maybe it should be compared to Vietnam, or to both. But to be precise, Eritrea has developed its own model of resistance. Its courage, its struggle, is its own. It is a totally unique place, and its people are proud to be distinctive.

But can Eritrea survive, while much bigger and richer countries, like Libya, Iraq, and Syria are falling one after another, simply because the Empire decided that they were giving too much to their own people, and too little to its corporations?

***

"We do not want to be boxed", I am told over and over again, whenever I ask whether Eritrea is a socialist country.

"Look at Amílcar Cabral, from Guinea-Bissau", I am told by Elias Amare, one of the most accomplished writers and thinkers of Eritrea, who is also a Senior Fellow at the 'Peace building Center for The Horn of Africa' (PCHA). "Cabral always said: 'judge us on what we are doing on the ground'. The same can be applied to Eritrea."

Most of the leaders of Eritrea, most of its thinkers, are either Marxists, or at least their hearts are very close to socialist ideals. But there is very little talk about socialism here, and there are almost no red banners. The Eritrean national flag is in the center of all that is happening, while independence, self-reliance, social justice and unity could be considered as basic pillars of the national ideology.

According to Elias Amare:

"Eritrea registered success, substantial achievements, in what the United Nations defines as 'Millennium Development Goals', in particular ensuring primary education for all, free-of-charge; ensuring women's emancipation and equality of women in all fields. In healthcare – it achieved a dramatic reduction of infant mortality, as well as the reduction of maternal mortality. In this regard, Eritrea is considered exemplary in Africa; few other countries have attained that much. So, despite all the obstacles that the country faces, the picture is positive."

"Eritrea continues on the national independent path. It has progressive view in building national unity. Eritrea is a multi-ethnic, multi-religious society. It has 9 ethnic groups, and two major religions: Christianity and Islam. Two religions co-exist harmoniously, and this is mainly due to the tolerant culture, that the society has built. There is no conflict or animosity between the ethnic groups or religious groups. The government and the people are keen to maintain this national unity."

This is in stark contrast to the rest of Africa. Ethnic and religious conflicts are plundering Sudan, Kenya, Congo, Uganda, Rwanda, Burundi and many other nations. Behind them often stand the old colonialism and neo-colonialism.

What Eritrea has accomplished is not some minor achievement, but an essential breakthrough.

Then why, I ask Elias, is the West so aggressively against the Eritrean path? He replies:

"I go back to Noam Chomsky's view on this: whenever a small country tries to pursue an independent national path, and does credible work on development, Western countries do not like it. They want their 'client states'. They want states that are submissive to the global capitalist interests.... All this is no-no in the eyes of the Western imperialist countries. They want neo-colonial regimes that obey the diktats of the World Bank, IMF, WTO, and so on."

***

The port of Massawa, is still in ruins. Ethiopia bombed this historic city to the ground, during the last stage of the Eritrean war for independence.

Since then, the reconstruction work is progressing, slowly but surely. And the port is now functioning well; it is modern and efficient. Cargo vessels are sailing to all corners of the globe, while passenger ferries are connecting the mainland with the Dahlak Islands.

Still, in this city itself, the horror of war is visible at every step. Many historic buildings stand like ghosts, with nothing inside. At the entrance to the port, there is a massive stand. I ask, what statue used to be placed on it, in the old days? "Haile Selassie", I am told.

We stop at the ancient coffee shop, which is known for its lengthy coffee ceremonies. Life is slowly returning to normal. People are drinking, and chatting.

Two ladies are cooking in front of their house. We approach them. I want to know whether their life has been improving.

Ms. Maaza, 55 years old, replies:

> *"It is definitely better than when the Ethiopians were here. Adults are being educated... Kids are being educated as well: all for free. Medical care is also provided, when we get sick. We are optimistic, hopeful about the future."*

Then she invites us home, for lunch.

Massawa is, once again, waking up to life. There is a new college (College of Marine Sciences and Technology), new international airport, and a free-trade zone.

Hotels are opening their doors.

The countryside is still dotted with war relics, with monuments, with destroyed tanks and armored vehicles.

What this country went through is mindboggling. The

fact that it is here, that it survived, that it won, managed to move forward, is itself a miracle. Or more precisely: it is proof of the heroism of its people.

***

In Asmara, I sit down for a talk with a senior Eritrean diplomat, Tesfamichael Gerahtu, a former Ambassador to the United Kingdom. But Mr. Gerahtu is not just a representative of Eritrea abroad; he is one of the national heroes, who fought, for long years, for the independence of this country, against all the odds. And he has been helping to build his nation, to this day:

> *"Eritrea is peaceful and stable because of the government's 'integrated development paradigm' – equal opportunities for all, with a special concentrated focus on rural areas and areas that were previously particularly disadvantaged. We are improving the general and overall quality of life... we are working on a cultural transformation that would lead to the creation of a 'knowledge society', where every person is an owner of the development process. We are trying to build cooperation based on dialogue, respect and ownership of the development programs and the process."*

I ask about the way the United States has been treating this country – this African rebel.

"The US pattern of behavior towards Eritrea over the years has been full of conspiracies."

He quoted the then US ambassador to the UN (later to become US Secretary of State) John Foster Dulles: "From the point of view of justice, the opinions of the Eritrean people must receive consideration. Nevertheless the strategic interest of the United States in the Red Sea basin and the considerations of security and world peace make it necessary that the country has to be linked with our ally Ethiopia."

I mentioned that the United States used and continues to use different pretexts and mechanisms to destabilize

Eritrea, to which Mr. Ambassador replied, passionately:

"They have actively promoted an economic blockade ... when that failed the US used Ethiopia to start the war in 1998 ... when that failed, it injected political dissent and tried to create divisions and cleavages along ethnic lines... when that failed, it used religion – Pentecostals ...when that failed, it actively began luring youth out of the country, even issuing visas, illegally, to people without the passports ... and then it turned around and accused the government of "human trafficking" ... when that failed, it actively pushed different neighboring countries to pick fights with Eritrea and also to encouraged them behind closed doors to encircle Eritrea out of IGAD ... It used the 'client' states to promote its own strategy for this region... And when that also failed, it used the infamous "terrorism" label to engineer illegal and unjust sanctions ... Finally, when everything failed, it used and continues to use "human rights" and "democracy" as a battle cry for intervention..."

***

"See what we are doing and tell us whether we are socialist country or not", is repeated to me, by many.

The more I see, the more I am convinced that the Eritrea's plan, its process, its revolution, are extremely close to what is being fought for in Cuba, in Venezuela or Ecuador.

But there is great pride and also great modesty, here. The Eritrean process is shy, unvocal. As a result, the world knows very little about this remarkable country.

***

Dr. Taisier Ali is a Sudanese who lives in Eritrea for 15 years. He is the director of PCHA. We sit down in his office, and try to analyze, why the Eritrean model is so misrepresented abroad, or why it is ignored by the Western mass media:

"When you talk about Eritrea, to the international community and the outside world, I think it is one of the

*most misunderstood countries on the whole globe...
After coming here, I soon realized that here, they have a
sense of purpose, a 'national project', conceived and
developed during the 30 years of struggle. We don't
have to accept it, but at least they are determined to
take their country from the point A to point B. They face
many challenges, but they have always stayed on
course. The rest of Africa is similar to my country –
Sudan – no sense of purpose."*

*"One disturbing factor in Sudan and in Africa in
general, is corruption. Eritrea is nothing like that. For
me it was always a reminder that if Eritrea could focus
on its development; bottom-up development, rising
from the real needs of its people, then why can't we, the
rest of us, do it, too?"*

I asked, "Is the national project and 'purpose', what is
actually bothering and scaring the West, the most? The fact
that Eritrea could influence, positively, the rest of the
region?"

*"The international community, imperialism, neo-
colonialism – they cannot perpetrate any society, unless
the society is divided, unless it is weak, and clueless
about where it wants to go; unless it does not have a
national project. The national project galvanizes all
natural resources, national actors, the human capital,
to achieve the level of development that would improve
the living standards of the people."*

"Like in Cuba?"

"Cuba is a very good example, yes! I also think that one
of the reasons for this misunderstanding of Eritrea has to
do with the self-reliance attitude of the party and the
ordinary citizens. It is simply not seen almost anywhere in
the world."

Mr. Ali says that many other countries have talked
about self-reliance, including Tanzania, but it was mainly
rhetoric. Eritrea did it. And when he speaks to local
comrades, they realize that with this approach, the journey
will take longer, but it will be achieved on Eritrean terms.

And that is definitely not what the West wants.

***

"Eritrea is not a neo-colonial state. Eritrea is an independent state. Eritrea does not host any military bases, any external forces. Eritrea has the vision, and not only for Eritrea, but also for the region. It is also promoting self-reliance and regional integration. It is also built on the ideal: 'let us use our own resources, and let us build our independence. It means elevating the life of Eritrean people, particularly those in the rural areas. This approach was considered in the West, as Chomsky said, as 'a rotten apple'."

There is Dr. Mohamed Hassan, again.

I ask him as well: Is it the main thing that the West is afraid of? A domino effect: an influence Eritrea could have on the rest of Africa?

"Of course", he replies. "Africa has some 50% of the world natural resources... Then consider this: the leadership of this country – they don't steal. They are living a normal life, that of normal people. No leadership in any other country in Africa lives like ours here. You go next door – the Prime Minister of Ethiopia who just died, left his family some 8 billion dollars."

I see the point: the lack of corruption could also considered be as 'very dangerous'. John Perkins explained to me, a long time ago, that corruption is one of the most effective tools used by the West in its quest to control the entire planet. It gives power to the elites, and it makes indebted and divided countries totally defenseless.

"Eritrea didn't attack anybody. But their views were considered very dangerous. And as you said, Eritrea is considered a virus contaminating much bigger nations," concludes Dr. Hassan.

A great Eritrean intellectual, Elias Amare, adds more, along the same lines:

"Eritrea has been insisting that its independence would be a genuine independence. It insists on self-reliance." It doesn't mean that Eritrea rejects direct foreign investment, for example. No. But when direct investment enters, Eritrea wants it to be on equitable terms. For example: Eritrea has huge natural resources. Gold, copper, zinc to name just a few. But it does not want to replicate what happened in DR Congo, or in Zambia. It wants an equitable partnership. Many Western countries do not see all this favorably. And that's the main reason for the hostility Eritrea is facing."

But Elias, the West is also constantly using the accusations that Eritrea is supporting terrorist movements all over the region.

Elias replies vehemently:

"That is totally baseless and false. First of all, because of the nature of how Eritrea gained its independence, the country is totally against any religious extremism. It has been actually targeted by Islamist extremist groups for many years. Eritrea is a secular state: it does not mix politics with religion. It had been proven by many credible investigative journalists, that there is no support for terrorism, coming from Asmara; no support for Islamic extremist groups, or for Christian extremist groups."

"Big powers do not want the Eritrean example to be replicated in Africa. I say again, Africa has huge natural resources. Big powers are now trying to grab these resources. What will happen if other governments in Africa were to try to follow Eritrea's example? It would definitely not be beneficial to great powers."

***

In the days that I am spending in Eritrea, I see dams and irrigation systems, villages working and the building of strategic food reserves. I see schools and medical posts, new roads.

I stop the car and talk to several girls walking on the new Domhina Road, some hundred kilometers from

Asmara. They are all from the 5th and 6th grades; cheerful, laughing, optimistic:

> *"In our village we already have an elementary school, and now we are walking to a secondary school, in a bigger village. We are good at school; we love English and math."*

The girls want to be teachers and doctors, but one resolutely aims at becoming an engineer, in order to build bridges, roads and power grids for her country.

Eritrea is still very poor, but it is neat, and orderly.

Crime is extremely low. I spoke to a Laotian eye surgeon, Dr. Soukhanthamaly Phonekaseumsouk, who has been performing cataract surgeries, for many years, in the deep countryside of Eritrea, where batteries that are charged using the solar system have been mainly powering her equipment. Eritrea is number 2 in the world, per capita, in terms of the use of solar energy. The Doctor explained that she never felt unsafe, living alone, in the countryside or in the city; she was never harassed.

The adviser to the Minister of Health, Dr. Ghebrehiwet Mismay, took me on visits to the hospitals in Asmara. The neat institutions were in shocking contrast to the monstrous hospitals that I saw in several turbo-capitalist countries like Kenya and Uganda.

In Eritrea, medical care, including medicine, is virtually free. Wards are clean; those hosting children are overflowing with stuffed animals.

The country has managed to dramatically reduce child mortality through vaccination programs and constantly improving medical care.

China has just completed several specialized blocks of the hospital in Asmara, including those for cancer treatment and for heart surgery. Several Cuban doctors are teaching here, and treating the patients.

New housing projects are going up in several parts of the capital city, as well as in Massawa and elsewhere.

The day before my departure I met 2 education experts from the government, Mr Tquabo Aimut and Ms Mehret Iyob, who explained to me, clearly, how seriously adult literacy is being taken here.

Eritrea is now one of very few African countries that will be able to meet many of the Millennium Development Goals.

At Independence, life expectancy stood at only 49 years, at the last census it was up to 63 (very high by African standards). In 1991 adult literacy stood at between 20% to 30% and only 10% for women. In 2008 it climbed to 65% and in 2010 to 74%, 2015's (realistic) goal being 80%.

We are talking about post-literacy and functional-literacy programs, but above all, about how democratic the system really is. Not 'democratic' in terms of the Western perception, but democratic in terms of the participation of the people in decision-making; in developing the curricula, and the blocking of projects that would bring no benefits to the communities.

Both ministries – those of Health and of Education – agree that while Eritrea is repeatedly praised by several UN agencies, including UNDP and UNESCO, very little of it is ventilated in the mainstream Western press.

***

For all these days, it has not always been a smooth ride. One evening I hold a round-table discussion with young intellectuals. We shout, argue: about socialism, about the fight against imperialism, about whether Eritrea should be more engaged; whether it should be closer to the socialist countries or not.

I film, photograph and record.

I am introduced to Mr. Zemhret Yohannes, Director of the Research and Documentation Center at PFDJ (People's Front for Democracy and Justice), and we have a long discussion about the turbulent Eritrean history and on the country's right to improve the life of its people. We talk into the night, until the tapes are gone and my memory cards are full.

During my last night I speak at a hall full of people. I address the local intellectuals and youth. And just few hours earlier, the ERI-TV interviews me.

It is all totally interactive; it is all one huge "process"; nothing is staged, everything spontaneous.

***

Eritrea is under fire; it is clearly on the hit-list of the West, because it serves its people, and because it is refusing to aid the Empire and the corporate world.

The West is using its toxic propaganda to the maximum, in order to smear the country.

It is also systematically boosting, financing and manufacturing 'the opposition', as it does all over the world.

Periodically, huge campaigns from the BBC and other sources of Western propaganda get pointed, directly, at Asmara.

For instance, at the height of the "coup" that never was (January 2012), African Strategies served as a defying force that helped patriots around the world counter the barrage of disinformation regarding Asmara and the Government of Eritrea spread by the so-called "experts".

That is the time when the Western news channels and Al-Jazeera were reporting on the 'rebellion' in the capital city.

My local camera-person, Mr. Azmera, summarized the event:

> "As the 'coup' was taking place, I was just leaving the Presidential compound, after working there for some time. I walked out, ate lunch... Then at 4PM I was called and told: 'Al-Jazeera is reporting that there was a coup in Asmara!' I just ignored them, and walked home."

***

After my intensive work in Eritrea, I testify: I came to my conclusion: the country is socialist!

It is socialist, if the definitions of Latin America were to be applied.

At the same time, it is socialist in its own way. It will never take any diktats from anybody: from the West, or even from the friendly countries of Latin America, South Africa, China or Russia.

Eritrea belongs to its own people.

I have worked in 150 countries of the world, and I never encountered a nation like this.

My first three days there were confusing. I tried to place Eritrea in a box, somewhere. Later, I just let go and smiled... And enjoyed the ride, so to speak.

What a beauty she is! And what strength, courage, and resilience she radiates!

As my plane was taking off, for Cairo, at 4 in the morning, I was humming some tune, happily. I was leaving behind a country that I truly could admire.

Inside, in my heart, I felt much richer than when I arrived.

If this was, for Western capitalism and imperialism, a virus – political and economic, social Ebola – then I was ready to be infected by it, gladly over and over again!

December 12, 2014

*****

9

2015 Will See Decisive Battles

THE EMPIRE IS CRUMBLING, THAT IS WHY IT NEEDS WAR

By Andre Vltchek

Last night in Beijing, I sat in a historic Szechuan restaurant with a friend who happens to be a Chinese diplomat. We exchanged some stories, ordered food, and then, suddenly, my throat felt dry and my eyes got misty.

I bowed and thanked her for the heartfelt offer China made to rescue Russia.

Just before leaving my hotel, I read the news on the RT:

> *"China's foreign minister has pledged support to Russia as it faces an economic downturn due to sanctions and*

a drop in oil prices. Boosting trade in Yuan is a solution proposed by Beijing's commerce minister.

'Russia has the capability and the wisdom to overcome the existing hardship in the economic situation,' Foreign Minister Wang Yi told journalists. China Daily reported Monday: 'If the Russian side needs it, we will provide necessary assistance within our capacity.'"

By no means was I representing the Russian Federation here, in Beijing, nor was my friend representing China that night, at the dining table. It was an informal meeting attended by just a few friends, nothing more.

Not to mention that I am not really, 'technically' a Russian. Yes, I was born in Leningrad but almost my entire life I spent elsewhere... all over the world, to be precise. And in my veins, not that it really matters; it is also all confused... there circulates an explosive mixture of Russian, Chinese and European blood.

But lately, to be Russian, to me and to many others, is much more than just about blood. 'I am a rebel; therefore I am Russian', to paraphrase Albert Camus. Or: 'I am Russian because I refuse to abandon the struggle.'

'Ya Russkii!' or 'Cubano soy!' It simply feels good, and makes one proud, and stronger.

***

The world is in turmoil. Like in the early 1940's, something tremendous is gaining shape, something irreversible.

Almost all of us who have been analyzing the Empire fighting against the propaganda and nihilism it spreads, and its venomous tentacles extending to every corner of the globe, know that 'appeasing' Western imperialism is clearly impossible, as it is impractical, and even immoral.

Just as George W. Bush (clearly borrowing from

fundamentalist Christian rhetoric), liked to say: "You are either with us or against us". Countries are now evidently put on the spot: 'they either accept the Western neo-colonialist doctrine', or they get destroyed, one after another, as were Iraq, Afghanistan, Libya and Syria.

No logic can help, no negotiations, no international mediation from the United Nations. The willingness to compromise is mocked. Appeals for simple human compassion do not move the rulers of the Empire even an inch.

It is clear that the Empire is preparing for the final assault. It will not back down. It will attack, destroy and annihilate. No idea when, but it will. And it will happen sooner rather than later, and with tremendous force.

Some would ask, why now? Why is there suddenly such a rush to fight the final battle for the total control over the planet?

The answer is very clear: for the first time disgust with the Empire is widespread, and worldwide. Many people are getting cured from blindness.

The mask of benevolence and rationality has been torn off by powerful media outlets based in the countries of Latin America, in Russia, China, Iran, but also in North America where the independent media is playing an increasingly important role. It is not even a matter of some elaborate 'objectivity', anymore. To get things right, it is enough to call fascism by its real name, as it is sufficient to identify mass murder perpetrated by the Empire on all continents!

The mask has fallen and what is now exposed is horrifying: the face of a monster, with blood and pus, a greedy grin and merciless fangs. It is a monster that is still in love with itself, unable to see its dreadfulness. It remains proud of its fundamental religious dogma, which it often doesn't even see as 'religious'. It dwells on self-righteousness, and at the same time, on its twisted market-fundamentalist faith that everything and everybody are for sale. It is a monster full of complexes – both those of superiority and inferiority.

It is not a happy monster and the people it produces are mostly miserable, lonely and scared. But it cannot change, it cannot back-up, it cannot let go. It would rather destroy its children and the world, than to admit that it went totally wrong, for years, decades and centuries.

Now many people have had enough, and some have even forgotten how to be scared! And the monster knows it, and it is actually scared itself, of those who are not scared of it.

The voices of the voiceless are now resonating louder and louder – we make sure that they are!

Except in the countries where the intellectuals and 'elites' have totally sold out, like in Indonesia or Malaysia, the horrendous deeds of the colonialism and neo-colonialism of Europe and North America, are finally being discussed, analyzed, and understood.

And the monster, the Empire, knows that it is the beginning of the end.

It cannot live as an equal. Therefore, it will fight its final battle. It will try to win. Or, it will try to destroy the world. Because life is not worth living for it, if it is not in full control; if its God is not in control, if it is not perceived as the enforcer of the divine manifesto.

***

When I visit a barbershop in Beirut or Amman, and am asked 'where are you from?' (It used to be a painfully confusing and complex question to answer, just a few years ago), I now simply reply: "Russia," and people come and hug me and say, "Thank you."

It is not because Russia is perfect. It is not perfect – as no country on Earth could or should be. But it is because it is standing once more against the Empire, and the Empire has brought so many horrors, so much humiliation, to so many people; to billions of people around the world... and to them, to so many of them, anyone who is standing against the Empire, is a hero. This I heard recently, first hand, from people in Eritrea, China, Russia, Palestine, Ecuador, Cuba, Venezuela, and South Africa, to name just a few places.

And that is why the Empire is now 'in such a hurry', unwilling to wait any longer, trying to provoke Russia, to bring it, metaphorically speaking, into yet another open epic battle, like the one that was fought in ancient times, on the thick ice, by Alexander Nevski.

The Empire is in too much of a rush, it is too scared to think, to understand, to remember, what every invader had to learn the hard way: Russia can be attacked and the Russian people can be murdered by millions. There can be devastation and fire; there can be ruins, tears and graves, graves, graves... Mothers burying their sons, and sons returning back home, to only encounter ashes. But Russia cannot be defeated. When the survival of the world is at stake, Russia stands up, enormous, powerful and frightening. And it fights as no other nation can; it fights for humanity, not only for itself. And it wins.

When such a moment comes, there is only one possible way how to defeat Russia: it is to destroy the entire world.

Are you ready for that, Mr. Obama? Are you ready for it, corporate America and Europe? Are you ready for it, Pentecostal Christians, Televangelists and other morally defunct beings?

Think twice. One more step, and you will find yourself facing two enormous nations, and dozens of smaller ones, ready to fight for the survival of mankind.

Your only strength is in your weapons of mass destruction, and therefore in spreading fear. And most of your arguments have no foundations in truth, only in deception and lies.

This year, I witnessed your deeds in Iraq, in Eritrea, China, Ukraine, all over Africa and the Middle East.

This year, somehow, it appears that you went too far, that the proverbial drop has fallen on Earth.

Stop! And stop torturing this Earth. Do not provoke, do not trigger yet another world war!

Stop, or there will be a fight. And you will lose, or we will all lose, but you will lose no matter what, because this time, Russia and China, Venezuela and Cuba, and others and many others, will not back down, anymore, while others will join.

***

Despite all of its terror, propaganda and brainwashing called 'education'—or news, or entertainment—the Empire is well aware that it is losing its grip on global power. And it is horrified, because it does not know how else to live, except with a whip in its hand. Planet Earth realizes that the ruler is sinister, ruthless and degenerate – some people realize it clearly using logic, others just sense it, intuitively. If there was really a global democracy, the people of our planet would throw the existing power structure straight to the dogs. But there isn't, there still isn't! Just look at the toothless, constantly humiliated United Nations. Almost everywhere, voting has become nothing more than an act of sticking a piece of paper into a box, and not much more.

***

The year 2015 is approaching. During that year, it will become clear who is fighting for the survival of our human race, and who is on the side of oppression, of imperialism, and of the Empire.

Next year, more and more countries will get destabilized or attacked. Perhaps millions of people will get killed, as they get killed every year, but most likely, this time, many more will. The 'opposition movements' manufactured by the West, as well as various Christian groups and other right-wing religious factions, will continue standing firmly on the side of imperialist oppression and market fundamentalism. The conservative petite bourgeoisie in the West and in almost all 'client states' will be battling to uphold their privileges. Fascist family structures and cultures will continue intimidating children and young people, preventing them from thinking, from rebelling and from living.

The Empire has many allies, all over the world, but most of them are of an extremely sinister nature. But their closest allies are always ignorance, servility and fear.

While our revolutions, the true ones, as well as the resistance and battles for a better world, are always based on knowledge, and in summary are nothing else other than an act of love.

***

The fight ahead of us will be extremely tough; it will be an epic struggle, involving great nation states, as well as groups and movements.

As the grungy Russian bear is being battered and provoked into a military conflict, great Chinese dragons are determined to form a protective circle, and this time, are declaring indirectly but clearly that they will come to the rescue of weaker nations attacked by the West. As even The New York Times reported:

> *"Mr. Xi did not mention the United States by name but took an unmistakable jab at Washington, saying, 'The growing trend toward a multi-polar world will not change', a reference to the Chinese view that America's post-Cold War role as the sole superpower is drawing to a close."*

The goal is to never allow Western imperialism and colonialism to take control over the planet again, as it mercilessly did at the end of the 19th century and at the beginning of the 20th, at the cost of tens of millions of human lives.

After centuries of plunder, rape and occupations, the

West has no mandate to govern the world.

After constantly justifying and glorifying its terrible deeds, brainwashing our planet into believing that it actually brings progress and rationality to the savages (the rest of the planet), it cannot be trusted with 'informing' and 'educating' the people.

That is why we now have independent media, as well as powerful state-controlled media outlets based in the countries that are not willing to succumb to European and North American propaganda and indoctrination.

These media and education institutions should and will redraw the entire historical and contemporary narrative.

Some examples?

Instead of glorifying the wisdom of Founding Fathers of the United States, we should recall that North America was created on the unimaginable suffering of the indigenous people, on Christian bigotry and forced conversions, on genocide, and on theft of the land. And that it was not done by some new and extraterrestrial breed or race called 'Americans', but by the same European puritans and religious hordes that had already murdered for centuries, all over Asia, Africa and the Middle East—not to mention each other.

'New America', both North and South, was predictably created on fear, violence, glorified superstition, and theft.

We should recall the slaves who were brought in shackles from Africa. Most of them died when traversing the Ocean, women raped and humiliated, children raped and marked forever, men with their dignity taken away from them.

Women and young girls were then chained in the fields, becoming sexual toys for those 'puritan' white farmers. Men and children, at least those who survived, were made to work days and nights, until falling dead from exhaustion.

All this done under the shadow of the cross, progress, and 'democracy'!

This is how America was built. This is the true story, the true narrative, of those 'great beginnings of the land of the free'!

And those theatres of Europe, cathedrals and churches, palaces and parks –far too many created from loot and genocides, colonialism and the Crusades, 'military adventures'.

This is how the regime, how the Western establishment always functioned. Rape is love. Indoctrination is education and information. Fear is belief. Slavery is freedom!

Do we want this kind of world for several more decades, even centuries?

I am not asking Parisians, Londoners or New Yorkers. I am not asking corrupt businessmen in Jakarta or deranged preachers in Kinshasa, top military brass in Kigali or the murderous feudal lords in Guatemala.

No humanist, no compassionate human being wants this sort of shit!

And for the first time, people are not afraid to say it, or at least to hear it, or read it!

I am not afraid to write this. Are you scared to read it? I don't think so.

***

The 'peace', we were told about again and again, is something that has to be achieved and upheld by all means.

But what kind of peace are we aiming at, and peace for whom?

The Empire wants a 'peace' arrangement, in which countries like Cuba and Russia, Venezuela and China, just back down, give up, and surrender. That is not peace!

We are asked, ordered, to live peacefully in a world ruled by European and North American masters, as some slaves crawling in filth.

Are we expected to succumb to the one and only religious dogma on which this entire racist, imperialist and capitalist system is built?

What a prospect, what a peace!

To them, to the imperialist West, peace means only one thing: unopposed rule over the planet.

If one fights for his people, he is a terrorist, a bandit. Then, it is a war!

The Nazis called resistance fighters in Ukraine or France, 'terrorists'.

The Israeli military calls Palestinian resistance by the same name.

The West calls any legitimate rebellion, 'terrorist'. Even MRTA in Peru was a 'terrorist group'; MIR resistance against Pinochet was 'terrorist'. The mainly social movement in Lebanon – Hezbollah – is defined as 'terrorist', and so is the entire proud Eritrean state.

Shia Muslims are 'terrorists', because the West is supporting Sunni monsters in the Gulf.

Che Guevara was a terrorist, and so were Fidel and sub-commandant Marcos. So was Lumumba.

To the West, to its lackey regimes and NGOs, true peace will come only if all natural resources were offered to the multi-national companies. All left-wing, Communist and socialist movements would be butchered, if Russia were to return to that humiliated and shapeless shit it was converted into, for a short time, under the sneaky and brutal alcoholic Boris Yeltsin, if China turned back to the Deng Xiaoping days of only providing cheap products, labor and almost no global fight against imperialism! If Venezuela was to supply crude and fuck its own people, as it used to, before the heroic revolution of Hugo Chavez, if

Cuba sold its women and booze and cigars for a pittance, before its most dignified revolution took place!

'Peace' would be, if billions of miserably poor people were quietly and un-confrontationally dying in their slums, while the capitalists, preachers and landowners several neighborhoods further were enjoying their private clinics and private schools!

But such peace will never again be accepted!

To fight for a better world, and for the oppressed, is like writing a poem.

War is when you plunder and rape, when you murder in order to oppress, and to control others!

Peace can only be based on justice, on social justice especially; otherwise it is not peace.

***

Russia and the Union of Soviet Socialist Republics fought for its survival on many occasions. Germans attacked it, then after the Revolution in 1917, the West Europeans and North Americans attacked, and then the Germans again. Tens of millions vanished defending the Motherland. Not one apology ever came from Washington or London!

China was forced open, humiliated, ransacked, including its capital city Beijing. Those who did it, the Brits and French, are now lecturing China about 'human rights' and 'freedom'. It is truly grotesque!

Look at the other nations that are now standing up against Western imperialism!

Iran, colonized, destroyed when it took a socialist path, and then infected by a Suharto-style maniac, the Shah, later attacked by Iraq, after the West had armed Baghdad.

Latin America – was ruined by colonial and neo-colonial expeditions, for centuries, reduced to nothing by the 'Monroe Doctrine', with death squads trained in the

US; trained how to kidnap and torture, and how to rape children in front of their parents.

Should we go on? Korea: tens of thousands of civilians were burned alive by US troops in tunnels. It was one of the most brutal wars in the history of mankind, aptly described by the most brilliant investigative journalist of the 20th century – Wilfred Burchett.

Indochina – 7 million were killed, bombed to death, or burned alive. Will we ever know how many? Vietnam is now an ally!

South Africa, Zimbabwe, Eritrea...

Yes, this is our alliance. Some 2 billion people who are living in the countries that were terrorized, brutalized, reduced to ashes, but that stood again and decided to fight, rather to live like slaves.

These are all imperfect countries, but countries peaceful to the core, countries that exist mainly in order to improve the lives of their men, women and children... and those all over the world.

And look at the other nations that are resisting Western attacks *against their sovereignty*– Cuba, North Korea, Eritrea – ostracized, surviving countless terrorist attacks, subversions, propaganda, and destabilizing campaigns. And then, when they mobilize, ready to protect themselves, they are designated, and defined as 'hermit states' or 'beastly dictatorships'!

Who forced them into a corner?

It is all twisted. Never again! Enough!

***

Do you hear that silence, after the US decided to 'normalize' its relationship with Cuba? We all know why there is such a terrible silence, don't we? Because we realize that, based on the centuries of US involvement in Latin America, this will be part of a new destructive tactic, a new attack: that Cuba may now actually be facing the greatest danger in decades! We don't know exactly what will happen, but we are somehow certain, that something very terrible will.

Is the West going to manufacture a 'Cigar Opposition Movement' in Cuba? Or is it going to be yet another color?

2015 will see many battles.

But the most important first step has just been made.

China made a great symbolic gesture: calmly, respectfully, but decisively. The message is clear: "You shall not be allowed to destroy others!" Not anymore.

The Empire is decomposing; it is sick, unsustainable.

But it is also toxic, and its illness is contagious. Its propaganda is mighty and its dogmas are violent.

Let us make sure that it goes away, crumbles, step by step, without destroying the world, without dragging it into WWIII.

Let us unite, individuals and nations, movements and parties. At least until the most dangerous period passes.

December 26, 2014

*****

10

The West is Manufacturing Muslim Monsters

WHO SHOULD BE BLAMED FOR MUSLIM TERRORISM?

By Andre Vltchek

A hundred years ago, it would have been unimaginable to have a pair of Muslim men enter a cafe or a public transportation vehicle, and then blow themselves up, killing dozens. Or to massacre the staff of a satirical magazine in Paris! Things like that were simply not done.

When you read the memoirs of Edward Said, or talk to old men and women in East Jerusalem, it becomes clear that the great part of Palestinian society used to be absolutely secular and moderate. It cared about life, culture, and even fashion, more about religious dogmas.

The same could be said about many other Muslim societies, including those of Syria, Iraq, Iran, Egypt and Indonesia. Old photos speak for themselves. That is why it is so important to study old images again and again, carefully.

Islam is not only a religion; it is also an enormous culture, one of the greatest on Earth, which has enriched our humanity with some of the paramount scientific and architectural achievements, and with countless discoveries in the field of medicine. Muslims have written stunning poetry, and composed beautiful music. But above all, they developed some of the earliest social structures in the world, including enormous public hospitals and the first universities on earth, like The University of al-Qarawiyyin in Fez, Morocco.

The idea of 'social' was natural to many Muslim politicians, and had the West not brutally interfered, by overthrowing left-wing governments and putting on the throne fascist allies of London, Washington and Paris; almost all Muslim countries, including Iran, Egypt and Indonesia, would now most likely be socialist, under a group of very moderate and mostly secular leaders.

***

In the past, countless Muslim leaders stood up against the Western control of the world, and enormous figures like the Indonesian President, Ahmet Sukarno, were close to Communist Parties and ideologies. Sukarno even forged a global anti-imperialist movement, the Non-Allied movement, which was clearly defined during the Bandung Conference in Indonesia, in 1955.

That was in striking contrast to the conservative, elites-oriented Christianity, which mostly felt at home with the fascist rulers and colonialists, with the kings, traders and big business oligarchs.

For the Empire, the existence and popularity of

progressive, Marxist, Muslim rulers governing the Middle East or resource-rich Indonesia, was something clearly unacceptable. If they were to use the natural wealth to improve the lives of their people, what was to be left for the Empire and its corporations? It had to be stopped by all means. Islam had to be divided, and infiltrated with extremists and anti-Communist cadres, and by those who couldn't care less about the welfare of their people.

***

Almost all radical rightwing movements in today's Islam, anywhere in the world, are tied to Wahhabism, an ultra-conservative, reactionary sect of Islam, which is in control of the political life of Saudi Arabia, Qatar and other staunch allies of the West in the Gulf.

To quote Dr. Abdullah Mohammad Sindi:

> "It is very clear from the historical record that without British help neither Wahhabism nor the House of Saud would be in existence today. *Wahhabism is a British-inspired fundamentalist movement in Islam. Through its defense of the House of Saud, the US also supports Wahhabism directly and indirectly regardless of the terrorist attacks of September 11, 2001. Wahhabism is violent, right wing, ultra-conservative, rigid, extremist, reactionary, sexist, and intolerant...*"

The West gave full support to the Wahhabis in the 1980s. They were employed, financed and armed, after the Soviet Union was dragged into Afghanistan and into a bitter war that lasted from 1979 to 1989. As a result of this war, the Soviet Union collapsed, exhausted both economically and psychologically.

The Mujahedeen, who were fighting the Soviets as well as the left-leaning government in Kabul, were encouraged and financed by the West and its allies. This horrible conflict, totally manufactured by Washington, was the "Soviets' Vietnam", in the words of Zbigniew Brzezinski, its principal architect. The Muslim faithful came from all corners of the Islamic world, to fight a 'Holy War' against "Communist infidels."

According to the US Department of State archives:

> "Contingents of so-called Afghan Arabs and foreign fighters who wished to wage jihad against the atheist communists. Notable among them was a young Saudi named Osama bin Laden, whose Arab group eventually evolved into al-Qaeda."

Muslim radical groups created and injected into various Muslim countries by the West included al-Qaeda, but also, more recently, ISIS (also known as ISIL). ISIS is an extremist army that was born in the 'refugee camps' on the Syrian/Turkish and Syrian/Jordanian borders, and which was financed by NATO and the West to fight the Syrian (secular) government of Bashar al-Assad.

Such radical implants have been serving several purposes. The West uses them as proxies in the wars it is fighting against its designated "enemies" – the countries that are still standing in the way to the Empire's complete domination of the world. Then, somewhere down the road, after these extremist armies 'get totally out of control' (and they always will), they can easily serve as scarecrows and as justification for the 'The War On Terror', or, like after ISIS took Mosul, as an excuse for the re-engagement of Western troops in Iraq.

Stories about the radical Muslim groups have constantly been paraded on the front pages of newspapers and magazines, or shown on television monitors, reminding readers 'how dangerous the world really is', 'how important Western engagement in it is', and consequently, how important surveillance is, how indispensable security measures are, as well as tremendous 'defense' budgets and wars against countless rogue states.

***

From a peaceful and creative civilization, that used to lean towards socialism, the Muslim nations and Islam itself, found itself to be suddenly derailed, tricked, outmaneuvered, infiltrated by foreign religious and ideological implants, and transformed by the Western ideologues and propagandists into one 'tremendous threat'; into the pinnacle and symbol of terrorism and intolerance.

The situation has been thoroughly grotesque, but nobody is really laughing – too many people have died as a result; too much has been destroyed!

Indonesia is one of the most striking historical examples of how such mechanisms of the destruction of progressive Muslim values really functions:

In the 1950s and early 1960s, the US, Australia and the West in general, were increasingly 'concerned' about the progressive anti-imperialist and internationalist stand of President Sukarno, and about the increasing popularity of the Communist Party of Indonesia (PKI). But they were even more anxious about the enlightened, socialist and moderate Indonesian brand of Islam, which was clearly allying itself with Communist ideals.

Christian anti-Communist ideologues and 'planners', including the notorious Jesuit Joop Beek, infiltrated Indonesia. They set up clandestine organizations there, from ideological to paramilitary ones, helping the West to plan the coup that in and after 1965 took between 1 and 3 million human lives.

Shaped in the West, the extremely effective anti-Communist and anti-intellectual propaganda spread by Joop Beek and his cohorts also helped to brainwash many members of large Muslim organizations, propelling them into joining the killing of Leftists, immediately after the coup. Little did they know that Islam, not only Communism, was chosen as the main target of the pro-Western, Christian 'fifth column' inside Indonesia, or more precisely, the target was the left-leaning, liberal Islam.

After the 1965 coup, the Western-sponsored fascist dictator, General Suharto, used Joop Beek as his main advisor. He also relied on Beek's 'students', ideologically. Economically, the regime related itself with mainly Christian business tycoons, including Liem Bian Kie.

In the most populous Muslim nation on earth, Indonesia, Muslims were sidelined, their 'unreliable' political parties banned during the dictatorship, and both the politics (covertly) and economy (overtly) fell under the strict control of a Christian, pro-Western minority. To this day, this minority has its complex and venomous net of anti-Communist warriors, closely-knit business cartels and mafias, media and 'educational outlets' including private religious schools, as well as corrupt religious preachers (many played a role in the 1965 massacres), and other collaborators with both the local and global regime.

Indonesian Islam has been reduced to a silent majority, mostly poor and without any significant influence. It only makes international headlines when its frustrated white-robed militants go trashing bars, or when its extremists, many related to the Mujahedeen and the Soviet-Afghan War, go blowing up nightclubs, hotels or restaurants in Bali and Jakarta.

Or do they even do that, really?

Former President of Indonesia and progressive Muslim cleric, Abdurrahman Wahid (forced out of office by the elites), once told me: "I know who blew up the Marriott Hotel in Jakarta. It was not an attack by the Islamists; it was done by the Indonesian secret services, in order to justify their existence and budget, and to please the West."

***

"I would argue that western imperialism has not so much forged an alliance with radical factions, as created them", I was told, in London, by my friend, and leading progressive Muslim intellectual, Ziauddin Sardar.

And Mr. Sardar continued:

> "We need to realize that colonialism did much more than simply damage Muslim nations and cultures. It played a major part in the suppression and eventual disappearance of knowledge and learning, thought and creativity, from Muslim cultures. The colonial encounter began by appropriating the knowledge and learning of

Islam, which became the basis of the 'European Renaissance' and 'the Enlightenment' and ended by eradicating this knowledge and learning from both Muslim societies and from history itself. It did that both by physical elimination – destroying and closing down institutions of learning, banning certain types of indigenous knowledge, killing off local thinkers and scholars – and by rewriting History as the history of western civilization into which all minor histories of other civilization are subsumed."

From the hopes of those post-WWII years, to the total gloom of the present days – what a long and terrible journey is has been!

The Muslim world is now injured, humiliated and confused, almost always on the defensive.

It is misunderstood by the outsiders, and often even by its own people who are frequently forced to rely on Western and Christian views of the world.

What used to make the culture of Islam so attractive – tolerance, learning, concern for the wellbeing of the people – has been amputated from the Muslim realm, destroyed from abroad. What was left was only religion.

Now most of the Muslim countries are ruled by despots, by the military or corrupt cliques. All of them closely linked with the West and its global regime and interests.

As they did in several great nations and Empires of South and Central America, as well as Africa, Western invaders and colonizers managed to totally annihilate great Muslim cultures.

What forcefully replaced them were greed, corruption and brutality.

It appears that everything that is based on different, non-Christian foundations is being reduced to dust by the Empire. Only the biggest and toughest cultures are still surviving.

Anytime a Muslim country tries to go back to its

essence, to march its own, socialist or socially-oriented way – be it Iran, Egypt, Indonesia, or much more recently Iraq, Libya or Syria – it gets savagely demonized, tortured and destroyed.

The will of its people is unceremoniously broken, and democratically expressed choices overthrown.

For decades, Palestine has been denied freedom, as well as its basic human rights. Both Israel and the Empire spit at its right to self-determination. The Palestinian people are locked in a ghetto, humiliated, and murdered—with almost complete impunity. Religion is all that some of them have left.

The 'Arab Spring' was derailed and terminated almost everywhere, from Egypt to Bahrain, and the old regimes and military are back in power.

Like African people, Muslims are paying a terrible price for being born in countries rich in natural resources. But they are also brutalized for having, together with China, the greatest civilization in history, one that outshone all the cultures of the West.

***

Christianity looted and brutalized the world. Islam, with its great Sultans such as Saladin, stood against invaders, defending the great cities of Aleppo and Damascus, Cairo and Jerusalem. But overall, it was more interested in building a great civilization, than in pillaging and wars.

Now hardly anyone in the West knows about Saladin or about the great scientific, artistic or social achievements of the Muslim world. But everybody is 'well informed' about ISIS. Of course they know ISIS only as an 'Islamic extremist group', not as one of the main Western tools used to destabilize the Middle East.

As 'France is mourning' the deaths of the journalists at the offices of the satirical magazine, Charlie Hebdo (undeniably a terrible crime!), all over Europe it is again Islam which is being depicted as brutal and militant, not the West with its post-Crusade, Christian fundamentalist doctrines that keeps overthrowing and slaughtering all moderate, secular and progressive governments and systems in the Muslim world, leaving Muslim people at the mercy of deranged fanatics.

***

In the last five decades, around 10 million Muslims have been murdered because their countries did not serve the Empire, or did not serve it full-heartedly, or just were in the way. The victims were Indonesians, Iraqis, Algerians, Afghanis, Pakistanis, Iranians, Yemenis, Syrians, Lebanese, Egyptians, and the citizens of Mali, Somalia, Bahrain and many other countries. Many of their homelands have been turned to rubble.

The West identified the most horrible monsters, threw billions of dollars at them, armed them, gave them advanced military training, and then let them loose.

The countries that are breeding terrorism, Saudi Arabia and Qatar, are some of the closest allies of the West, and have never been punished for exporting horror all over the Muslim world. The kept Western media naturally never mentions such an obvious fact.

Great social Muslim movements like Hezbollah, which is presently engaged in mortal combat against the ISIS, but which also used to galvanize Lebanon during its fight against the Israeli invasion, are on the "terrorist lists" compiled by the West. It explains a lot, if anybody is willing to pay attention.

Seen from the Middle East, it appears that the West, just as during the crusades, is aiming at the absolute destruction of Muslim countries and Muslim culture.

As for the Muslim religion, the Empire only accepts the sheepish brands – those that accept extreme capitalism and the dominant global position of the West. The only other tolerable type of Islam is that which is manufactured by the West itself, and by its allies in the Gulf – designated to fight against progress and social justice; the one that is devouring its own people.

9 January 2015

11

GENOCIDES, NOT WARS

By Andre Vltchek

In ancient times, even the greatest bandits such as kings and conquerors, deranged knights and simple arch-brigands, used to lead their armies into battle. It would be unthinkable for them to hide behind; it would be so shameful!

The Queen or a lady of his heart would embrace the warrior, or throw her scarf at his feet, or collapse in real or staged grief. And the warrior, often a nitwit and idiot, but a warrior nevertheless, would saddle his horse, salute his wife and his people, and go to battle, proudly leading his troops. And the chances were he would die during the battle. Therefore, he would think twice before leading his country to a war.

There used to be great pathos in all this, and also, great unpronounced rule: you want to murder, rape and steal, then be prepared to spill your own blood and brains!

Of course the priests and preachers hardly went to battles. While Christianity was behind most of the outrageous conquests and crimes against humanity, its leaders were living a safe life in tremendous palaces and villas. Only those who enjoyed the actual acts of torture and rape went to the field. But the Christian clergy almost always consisted of liars and cowards, and torture was done in safety, far from the trenches.

But the kings, their marshals and generals went, and often died, like soldiers, in a bath full of blood, puss and shit! At least they died properly, like their soldiers. They were brigands, but many of them were brave brigands, nevertheless.

***

Look at these cowards of nowadays, those modern-day crusaders, the leaders of the Empire! Where are their horses, their armor and where is their courage?

They don't even think twice about whom to fight. They can lead dozens of conflicts, simultaneously. Because today's wars are totally safe for them – they are like video games. Only those who are 'targeted' are at great risk. Attackers are akin to what Christians always thought God is: punishing, scary, spreading fear and demanding obedience, unpredictable.

So they turned themselves into gods, or demigods, along with their chosen race, culture and religion... and their self-proclaimed right to control and to punish others, those who want to believe in something else, and to live their own lives as they choose.

Yes, the Empire's leaders really believe that they have become gods. And now we only hear their twisted propaganda slogans, and their self-glorifying lies. They have become like those preachers and priests of the bygone eras: sadistic but constantly frightened, brutal and suspicious.

***

Mr. Obama, it is pity that we will never meet: that I will never have the chance to show you what your 'smart bombs' are doing near Mosul in Iraq, or what crimes the NATO-financed and trained ISIL are committing all over the Middle East.

But you have an inkling of everything that I would be showing you, anyway, at least theoretically, just as your predecessors were aware about all those millions of men, women and children, massacred all over Indochina, as well as in Indonesia, Latin America, Middle East and Africa.

But you are, forgive me for saying this, a fundamentalist, a Christian Western supremacist, as all your predecessors were. And a fundamentalist has extremely thick skin, and he is incapable of feeling compassion. A fundamentalist has to impose his will and his beliefs on others. He may suspect something, he may even 'know', but he is unable to convert this knowledge into respect and support for other people and for other opinions.

This is also actually what Western Christian fundamentalists converted Islam into – they kidnapped it and re-created it into a reflection of their own image. The reason was to have some worthy enemy to fight against, and to have some justification for those war games. And, most importantly, to have an ally in its most important war: against Communism, against Socialism, against social justice and against real progress!

A fundamentalist can easily become a killing machine, if he is not stopped.

***

The Second World War was really the last war in which Western troops were fully engaged, where they actually fought, although even then, whenever civilians could have been bombed, they were. Millions of women and children died during the carpet-bombing of Tokyo, Dresden, as well as the nuclear bombing of Hiroshima and Nagasaki.

The bombing of civilians is the true Western way of conducting war! Even the Japanese, I was told in Oceania, would always evacuate the civilians before getting engaged in the terrible 'final battles' against the US troops! Not to speak of the fact that Pearl Harbor was a 'surgical strike' against the US Navy, in which no civilian object was bombed by the Japanese, and as the old people who can still remember told me, repeatedly, the only civilian casualties there, were those inflicted by the Japanese planes that were shot down and crashed into the ground.

What followed WWII were not really true wars, anymore, but genocides; holocausts. All perpetrated mainly through carpet-bombing, through poisonous chemicals, later by enlisting corrupt foreign military, US-trained and financed death-squads, and most recently by using 'smart bombs', stealth fighters, cruise missiles and drones, as well as 'Muslim terrorists' (created in NATO camps).

In this way, new-era crusaders sit in their comfortable offices and war-rooms, and play games that are destroying hundreds of thousands of lives. After they are done murdering, they drive home, eat their burgers and watch sports on television. Long distance wars, as well as long distance killing, are like any other job: it is like selling insurance policies or cutting someone's hair.

Except that countless human beings get torn to pieces.

***

There is no ideology in all this, no risk, and no pathos. It is all extremely pragmatic. The Empire wants to control the world, therefore it murders, surgically, quietly and mainly without witnesses.

Those of us, who go to the places where all this is happening, now face countless obstacles, intimidation, or at the least, red tape. There is an almost complete media black-out. We go without any backup, without any cover, or support. We are out on our own. If we fall, then we fall – we have no organization to call, nobody to pick us up off the ground. We die, regularly. Selena, my colleague from Press TV died, covering the same story as I was: ISIL, and how NATO manufactured them. I survived. After that, someone called me 'an armchair revolutionary' and a coward... because I 'only' stayed in the Mosul area for two days...

Sometimes, we get humiliated, insulted by our own readers whom we serve faithfully, or even by those whom we considered to be the closest people on Earth.

Just as in ancient times, those few of us, are at the forefront, like Don Quixote, or like the scribe of Saladin.

We document all that is done to the world and to those poor people of the planet. We often work 8 days a week, 25 hours a day. Because there are fewer and fewer of us... Because what we do, has to be done, somehow; by someone...

***

And the Empire keeps on killing. And the citizens of the Empire have mostly no clue how it is done, or how a dead body really looks like. Or how the village bombed to the ground looks like. Or how it feels when some country loses all hope after being overrun by those button-pushing invincible boys sitting several thousands of miles away.

What cowardice it is to kill defenseless children and women, what a shame!

***

But it is not just children and women the Empire kills: it kills everything that stands in its way.

A few months ago I was almost killed by a unbalanced preacher in Surabaya, Indonesia. He said that he would, and he tried to liquidate me. These dudes are particularly malicious, as they or their ancestors, had already betrayed China after the revolution, and then they betrayed again, this time Indonesia, during and after the 1965 massacres. They have been serving foreign interests, they have been brainwashing people, and now many of them are going back to China, obeying orders from their foreign handlers to implant the 'prosperity gospel' and all sort of deranged Protestant crap.

Killing with bombs is not the only way that the Empire destroys entire countries. It also kills through religion, propaganda and ideology.

Its Pentecostal and Protestant implants have already caused great damage all over Africa, in Asia and all over Latin America, spreading corruption, ignorance and gloom. Only the strongest countries like Vietnam, China and Eritrea have stood firm and defined those religious inserts as weapons of imperialism and fundamentalist capitalism.

Entire nations have been ruined by the anti-Communist and anti-socialist propaganda, by dark nihilism and commercialism, by pop culture and by the manufactured 'opposition movements', those that are serving directly or indirectly the interests of the Empire.

All this has been done 'remotely' – entire parts of the world have collapsed without almost any Western lives being lost or even risked.

***

I have already survived several attempts on my life, by those 'proxy' fanatics. The latest try being by above-mentioned deranged Surabaya preacher and a businessman ('two in one' human projectile), and much earlier, by Indonesian intelligence, while being savagely tortured in occupied East Timor. I had been condemned to death by Peruvian military, camouflaged as Shining Path guerillas in 1992. I was captured and almost killed by that modern-day Ustaše during the Yugoslav War. I survived the Israeli shelling of Gaza during the Intifada, and all sorts of sniper and artillery barrages. And more recently, I survived the depths of an intelligence bunker in Goma, the Democratic Republic of Congo, as well as a Kenyan jail. Of all of this, the Surabayan preacher was the most toxic, the vilest... But even him, I survived.

All these were proxy attacks – proxy operations, all conducted by traitors, by the lackeys of the Empire and of its ideologies, and religions.

I survived, but others didn't. But at least those of us, who didn't, including Selena Shim (covering ISIL for Press TV) or Hiroyuki Muramoto (covering a murderous attack by the Thai military against 'Red Shirt' protesters in 2010 Bangkok), received some recognition. Millions, tens of millions of ordinary, mostly 'local' people, slaughtered like cattle, have never even been mentioned by their names in any mainstream reports.

***

President Obama was certainly perfectly aware of all those 'proxy wars' and maneuvers, for years and decades before he became the President of the United States. His father, a Kenyan economist, was recruited by 'Tom Mboya' (Thomas Joseph Odhiambo), then flown to Hawaii, indoctrinated/educated there, and finally sent back to Kenya, in order to steer his country away from the possibility of a socialist path.

His mother's second husband, Obama's stepfather, and an Indonesian officer, Lolo Soetoro was yet, another recruit and a traitor/collaborator, serving the West. When he met Obama's mother, he was undergoing training in Hawaii. Then, after the horrid 1965 US-sponsored coup took place, he was flown back to Indonesia (1966), and Obama and his mother followed him just one year later. They lived in the upscale Menteng neighborhood of Jakarta, where Obama is still remembered 'with love' by the children of other Indonesian anti-Communist cadres, as 'our Barry from Menteng'.

I have lived in both countries – Kenya and Indonesia – and can testify that both of them have thoroughly collapsed, socially and morally, as they have pioneered some of the most shameful models of corruption and unbridled capitalism in the world. Not one Western soldier has died destroying them. They were conquered, plundered and made into submissive client-states thanks to great planning by the Empire, and because of the tremendous cynicism and greed of local collaborators: the military, the religious clergy, the 'educators' and the business 'leaders'.

***

And so the drones are flying, stealth fighters are bombing, cruise missiles are crashing into cities and villages, and the collaborators with Western fascism are helping to oppress their own people, keeping them in darkness and in constant fear.

It has all been effective until now, but will not be, forever.

This system will not survive for long, because the arrangement is simply too appalling, and even the massive propaganda in the 'client' states, by corporate media and by private schools, that manufactures unanimity, cannot keep people from noticing, that something has gone terribly wrong, that they had been robbed, humiliated and fooled.

In stark contrast to the cowards sitting in their gated communities or in their 'war rooms', all great leaders of progress and resistance, from Che, Mao, Ho Chi Minh, Fidel, Chavez, Morales, to Al-Sadr or Nasrallah, always stood at the forefront, leading their people in the fight against oppression, for independence and justice. They never hid behind civilians, behind women and children. That is what people expect; this is what is demanded.

President Salvador Allende of Chile tried it the peaceful way. But when, on 9-11-1973, the military junta provoked by the war criminal Henry Kissinger, by ITT, by Chase

Manhattan and the Chicago School of Economics, as well as by several other institutions, sent its jets and combat helicopters against the Presidential Palace 'La Moneda', he did not run away to Havana or Moscow. Allende stood up, and marched towards the rockets and the explosion, towards his certain death. It is because President Salvador Allende was not a traitor or a coward. He was a Chilean man, a patriot, a socialist. And if his country, his beloved Chile, was going to die, to go up in flames that day, so was he.

Ask in the villages of West Bengal or in towns in Amazonia, whether the people want to be controlled by cowardly and greedy corporate tycoons and by the governments in Washington or Europe, governments that are simply serving those corporate interests, while hiding behind cordons of armed guards and security apparatchiks. We all know what the answer would be!

***

The world has almost forgotten what a real war is. But let us recall something: it is when two armies fight against each other, bravely or mostly stupidly, but fight. In a real war, each man in those trenches, rightly or wrongly, thinks about his city or his village, about his dear ones, about his girlfriend, wife, mom, children. Behind their backs are rivers and forests, beaches, mountains and meadows. For them, they are ready to die for, defending them.

But this, what we have now? The aggressor is defending nothing. There is just the hard back of a chair behind his back, and perhaps a few communication modules.

And those victims! How could they defend anything if they don't even know what, and when, it is going to fall on them? One second, and entire blocks of houses go up in flames. There is no warning.

These are not wars, but genocides! These are persistent, constant genocides perpetrated by the market, Christian, Western fundamentalists.

***

On 1st May 2004, when it appeared that the United States might once again attack Cuba, President Castro spoke in Havana, addressing then President G.W. Bush:

"You have neither the morality nor the right, none whatsoever, to speak of freedom, democracy and human rights when you hold enough power to destroy humanity and are attempting to install a world tyranny, side-stepping and destroying the United Nations Organization, violating the human rights of any and every country, waging wars of conquest to take over world markets and resources and installing decadent and anachronistic political and social systems which are leading the human race into the abyss."

At the end, Fidel declared that if Cuba is attacked, he would do what he was expected to do, and what he already had done on several previous occasions – he would go and fight! And none of us had any doubt that he would. But he had one regret, in regard to President Bush:

"My only regret is that I would not even see your face because in that case you would be thousands of miles away while I shall be on the frontline to die fighting in defense of my homeland."

Januari 22, 2015

France Now an Obedient, Cowardly Nation

THE COLLAPSE OF FRENCH INTELLECTUAL DIVERSITY

By Andre Vltchek

There are several machine gunners in front of the Charlie Hebdo building in Paris. These are cops, wearing bulletproof vests, carrying powerful weapons. They stare at occasional pedestrians in their special, revolting and highly intimidating way. Charlie Hedbo editors are well protected, some of them postmortem.

If you think that France is not as much a police state, as the UK or the US, think twice. Heavily armed military and police are visible at all train stations and many intersections, even at some narrow alleys. Internet providers are openly spying on their costumers. Mass media is self-censoring its reports. The regime's propaganda is in "top gear"

But the people of France, at least the great majority of them, believe that they live in an 'open and democratic society.' If asked, they cannot prove it; they have no arguments. They are simply told that they are free, and so they believe it.

***

Employees of Charlie Hebdo go periodically out of the building for a smoke. I try to engage them in a conversation, but they reply in very short sentences only. They do their best to ignore me. Somehow, intuitively, they sense that I am not here to tell the official story.

I ask them why don't they ever poke fun at the Western neo-colonialism, at the grotesque Western election system, or at the Western allies that are committing genocides all over the world: India, Israel, Indonesia, Rwanda, or Uganda? They impatiently dismiss me with their body language. Such thoughts are not encouraged, and most likely, they are not allowed. Even humorists and clowns in modern France know their place.

They soon let me know that I am asking too many questions. One of the employees simply looks, meaningfully, in the direction of armed cops. I get the message. I am not in the mood for a lengthy interrogation. I move on.

In the neighborhood, there are several sites carrying outpours of sympathy for the victims; 12 people who died during the January 2015 attack on the magazine. There are French flags and there are plastic white mice with Je Suis Charlie written on their bodies. One big poster proclaims: Je suis humain. Other banners read: "Islamic whores", with red color correction, replacing Islamic with "terrorist" – Putain de terroristes.

There is plenty of graffiti written about freedom, all over

the area. "Libre comme Charlie", "Free like Charlie"!

A woman appears from the blue. She is very well dressed; she is elegant. She stands next to me for a few seconds. I realize that her body is shaking. She is crying.

"You're a relative...?" I ask her, gently.

"No, no", she replies. "We are all their relatives. We are all Charlie!"

She suddenly embraces me. I feel her wet face against my chest. I try to be sensitive. I hold her tight, this stranger – this unknown woman. Not because I want to, but because I feel that I have no other choice. Once I fulfill my civic obligation, I run away from the site.

***

Fifteen minutes walk from the Charlie Hebdo building, and there is the monumental National Picasso Museum, and dozens of art galleries. I make sure to visit at least 50 of them.

I want to know all about that freedom of expression that the French public is so righteously longing for and 'defending'!

But what I see is endless pop. I see some broken window of a gallery and a sign: "You broke my art". It is supposed to be an artwork itself.

Galleries exhibit endless lines and squares, all imaginable shapes and colors.

In several galleries, I observe abstract, Pollock-style 'art'.

I ask owners of the galleries, whether they know about some exhibitions that are concentrating on the plight of tens of thousands of homeless people who are barely surviving the harsh Parisian winter. Are there painters and photographers exposing monstrous slums under the highway and railroad bridges? And what about French military and intelligence adventures in Africa, those that are ruining millions of human lives? Are there artists who are fighting against France becoming one of the leading centers of the Empire?

I am given outraged looks, or disgusted looks. Some looks are clearly alarmed. Gallery owners have no clue what am I talking about.

At the Picasso Museum, the mood is clearly that of 'institutionalism'. Here, one would never guess that Pablo Picasso was a Communist, and deeply engaged painter and sculptor. One after another, groups of German tourists consisting mainly of senior citizens are passing through well-marked halls, accompanied by tour guides.

I don't feel anything here. This museum is not inspiring me, it is castrating! The longer I stay here, the more I feel that my revolutionary zeal is evaporating.

I dash to the office and summon a junior curator.

I tell her all that I think about this museum and about those commercial galleries that are surrounding it.

"Those millions who were marching and writing messages around Charlie Hedbo... What do they mean by 'freedom'? There seems to be nothing 'free' in France, anymore. Media is controlled, and art has just became some sort of brainless pop."

She has nothing to say. "I don't know", she finally replied. "Painters are painting what people want to buy."

"Is that so?" I asked.

I mention "798" in Beijing, where hundreds of galleries are deeply political.

"In oppressed societies, art tends to be more engaged", she says.

I tell her what I think. I tell her that to me, and to many creative people I met in China, Beijing feels much more free, much less brainwasher or oppressed, than Paris. She looks at me in horror, then with that typical European sarcasm. She thinks I am provoking, trying to be funny. I cannot mean what I say. It is clear, isn't it, that French artists are superior, that Western culture is the greatest. Who could doubt it?

I give her my card. She refuses to give me her name.

I leave in disgust, as I recently left in disgust the Peggy Guggenheim Collection in Venice.

At one point I walk into a cafe, to drink a cup of coffee and a glass of mineral water.

A man and his enormous dog walk in. Both park at the bar, standing. A dog puts its front paws on the bar table. They both have a beer: the man from a glass, his dog from a saucer. A few minutes later, they pay and leave.

I scribble into my notepad: "In France, dogs are free to take their beer in cafes."

***

In the same neighborhood, I rediscover an enormous National Archive, a beautiful group of buildings with gardens and parks all around.

The place is holding a huge exhibition: on how France collaborated with the Nazi Germany during the WWII. The retrospect is grand and complete: with images and texts, with film showings.

For the first time in days, I am impressed. It all feels very familiar, intimately familiar!

***

At night I found myself in that enormous new Philharmonic, at the outskirts of Paris, near Porte de Pantin. I managed to smuggle myself to the invitation-only-opening of an enormous exhibition dedicated to French composer, conductor and writer – Pierre Boulez. That same Pierre Boulez who has been promoting, for ages, the idea of a public sector taking over French classic music scene!

Nobody protested at the exhibition, and I did not hear any jokes directed at Pierre Boulez. It was all brilliantly orchestrated. Great respect for the establishment cultural figure, for the cultural apparatchik!

I heard a technically brilliant concert of contemporary classical music, with new instruments being used.

But nowhere, in any of those tremendous spaces of the Philharmonic, did I hear any lament, any requiem, for the millions of people literally slaughtered by the Empire, of which France is now an inseparable part. No new symphonies or operas dedicated to the victims of Papua, Kashmir, Palestine, Libya, Mali, Somalia, the Democratic Republic of Congo, or Iraq.

My new friend, Francois Minaux, is writing an opera about the US carpet-bombing of the Plane of Jars, during the 'Secret War' conducted by the West against Laos. I am helping him with this enormous and noble project. But paradoxically (or logically?), Francoise is not living in France, but in the United States.

When I shared my thoughts with him, on Charlie Hebdo, and on freedom of expression in France, he summarized:

"It's terrible. The art scene sucks. People are zombies. The mass reaction to the Charlie H attack is disgusting and depressing. '1984' is happening but people are too blind to see it."

A few hours later, I received an email in which Francoise reflected on his complex relationship with his native land, and its culture:

"Being French nowadays and being free to express yourself is impossible. Back in the early 2000, I could not accept the frame that culture would impose on its artists, and they could not accept my questioning and different approach to art making. They either spat on me or even worse, went mute. So, I left. You must travel outside of Europe and live and work outside, to feel the world.

I felt also that politically engaged works of art were not considered real art in Paris. There is this thing in France: any political engagement is seen either as propaganda or as advertisement. Back in the early 2000's, we were supposed to make art for art's sake. We were living under the glass dome of the conservatory. We were 'protected by the government'.

They let us know that we should not talk about politics or religion in public. Maybe French secularism was a good idea but not to the present extent, when politics and religion became taboo. There is this climate of fear: our elders and teachers hardly discuss politics and religion. And so we didn't know! Certain things are forbidden to be known in France.

Life in Paris became suffocating. Opinions were not expressed. We were not allowed to understand others. Live became boring: we had nothing substantial to talk about. And so we discussed greasy food and French wine. Economists describe French economy as "austere", but I would go further by saying that French behavior as well as French identity is austere. But the French people can't see it because they now all think the same. They are trying so hard to stay French but they are forgetting, how the world has bled, so their French-ness could be preserved. Their culture was built from the blood flowing from the French colonies, and on the foundations of the modern-day French Empire."

***

So where are those brave French minds now; people so many of us were admiring for their courage and integrity?

They were never 'perfect', and they erred, like all humans do, but they were often standing on the side of oppressed, they were calling for revolutions and some even for the end of colonialism. They were holding Western culture responsible for the horrors our planet has been facing for centuries.

Emile Zola and Victor Hugo, then later Sartre, Camus, Malraux, Beauvoir, Aragon...

What do we have now? Michel Houellebecq and his

novels, full of insults against Islam, as well as of 'tears of gratitude' felt after each blowjob his characters get from their girlfriends.

The legacies of Houellebecq and Charlie are somehow similar. Is this the best France can do, these days? Is kicking what is on the ground, what was already destroyed by the West, what is humiliated and wrecked – called courage?

Are pink poodles on silver leashes, exhibited in local galleries, the essence of what is called the freedom of speech? Such stuff would pass any censorship board even in Indonesia, or Afghanistan! No need for the freedom of expression. It is cowardly and it is selfish – exactly what the Empire is promoting.

***

Christophe Joubert, a French documentary filmmaker, told me over a cup of coffee:

> "First I was sad, when I heard about what happened to people at Charlie Hedbo. Then I got scared. Not of terrorism, but of the actions of the crowd. Everybody was indoctrinated: thinking the same way, acting the same way. Like Orwell and his 1984! More precisely, 'the 8th day.'"

"People in France know nothing about the world", continues Christophe. "They believe what they are told by propagandist mass media".

"I am not allowed to speak", the Eritrean Ambassador to France, Hanna Simon, explained to me. "They invite me to some television show where they present a film criticizing my country. They speak openly, but when I try to respond, they shut me up."

"I know nothing about what you are saying", my good Asian friend replies, with sadness, after I tell him about the tremendous global rebellion taking place against the West, in Latin America, China, Russia, Africa... He is a highly educated man, working for the UNESCO. "You know, here

154

we hear only one side; the official one."

I am wondering whether, perhaps in 70 years from now, the National Archive will have another huge exhibition: one on France's collaboration with neoliberalism, and on its direct involvement in building the global fascist regime controlled by the West.

But for now, as long as dogs can have a beer at the bar, fascism, imperialism and neoliberalism do not seem to matter.

March 20, 2015

Andre Vltchek – Christopher Black – Peter Koenig

13

Czechs Are Welcoming Dear American Soldiers!

THE CZECH REPUBLIC AND THE FINE ART OF COLLABORATION

By Andre Vltchek

The US military convoy will soon be passing through the Czech territory, from the Baltics and Poland, to its permanent base in Bavaria, Germany.

That is bad enough. The Czechs should not have allowed the convoy to pass. Provoking Russia and moving closer and closer to the fascist Empire is a shameless and cowardly act.

But they would not be Czechs, if they would not go that extra mile; if they would not take their collaboration with the present masters to an absolutely bizarre, ridiculous, and Kafkaesque extreme:

Several Czech groups are now using social media to organize in advance what is called 'a grand welcome' for the Americans. Plans include beer stands with cold Pilsner beer accompanied with loud cheers, as well as 'expressions of solidarity' with the GI's and member states of NATO.

There are several planned initiatives, with the most vocal called "Welcoming of the American Army" (Vitani americke armady).

"Freedom Forum", organized by a journalist named, Pavel Safr, claims: "At the points through which the American convoy will be passing, and where there is a danger of shameful actions of pro-Russian extremists, posts will be erected. We call them "czechpoints" and they will be similar to the military checkpoints. There, Czech supporters of the US army will be gathering, supporting our allies."

Pro-American and pro-NATO elements are sending warnings that those who dare to protest against the US military presence on Czech territory could face consequences, including physical attacks.

***

Is this some sick, pathetic ass kissing? Of course, but it did not fall from the sky.

Czechs have long history of grotesque collaboration. They are also known for outbursts of "delayed wrath" towards those whom they fatefully and excessively served in the past.

In modern history, the Czechs were the trusted and determined allies of Nazi Germany. Soldiers of the "3rd Reich" were enthusiastically welcomed by the Czech masses, waving Swastikas, in Prague and elsewhere. Czech workers, some of the most skilled in Europe, began producing weapons for German army right from the first days of the occupation. The Germans, in turn, left the Czech population alone, and even forced local banks to write off their housing loans.

There was virtually no resistance against Nazis during the WWII, and the assassination of Reichsprotektor Reinhard Heydrich, by Czech paratroopers in 1942 had to be planned and organized from London.

While the Germans were rounding up Czech Jews and deporting them to concentration camps, the Czech people were busy liquidating their Roma (Gypsy) citizens, with full German blessing, but little help. The Germans did not bother getting involved. They knew that the Czechs were racist and loyal to any master, and they trusted them with running their own Roma concentration/extermination camps, particularly that at the village of Lety.

Just a few days before the end of the war, when the victory of the Allies became imminent, the Czechs launched their 'uprising' and the Soviet army had to accelerate its push towards Prague. 150,000 Soviet lives were lost liberating the country.

After the war, the Czechs deported, literally kicked out, millions of minority Germans from the border region. Countless women were raped, houses were looted, people killed. The more shamelessly the Czechs collaborated with the Nazis, the more vindictive they were after the war!

Those eerie villages and towns, left empty after the German families were deported, were eventually 'repopulated' by Roma/Gypsies, who were forcefully brought from Eastern and Southern Europe (as there were not enough 'Czech gypsies' left after the war).

What a history! But even those unfortunate and tortured Gypsies, who managed to survive the WWII, or those who were later brought to the Czech lands and forced to settle down right on the Cold War frontier, were soon discriminated against brutally, humiliated, and forced to 'assimilate'. The discrimination, in fact Czech-style apartheid, is practiced until now, all over the country.

At one point, there were even walls built around Czech

Gypsy settlements – not unlike those now separating Jewish and Israeli settlements (the state of Israel and its racist policies are full heartedly supported and greatly admired in the Czech Republic). Most of the Gypsy kids are forced to attend 'special schools' for retarded children.

But back to those post-WWII days! After the war, the Communist Party came to power and things somehow improved. Many Czechs and Slovaks joined the new system enthusiastically, and Czechoslovakia, historically one of Europe's powerhouses of industry and knowledge, embarked on an extremely exciting journey. It began supporting deprived nations all over the world, educating people, and demanding the end of colonialism. It gave scholarships to tens of thousands of students from Asia, Africa and the Middle East. It built steel mills and sugar mills. For the first time in its history, Czechs abandoned their selfish essence and stood on the side of the oppressed.

The Czechoslovak Socialist Republic! It had a proud sound to it. It was suddenly respected and admired all over the world!

But was it all done 'voluntarily'?

Before, and during 1968, during the so-called 'Prague Spring', or 'socialism with human face', the direction towards which the country marched began to be internally criticized.

The Soviet Union panicked, convinced that Czechoslovakia could leave its orbit in the foreseeable future. The Soviets, backed by other East European countries, invaded.

It was, arguably, the most bloodless occupation in human history, with only few casualties, mostly caused by accidents. But, it is argued; the enthusiasm of Czech and Slovak people was broken as the country felt humiliated, derailed and suddenly full of Soviet troops.

What is of course not mentioned in the Western propaganda (and in the present-days Czech propaganda) is that 1968 did not happen outside of a historical and political context. The Allies – the US, France, Soviet Union and the UK, decided that Czechoslovakia would belong to the Soviet orbit, at the end of the WWII. It was definitely not the Soviet Union alone, which made the decision.

The UK and US committed incomparably more brutal crimes to keep many countries in their own 'sphere of influence'.

To prevent West Germany, France, Italy, Greece and other countries from electing the Communist Parties (and from leaving the Western orbit) after the WWII, the US and British intelligence agencies 'employed' countless Nazi cadres, who then began intimidating, murdering and torturing Left wing politicians and activists.

Those Nazi criminals were later allowed to leave, some with great booty of gold from Jewish victims in their bags. They were expedited to South America, particularly to Paraguay, Argentina and Chile, but also elsewhere. I spoke to several of them, two decades ago, in Asuncion. They were proud and open about what they had done.

If the US and UK failed to break the spine of the West European Left, the Communist parties would win the elections. Such a scenario would be unacceptable for both Washington and London. To prevent it, a bloodbath was administered. And then, of course, the most horrific oppression was saved for Greece and Turkey.

The terror used by the Western block countries against the Left was incomparably more horrific than the actions taken by the Soviet Union in Hungary and Czechoslovakia.

At some point, it was Czechoslovakia, which provided political asylum to many West European dissidents, particularly those fleeing Greece.

But Western and now Czech propaganda have a very selective memory!

***

After 1968, many Czechs departed for the West. Several months after the invasion, the borders remained open, another 'courtesy' of the Soviet Union.

In occupied Czechoslovakia, there was absolutely none of the savagery that takes place regularly after the West occupies some territory or orchestrates a coup: death squads murdering opposition, mass rapes, beastly torture, disappearances...

But the Western propaganda went to work, almost immediately. 1968 became a symbol, a rallying cry, and an anti-Communist dogma.

Czech and Slovak population was bombarded, day and night, by elaborate and powerful brainwashing, coming from several dedicated radio stations like Radio Free Europe, Voice of America, and the BBC (Czech and Slovak desks). Propaganda flowed in German from the television stations broadcasting from Austria and West Germany.

"The more propaganda the West spread, the more they accused the Czech and Slovak state media of actually being the ones spreading lies", explained, Milan Kohout, during my recent visit to Prague. A renowned performer and a professor at the Faculty of Philosophy at the West Bohemian University in Pilsen, Mr. Kohout was a signatory of the 'Charter 77', the major dissident movement during the 70's and 80's, but he later turned around and attacked Western neoliberalism and imperialism. "Actually, looking back, the Czech Communist media was very correct, in all that it wrote about Western imperialism, colonialism, and capitalism."

Even after the 1968 occupations, Moscow allowed the standard of living in Czechoslovakia to remain substantially higher than that in the Soviet Union, something unthinkable in the countries colonized or occupied by the West.

Still, Czechs were angry. They dreamed about joining the West. Building an egalitarian, just world was simply not something that they fantasized about. Internationalism was an extremely foreign concept for Europeans, and Czechs were no exception.

As my uncle, a true Communist and engineer who worked on construction of heavy industry facilities in several 'developing countries' like Syria, Lebanon, and Iraq, once told me: "We had some people in our teams, some Czechs who believed in social justice and internationalism, but most of them were there only for the money. Remember that in essence, Czechs are very racist and unpredictable individuals. In the Middle East, which I always loved so much, they were building industry, while they actually hated Arabs. Simultaneously, while hating them, they were pimping their own wives to the locals."

Many Czechs not only hate the concept of the Soviet Union but they also hate the Russian people. A few years ago, I heard hate speeches against Russians even from one of the editors of "A2", a progressive intellectual magazine.

Located in Asia and Europe, multicultural and constantly battered by the West, Russia is definitely not the ideal 'colonizer' for the nation obsessed with the superiority of the white race and the greatness of 'European culture'.

Russians are seen as a 'lower', Asian nation, unfit to rule over a Western, European and therefore 'civilized' country, the notion so frankly expressed in the novel by Josef Skvorecky "The Cowards".

***

After 1968, Russians soldiers did not mingle with the locals; they mainly stayed in the barracks. They did not harass or rape Czech women (unlike Czechs during the WWI, when their brutal 'legions' occupied huge part of the Trans-Siberian Railway, plundering, murdering and raping in the villages and towns all alone the railroad).

But despite their hatred, Czechs were still ready to do what they always do best: to collaborate.

Except for those few signatories of the above-mentioned 'Charter-77', there was hardly any opposition worth mentioning. And both Czechs and Slovaks kept flocking into all sorts of collaborative clubs, including the 'Club of Czechoslovak – Soviet Friendship'.

Hundreds of thousands became snitches, denouncing each other to the STB – the secret police. They were spying on each other, as they were doing during the Austro-Hungarian Empire and German occupation; and now.

"Why do they actually hate Russians so much?" I asked Milan.

"Because they were kissing their asses so intensively", he replied. "It is embarrassing how Czechs were behaving, when Soviets were in charge. Nobody asked them to go to such extremes. And since they are unable to hate and ridicule themselves, they now blame everything on the Russians and Communism."

***

As I was strolling towards the Visehrad Castle, an Iranian man approached two young women pushing their baby carriages. He was well dressed, he was smiling, holding tourist map in his hands. "Could you please help me to find Visehrad?" he asked in passable English, very politely.

Both women waved him away, as if he would be a fly or an annoying mosquito.

They left him standing there, in the middle of the road, terribly hurt, tears in his eyes.

I ran towards him. I showed him how to get to the castle. He thanked me, then asked: "Why did they treat me like that?"

"Do you want pre-edited answer, or do you want to know the truth?"

"The truth", he insisted.

"Because they are damned racists", I replied. "Because

they think that you are a Muslim, which in this society is something absolutely terrible. Because they think that you are Arab, and they see no distinction between Arabs and Iranians and Pakistanis. They despise everyone who has dark skin."

"Are you Czech?" he asked.

"No", I replied. "My mother is half Chinese, half Russian. But I had very bad luck spending a few years here, during my childhood. When I was a little boy, they used to beat me like a dog, after each class. For having 'Asian mother', for having 'Asian ears', for being born in Russia. As if I could choose where to be born."

No doubt, my short biography made him feel better. We shook hands. I gave him a hug and suggested he sticks to well-lit streets, especially after dark. I ran back to my hotel, where I met a publisher of 'Broken Books', which recently translated and published my discussion with Noam Chomsky: "Western Terrorism: From Hiroshima to Drone Warfare".

Peter, the publisher, had much to add to the topic: "In Olomouc, the city where I live and teach, there is not one single Muslim there, but everyone is anti-Islamic. In this country, people know very little about the world, but they all have strong opinions. Students are brainwashed by Western propaganda, but at least they know something. But if you go to the countryside, it is total disaster. Like in my family... They never saw a Muslim, but they hate them, and they hate Islam."

***

The Czechs waited to start their 'Velvet Revolution' until the very end. They made sure that there would be no risks. That is how it always is here. Then they flooded the streets of all major cities, ringing keys, demanding 'freedom'. By then, everything was already over in the Soviet Union and in almost all countries of the Eastern block.

Washington and NATO fooled Gorbachev, and the imperfect and complex group of socialist countries collapsed, from the pressure, weight and deception coming from the West. Thanks to this group, fascism was defeated and colonialism smashed.

Western Europe and North America – the gang of countries that plundered the world for centuries, murdering hundreds of millions of innocent people on all continents – was shouting: "Victory of freedom and democracy. The Berlin Wall Fell!"

For the West, there was plenty to celebrate. The Eastern block – the last serious adversary, the deterrence to their total, dictatorial and monstrous control over the planet, was collapsing, destroyed by Western propaganda, by the dissident movements financed from Washington and London, and by Western-trained Mujahedeen in Afghanistan.

From now on, it was going to be one uninterrupted bloodbath, true fun for neo-colonialists, a party with no restrains and no opposition: in Iraq and Afghanistan, Pakistan, Palestine, Kashmir, Papua, the Democratic Republic of Congo, Syria, Somalia, Sudan, Mali, Ukraine; wherever the Empire was ready to plunder and to experiment on human beings.

In the following years, as a result of the collapse of the 'Eastern block', tens of millions died, victims of the unopposed Western terror.

The Czechs grabbed the opportunity! With each ring of their keys, the message was getting clearer and clearer: "To hell with the world and with that ridiculous aim for justice! We are back! We are Europeans! We want to be part of the Empire, right hands of the oppressors! Get us away from those lunatics who are dreaming about better world. We want even bigger houses and better cars, no matter who will pay for them. We want to embrace new masters, true masters of the world – the Empire!"

Soon after, tens of thousands of Western liberals

flooded Prague. Sex was easily available, and beer was cheap. That was all that mattered. Prague became synonymous with countless one-night stands and with late night puking on the streets, after innumerable pints of beer.

***

After Velvet Revolution, the Czechs bent more than they ever did in the past, even more than during the rule of the Nazis. They began collaborating with full force with the Empire.

Czech politicians began attacking and ridiculing Cuba and China; they supported attacks on Iraq and Afghanistan. They joined NATO and sent troops wherever the Empire decided to spread terror. They moved extremely close to Israel.

Czechoslovakia disintegrated. The industrial powerhouse that used to provide much of the developing world with the knowhow, while building factories and power plants, disappeared not long after so-called 'Velvet Revolution' in the shameful 'Velvet Divorce'. Two states emerged – The Czech and Slovak Republics. The people were never consulted; it was all done behind their backs and done very quickly – an unconstitutional, undemocratic surgical strike of nationalist politicians.

And Vaclav Havel, the Czech President, the beloved symbol of the Western liberals, was too busy getting standing ovations in Washington, riding pushbikes with the religious bigot and former CIA agent, the Dalai Lama, glorifying 'Western values' and supporting US invasions and acts of terrorism. Originally from one of the richest families in Prague, Havel gained back in 'restitutions' his family's countless estates and properties, literally forcing hundreds of people onto the street.

Oh those restitutions: Czech aristocrats and the Church stealing houses and flats from the poor, all over the country. Families of Czech businessmen and the bourgeoisie returning back and grabbing all they could: a plunder and yes, a true counter-revolution!

Then came 'lustration laws', stating that those who collaborated during the Soviet era cannot hold government jobs. This, in the height of Czech collaboration with the Empire; with the fascist West! What a shame, Czech Republic – what an embarrassment!

While purging Communists, the new masters of the land began selling Czech industry, which was once one of the mightiest on Earth. Western companies began buying everything – from nuclear reactor factories, to electric locomotive plants – in order to destroy it, to get rid of the competition. Siemens degraded locomotive production to the building of carriages. LET stopped making civil aircraft, and Volkswagen bought the huge Skoda car factory. The country's industry was soon reduced to a *maquilladora* level.

The huge privatization campaign was quick and lacking any transparency, murky. The goal was clear – to create a new bourgeoisie, as quickly as possible, at the expense of Czech people, and to redistribute wealth – from socialist ownership to the ownership of private individuals.

Imagine this: the whole nation was told, for decades, that it is building a socialist fatherland, which belongs to all. Then, in just a few months, the factories, farms, other companies, fell to the hands of new capitalists (who became rich over night, and who did nothing to gain extra privileges), and then were often sold to foreigners.

***

Prague was sold and ravished too. Once one of the most beautiful and cultural cities on Earth, Prague now resembles some tourist resorts like Pattaya, of course in a glorious architectural gothic and baroque setting.

Prague's streets are lined with horribly kitschy crystal stores, with pathetic souvenir stalls, with several 'museums of torture' (oh, Europeans love to watch torture!). The oldest opera house in the city, the one that premiered

Mozart's Don Giovanni, is now showing a British pop play. World famous Laterna Magica lost all artistic aspirations and converted itself into a tourist trap. And the Museum of Jan Saudek, who was one of the greatest European photographers, closed down, and where it stood, a new shiny Thai massage parlor has opened.

Almost no one lives in the old city, now. Restitutions kicked out most of the families and individuals. Those few who stayed cannot afford astronomic prices.

I stopped an old lady, near the Old City Square.

"Yes, I still live here", she explained. "But it is a miracle. I was allowed to stay in my old apartment. It is sort of charity. But I have no rights and the new owner can kick me out any moment. Almost nobody lives here, anymore. There are no supermarkets here, no basic services. It is all geared to tourists and companies. I travel by metro to get to a food store."

What used to be a pride of socialist Prague – its metro, the Palace of Culture, the museums, theatres, art cinemas – is all deteriorating, covered by graffiti, abandoned, even closed down.

To speak Czech means to get terrible service. I tried in my hotel but was ignored, even humiliated. I switched to English and got room upgrade and loving smiles. The same happens in fascist Indonesia, a client state of the West. I speak the language, but if I want to be treated with respect, I have to use English.

Over all this, Vaclav Havel presides. His huge poster/portrait is hanging from the facade of the National Museum. It reads "Havel Forever". After his death, the arch Czech collaborator was elevated to sainthood.

***

Monika Horeni, editor of the Left Wing Czech daily Haló noviny, summarized interaction of the Czechs with the Empire:

"During the so-called Velvet Revolution, ex-President Václav Havel, darling of the American politicians, was promising that both military alliances – Warsaw Pact and NATO – will cease to exist. He was promising the world without arm races and wars – absolute utopian dream. Our citizens believed him. Of course, after he and his people grabbed power, his promises diminished – suddenly it was enough to destroy Warsaw Pact. NATO stayed, and Czech Republic actually joined it, in March 1999, and politicians did not even bother to consult its citizens.

Vaclav Havel and others laid foundations for collaboration of Czech Republic with the US. Few days after entering NATO, CR participated in deplorable bombing of fellow Slavic country – Yugoslavia. It allowed NATO planes to use its airspace. I feel shame that my country belongs to the pact led by the United States – country that is responsible for increase of tensions in the world, for provoking other nations, for invasions, for spreading death all over the world, and now for creating the Islamic State/ISIS. Only the Communist Party openly declared that it demands that Czech Republic leaves NATO.

I see it this way: those who are defending Czech membership and activities in NATO are co-responsible for spreading the conflicts in the world. Present expression of collaboration is that the entire Czech government – all ministers from the right-wing and from the Social Democratic Party – agreed with the provocative passing of the US military column through Czech Republic, which will take place between 29 March and 1 April.

Unfortunately, part of Czech public collaborates as well.

Nobody with his or her sane mind can understand why is column not moving through the railways – why is it going to provoke by its presence in our cities. It is simply a show of force – exactly as the US representatives described it.

For me it is essential how many foreign bases have the US outside its territory – several hundreds. And Russians: only 2 or 3. It is therefore clear who is the global aggressor!"

***

Walking through Prague, I felt deeply depressed. I saw beggars kneeling in front of Czech police.

I heard stories about homeless people being deported to the outskirts of the city.

I felt a generally bad mood, a resignation, an acute lack of optimism, wherever I went.

The country was robbed, but people were lining up to applaud the thieves.

"This must be the only country on earth where students are demanding introduction of tuition fees"; my publisher explained to me.

Why has this place been so messed up? Where did such cynicism, such lack of pride come? I never understood.

Many years ago, during the Yugoslav War, I returned to Czech Republic, just for a few months. Then, once again, the country mentally destroyed me.

I ended up drinking, night after night, with the then Argentinian Ambassador to the Czech Republic, the great novelist and thinker, Abel Pose. We hit hard on the embassy's wine reserves, often lying down on a thick carpet, discussing Kafka, Hasek and Western imperialism and colonialism.

Abel was some 30 years older than I, and in terrible pain: he had just lost his beloved son. I lost a lot, too.

Then, he told me the story he was then writing – a story, which was eventually published as a book – Los Cuadernos de Praga:

As Argentinian Ambassador, he succeeded in convincing the Czech secret service to open files on his great compatriot – Ernesto "Che" Guevara. Between his failed campaign in Congo and the final and fatal fight in Bolivia, "Che" spent several months in Czechoslovakia.

Sick, his body full of parasites, he was treated by Czech doctors, in those years, some of the best on Earth. But the Czech security services could not figure out how to perceive this great revolutionary. They were 'protecting' him and spying on him at the same time. Was he a friend or a foe? They considered him to be both.

I was shocked. Pose was shocked, too.

Czechs collaborated, pretended to be the greatest revolutionaries and supporters of the liberation struggles worldwide. But deep inside, they felt no attachments; they had no allegiances.

"I felt betrayed", said Pose. "'Che' came here. He trusted them, with all his big heart. But they can never be trusted."

***

I asked Milan Kohout, great performer, former friend of Vaclav Havel, and his fellow dissident, to stage a short protest play at the outrageous "Memorial to the victims of Communism" in Prague. Before we went, I renamed the place to "The Monument to Czech Collaboration with Western Imperialism".

The monument is located only two minutes walk from the Palace of Justice. There are some stones in front of the palace. "This used to be a Monument to Soviet soldiers who died, liberating Prague from the Nazis, in 1945", explained Milan. "There used to be old Soviet tank. After the Velvet Revolution, the monument was desecrated – the tank was repainted to pink color. It was done officially. Then, few years later, the tank was taken away. Now, as you can see, there is nothing. 'Only' 150.000 Soviet people died, liberating Prague. Not worth mentioning, right?"

We move to the "Memorial to the Victims of Communism". It is quite a bizarre place, and piece of very bad art: a decomposing naked man, with semi-erect penis. And right behind the monument, there is a wall consisting of barbed wire. It is not there for any symbolic reason, just to protect some public property.

Even according to this propaganda venue, a grand total of 248 people were killed during the entire long period of Czech Communism. To compare it to some Western onslaughts that got away with no monuments at all (in the West): 2-3 million killed during the anti-Communist coup in Indonesia, 8 million in the Democratic Republic of Congo, and some 8 million in Indochina.

Milan began performing, by first stuffing the place with several symbols of the Western consumerism – empty cigarette boxes, coffee cartons and other junk.

We managed to provoke both shouts from supporters and from protesters.

Afterwards we felt better, just marginally better.

But still, the US convoy was just about to enter Czech Republic.

And the country was hanging in a vacuum, aimlessly, with no goal and no purpose, spreading toxic propaganda and lies.

And I felt suddenly terribly sad, because it was not only bitterness that I felt towards this land, not only bitterness and disgust... I felt many other things... But this country and I suddenly stood facing each other, at two sides of the barricade, ready for an inevitable showdown.

March 27, 2015

14

Shattered

NOTHING IS RIGHT IN THE MIDDLE EAST

By Andre Vltchek

There is nothing, absolutely nothing right in the Middle East these days. There seems to be no hope left, and no fervor. All that was pure was dragged through filth. All that was great here was stolen or smashed by the outsiders. Enthusiasm had been ridiculed, then drowned, or burned to ashes, or shattered by tanks and missiles.

Corruption thrives – corruption that inundated this entire region since the early days of Western colonialism, and then was sustained through the present-day imperialist global regime.

The land of the Middle East is tired; it is crying from exhaustion. It is scarred by wars. It is dotted with oil wells and rotting armor vehicles. There are corpses everywhere;

buried, turned into dust, but still present in minds of those who are alive. There are millions of corpses, tens of millions of victims, shouting in their own, voiceless way, not willing to leave anyone in peace, pointing fingers, accusing!

This land is where so much began. Europe was nothing, when Byblos and Erbil stood tall, when a fabled civilization was forming in Mesopotamia, when Aleppo, Cairo and Al-Quds could only be rivaled by the great cities of China...

And this is where greatness, progress, decency and kindness were broken and bathed in blood by the crusaders, and later by the colonialist scum.

Europeans like to say that this part of the world is now 'backward', because it never experienced renaissance, but before it was broken and humiliated; it went much farther than renaissance, following its own way and direction. A primitive and aggressive medieval Europe took most of the knowledge from here.

All this means nothing now. Almost nothing is left of the glorious past. Grand Arab cities, once exhibiting their fabulous socialist concepts, including public and free hospitals and universities, even several centuries before Karl Marx was born, are now choking in smog, polluted, with almost nothing public remaining. Everything is privatized, and corrupt monarchs, generals and mafias are firmly in charge, from Egypt to the Gulf.

People wanted to have it exactly the opposite way. After the WWII, from North Africa to Iran, they were opting for various socialist concepts. But they were never allowed to have it their own way! Everything secular and progressive was smashed, destroyed by the Western masters of the world. And then came the second wave of semi-socialist states: Libya, Iraq and Syria, and they were bombed and destroyed as well, as nothing socialist, nothing that serves the people is ever allowed to survive in the 'third world' by Washington, London and Paris.

Millions died. Western imperialism orchestrated coups, sent brothers against brothers, bombed civilians and invaded directly, when all other means to achieve its hegemonic goals failed.

It created, it 'educated' a substantial layer of cynical servers of the Empire, the layer of new elites who are accountable to the governments in Washington, London and Paris, and treat their own people with spite and brutality. This layer is now ruling almost entire region, is fully backed by the West, and therefore there is extremely difficult to remove it.

Recently, at the "American University" in Beirut, one of the local academics told me "this region is doomed because of corruption". But where did corruption come from, I wondered aloud. One after another, secular and socialist leaders in the Arab world were removed, overthrown. The Empire put the lowest grade of thugs, the most regressive monarchs and dictators, on the thrones.

The truth is, like in Africa, the people of the Middle East lost all hope that they could ever be allowed to elect the governments that would defend them and represent their interests. They sank to bare 'survival mode', to extreme individualism, to nepotism and to cynicism. They had to, in order to survive, in order to make their families and clans to stay afloat in the world forced on them by the others.

The result is atrocious: one of the most advanced civilizations on earth was converted into one of the most regressive.

***

And as a result, there is bitterness, humiliation and shame in the entire Middle East. There is an unhealthy, unnatural mood.

The thugs in Beirut, Amman, Erbil, Riyadh and Cairo are driving their shiny SUV's and latest European sedans. New and newer luxury malls are offering top designer brands for those who make huge profits from the refugee crises triggered by the Empire, or from the crude which is being extracted by mistreated migrant workers. Humiliated Southeast Asian maids, often tortured, raped and abused, are sitting on the marble floors of the shopping centers, waiting for their masters who are engaging in unbridled food and shopping orgies, spending money that they never had to work for.

Collaborators are extremely well rewarded, for serving the Empire directly, for keeping business rolling and oil wells pumping, for staffing the UN agencies and through them providing legitimacy to this grotesque state of things, for brainwashing local youth in West-sponsored schools and universities.

All this is extremely hard to observe and to stomach, unless one is on a certain 'wave', immunized and indifferent, lobotomized, resigned to this state of the world.

The Middle East is of course not the exception – it is just a part of what I often describe as the 'belt' of client states of the West; a belt that winds from Indonesia through almost the entirety of Southeast Asia, then via the sub-Continent and the Middle East, down to Kenya, Rwanda and Uganda.

***

Now Saudi Arabia is bombing Yemen. It does it in order to give full support to the outgoing pro-Western regime, and in order to damage Shi'a Muslims. Recent Saudi actions, as so many previous actions by that brutal client state of Washington, will open the doors to terrorism, and will kill thousands of innocent people. Shockingly, that is probably part of the plan.

I am now constantly invited to talk shows and radio and television interviews, to speak on the topic. But what more could be said and added?

The horrors of Western, Israeli, Saudi and Turkish aggressions (direct and indirect) are repeating themselves, year after year, in various parts of the Middle East. People are killed, many people, even children. There are some protests, some accusations, some 'noise', but at the end, the aggressors get away with everything. It is partially because the mass media in the West is twisting all the facts, again and again, and it does it extremely successfully. And most of the Arab media outlets are taking Western propaganda directly from the source, feeding it to their own people, shamelessly.

It is also because there is no effective international legal system in place that could punish aggressors.

The UN is nowhere to be found, when the acts or real terror are committed. Once in a while it is 'concerned', it even 'condemns' aggressors. But there are never any sanctions or embargos imposed against Israel or the United States, even Saudi Arabia. It is understood that the West and its allies are 'above the law'.

This sends powerful signals to the rulers of the Middle East. The Egyptian military, which killed thousands of poor people right after it grabbed the power in a 2014 coup (which is commonly not defined as a coup, there), is now once again 'eligible for US military aid'.

Fully prostituted Egyptian elites danced on the streets of Cairo when the coup took place, as did the elites in Chile, in 1973. I saw them, when I was making a documentary film for the South American Telesur, a film on how the West derailed the Arab Spring. They were posing for my cameras, cheering and hugging me, thinking that I am one of their handlers from the US or Europe.

Recently, I found an Egyptian UN staffer staring threateningly into my face:

"A coup?" she whispered. "You call it a coup? Egyptian people don't call it a coup."

How would I dare to argue with such a respectable representative of the Egyptian nation? I noticed that the pro-Western Egyptian elites love to pose as 'Egyptian people', as those species that are far removed from their mansions and chauffer-driven limousines.

***

There are tens of millions of people displaced in this part of the world. They come from Iraq and Syria, and from Palestine. There are new refugees and decades old refugees. Now, most certainly, there will be millions of Yemeni refugees.

In Lebanon alone, 2 million Syrian refugees live all over the place, some renting huts and houses, others, if the can afford it, leasing apartments in Beirut. But the UN and local authorities do not even register hundreds of thousands of them, those in Bekaa Valley and elsewhere. Refugees told me that many of them get turned away. If there is no registration, there are no food rations, no education for children and no medical care.

I saw refugees from several Iraqi cities, in Erbil, in Iraqi administered Kurdistan. They were escaping from the ISIS, which were created by the West.

A nuclear scientist Ishmael Khalil, originally from Tikrit University, told me: "All that I had was destroyed... Americans are the main reason for this insanity – for the total destruction of Iraq. Don't just just me, ask any child, and you will hear the same thing... We all used to belong to a great and proud nation. Now everything is fragmented, and ruined. We have nothing – all of us have become beggars and refugees in our own land... I escaped five months ago, after ISIS devastated my university. And we all know who is behind them: the allies of the West: Saudi Arabia, Qatar and others..."

Then I stood by what was left of a bridge, connecting the two shores of the Khazer River, just a few kilometers from the city of Mosul. ISIS blew up the bridge. A few villages around it were flattened by the US bombing. A Kurdish colonel who was showing me the area was proud to mention that he was trained in the UK and US. It felt like total insanity – all forces united in destroying Iraq, had the same sources: the US, the NATO, and the West!

A few kilometers from the frontline were oil fields, but local people said that oil companies were just stealing their land; nothing was coming back to local communities. As the flames of the oil refineries were burning, local people were digging out roots and herbs, in order to survive.

And there was a camp for Syrian refugees, too, nearby. But refugees were screened. Only those who expressed their hatred for the President al-Assad were allowed to stay.

***

Beirut is symbolic to what is happening in the entire Middle East.

Once glorious, the city now ranks near the bottom of quality of life indexes. With basically no public transportation, it is choking, polluted and jammed. Electric blackouts are common. Miserable neighborhoods are all around. Education and medical care are mostly private and unaffordable to the great majority. Dirty money propels construction of expensive condominiums, posh malls and overpriced restaurants.

Luxury cars are everywhere. Expensive condominiums, yachts, vehicles and designer clothes are the only measure of worth.

It is all thoroughly grotesque, considering that there are 2 million Syrian refugees struggling all over this tiny country. There are old Palestinian refugees in depressing camps. There are the hated and discriminated Bedouins, there are the abused Asian and African maids...

"Work is punishment", says local credo. Nobody bothers to work too much.

There is plenty of money, but most of it does not come from work. Huge amounts come from drugs, from 'accommodating refugees', from business in Africa and elsewhere, from remittances of those who work in the Gulf.

Israel is next door. It is threatening, and periodically it attacks.

Hezbollah is the only large movement in the country that is fighting for social welfare of the people. It is also fighting Israel whenever it invades. And now, it is locked in an epic battle with ISIS. But it is on the terrorist list of the West, because it is Shi'a, and because it is too 'socialist' and too critical of the West.

In Beirut, everything goes. The rich are burning their money like paper. They ride their luxury cars and bikes without mufflers, run people over on pedestrian crossings, and never yield. They are mostly educated in the West and trilingual (Arabic, French and English). They commute back and forth to Europe as if it is a next-door village.

The need of the upper classes to show-off is all that matters in Beirut.

The poor – the majority of the Lebanese people – do not exist. One never hears about them. They are irrelevant.

***

Those who rule over the Middle East are corrupt, cynical, and unpatriotic.

And they are scared, because they know that they have betrayed their own people.

The more scared they are, the more brutal are their tactics. I see them in action, in Bahrain, Egypt, Iraq and elsewhere.

Most of the left-wing movements and parties in the Middle East were destroyed, bought or derailed. Politics are about clans and religious sects and money. There is hardly any ideology left. There is no knowledge about Venezuela and Ecuador, China and Russia. The poor people love Russia, because "it stands against the West", but there is very little understanding of the world outside the Middle East and the old colonial master – Europe.

Nothing feels right in the Middle East, these days.

New reports are coming in, alleging Israel of interrogating, torturing young Palestinian children.

Yemen, that ancient land with which I fell in love with from first sight, many years ago, is bleeding and burning.

Two cradles of civilization – Iraq and Syria – are totally torn to pieces, devastated.

Libya is breaking apart, most likely beyond repair, absolutely finished as a country.

Egypt is once again squeezed in an horrendous military grip.

Shi'a people in Bahrain and Saudi Arabia are suffering great discrimination and violence.

People are dying; people are displaced, discriminated against. There is no justice, no social justice for the majority, the same scenario like in Indonesia, like in sub-Continent, like in East Africa, like everywhere where the Western imperialism and neoliberalism managed to have their way.

The West worked very hard to turn the Middle East into what it is now. It took centuries to transfigure this culturally deep and great part of the world into the horror show. But it is done!

The rest of the world should watch and learn. This should not be allowed to happen elsewhere. The "Southeast Asia – East Africa Corridor" is what the West wants to convert entire planet into. But it will not succeed, because there is Latin America, China, Russia, Iran, South African, Eritrea and other proud and determined nations standing on its way.

And the Middle East, one day, will stand up, too! The people will demand what is theirs. They will demand justice. Recently, they tried but they were smashed. I have no doubt that they will not give up – they will try again and again, until they win.

CHRISTOPHER BLACK

1

LOUISE ARBOUR: UNINDICTED WAR CRIMINAL

by Christopher Black and Edward S. Herman

Among the many ironies of the NATO war against Yugoslavia was the role of the International Criminal Tribunal and its chief prosecutor, Louise Arbour, elevated by Canadian Prime Minister Jean Chretien to Canada's highest court in 1999. It will be argued here that that award was entirely justified on the grounds of political service to the NATO powers, but a monumental travesty if the question of the proper administration of justice enters the equation. In fact, it will be shown below that as Arbour and her Tribunal played a key role in EXPEDITING war crimes, an excellent case can be made that in a just world she would be in the dock rather than in judicial robes.

Arbour To NATO's Rescue

The moment of truth for Arbour and the Tribunal came in the midst of NATO's 78-day bombing campaign against Yugoslavia, when Arbour appeared, first, in an April 20 press conference with British Foreign Secretary Robin Cook to receive from him documentation on Serb war crimes. Then on May 27, Arbour announced the indictment of Serb President Slobodan Milosevic and four of his associates for war crimes. The inappropriateness of a supposedly judicial body doing this in the midst of the Kosovo war, and when Germany, Russia and other powers were trying to find a diplomatic resolution to the conflict, was staggering.

At the April 20 appearance with Cook, Arbour stated that "It is inconceivable...that we would in fact agree to be guided by the political will of those who may want to advance an agenda." But her appearance with Cook and the followup indictments fitted perfectly the agenda needs of the NATO leadership. There had been growing criticism of NATO's increasingly intense and civilian infrastructure-oriented bombing of Serbia, and Blair and Cook had been lashing out at critics in the British media for insufficient enthusiasm for the war. Arbour's and the Tribunal's intervention declaring the Serb leadership to be guilty of war crimes was a public relations coup that justified the NATO policies and helped permit the bombing to continue and escalate. This was pointed out repeatedly by NATO leaders and propagandists: Madeleine Albright noted that the indictments "make very clear to the world and the publics in our countries that this [NATO policy] is justified because of the crimes committed, and I think also will enable us to keep moving all these processes [i.e., bombing] forward" (CNN, May 27). State Department spokesman James Rubin stated that "this unprecedented step...justifies in the clearest possible way what we have been doing these past months" (CNN Morning News, May 27).

Although the Tribunal had been in place since May 1993, and the most serious atrocities in the Yugoslav wars occurred as the old Federation disintegrated from June 1991 through the Dayton peace talks in late 1995, no indictment was brought against Milosevic for any of those atrocities, and the May 27 indictment refers only to a reported 241 deaths in the early months of 1999. The indictment appears to have been hastily prepared to meet some urgent need. Arbour even mentioned on April 20 that she had "visited NATO" to "dialogue with potential information providers in order to generate unprecedented support that the Tribunal needs if it will perform its mandate in a time frame that will make it relevant to the resolution of conflict...of a magnitude of what is currently unfolding in Kosovo." But her action impeded a negotiated resolution, although it helped expedite a resolution by intensified bombing.

Arbour herself noted that "I am mindful of the impact that this indictment may have on the peace process," and she said that although indicted individuals are "entitled to the presumption of innocence until they are convicted, the evidence upon which this indictment was confirmed raises serious questions about their suitability to be guarantors of any deal, let alone a peace agreement." (CNN Live Event, Special, May 27). So Arbour not only admitted awareness of the political significance of her indictment, she suggested that her possible interference with any diplomatic efforts was justified because the indicted individuals, though not yet found guilty, are not suitable to negotiate. This hugely unjudicial political judgment, along with the convenient timing of the indictments, points up Arbour's and the Tribunal's highly political role.

Background of the Tribunal's Politicization

Arbour's service to NATO in indicting Milosevic was the logical outcome of the Tribunal's de facto control and purpose. It was established by the Security Council in the early 1990s to serve the Balkan policy ends of its dominant members, especially the United States. (China and Russia went along as silent and powerless partners, apparently in a trade-off for economic concessions.) And its funding and interlocking functional relationship with the top NATO powers have made it NATO's instrument.

Although Article 32 of its Charter declares that the Tribunal's expenses shall be provided in the general budget of the United Nations, this proviso has been regularly violated. In 1994-1995 the U.S. government provided it with $700,000 in cash and $2.3 million in equipment (while failing to meet its delinquent obligation to the UN that might have allowed the UN itself to fund the Tribunal). On May 12, 1999, Judge Gabrielle Kirk McDonald, president of the Tribunal, stated that "the U.S. government has very generously agreed to provide $500,000 [for an Outreach project] and to help to encourage other states to contribute." Numerous other U.S.-based governmental and non-governmental agencies have provided the Tribunal with resources.

Article 16 of the Tribunal's charter states that the Prosecutor shall act independently and shall not seek or receive instruction from any government. This section also has been systematically violated. NATO sources have regularly made claims suggesting their authority over the Tribunal: "We will make a decision on whether Yugoslav actions against ethnic Albanians constitute genocide," states a USIA Fact Sheet, and Cook asserted at his April 20 press conference with Arbour that "we are going to focus on the war crimes being committed in Kosovo and our determination to bring those responsible to justice, " as if he and Arbour were a team jointly and cooperatively deciding on who should be charged for war crimes, and obviously excluding himself from those potentially chargeable. Earlier, on March 31, two days after Cook had promised Arbour supportive data for criminal charges, she announced the indictment of Arkan.

Tribunal officials have even bragged about "the strong support of concerned governments and dedicated individuals such as Secretary Albright," further referred to as "mother of the Tribunal" (by Gabrielle Kirk McDonald). The post-Arbour chief prosecutor Carla Del Ponte at a September 1999 press conference thanked the US FBI for helping the Tribunal, and expressed general thanks for "the important support the U.S. government has provided the Tribunal." Arbour herself informed President Clinton of the forthcoming indictment of Milosevic two days before the rest of the world, and in 1996 the prosecutor met with the Secretary-General of NATO and its supreme commander to "establish contacts and begin discussing modalities of cooperation and assistance." Numerous other meetings have occurred between prosecutor and NATO, which was given the function of Tribunal gendarme. In the collection of data also, the prosecutor has depended heavily on NATO and NATO governments, which again points to the symbiotic relation between the Tribunal and NATO.

Serb-Specific Focus

The NATO powers focused almost exclusively on Serb misbehavior in the course of their participation in the breakup of Yugoslavia, and the Tribunal has followed in NATO's wake. A great majority of the Tribunal's indictments have been of Serbs, and those against Croatians and Muslims often seemed to have been timed to counter claims of anti-Serb bias (e.g., the first non-Serb indictment [Ivica Rajic], announced during the peace talks in Geneva and bombing by NATO in September 1995).

Arbour herself did state (April 20) that "the real danger is whether we would fall into that [following somebody's political agenda] inadvertently by being in the hands of information- providers who might have an agenda that we would not be able to discern." But even an imbecile could discern that NATO had an agenda and that simply accepting the flood of documents offered by Cook and Albright entailed advertently following that agenda. Arbour even acknowledged her voluntary and almost exclusive "dependencies...on the goodwill of states" to provide information that "will guide our analysis of the crime base." And her April 20 reference to the "morality of the [NATO's] enterprise" and her remarks on Milosevic's possible lack of character disqualifying him from negotiations, as well as her rush to help NATO with an indictment, point to quite clearly understood political service.

In a dramatic illustration of Arbour-Tribunal bias, a 150 page Tribunal report entitled "The Indictment Operation Storm: A Prima Facie Case," describes war crimes committed by the Croatian armed forces in their expulsion of more than 200,000 Serbs from Krajina in August 1995, during which "at least 150 Serbs were summarily executed, and many hundreds disappeared." This report, leaked to the New York Times (to the dismay of Tribunal officials), found that the Croatian murders and other inhumane acts were "widespread and systematic," and that "sufficient material" was available to make three named Croatian generals accountable under international law. (Raymond Bonner, "War Crimes Panel Finds Croat Troops 'Cleansed' the Serbs," NYT, March 21, 1999). But the Times article also reports that the United States, which supported the Croat's ethnic cleansing of Serbs in Krajina, not only defended the Croats in the Tribunal but refused to supply requested satellite photos of Krajina areas attacked by the Croats, as well as failing to provide other requested information. The result was that the Croat generals named in the report on Operation Storm were never indicted, and although the number of Serbs executed and disappeared over a mere four days was at least equal to the 241 victims of the Serbs named in the indictment of Milosevic, no parallel indictment of Croat leader Tudjman was ever brought by the Tribunal. But this was not a failure of data gathering--the United States opposed indictments of its allies, and thus the Tribunal did not produce any.

Tribunal's Kangaroo Court Processes

Arbour has claimed that the Tribunal was "subject to extremely stringent rules of evidence with respect to the admissibility and the credibility of the product that we will tender in court" so that she was guarded against "unsubstantiated, unverifiable, uncorroborated allegations" (April 20). This is a gross misrepresentation of what John Laughland described in the Times (London) as "a rogue court with rigged rules" (June 17, 1999). The Tribunal violates virtually every standard of due process: it fails to separate prosecution and judge; it does not accord the right to bail or a speedy trial; it has no clear definition of burden of proof required for a conviction; it has no independent appeal body; it violates the principle that a defendant may not be tried twice for the same crime (Article 25 gives the prosecutor the right to appeal against an acquittal); suspects can be held for 90 days without trial; under Rule 92 confessions are presumed to be free and voluntary unless the contrary is established by the prisoner; witnesses can testify anonymously, and as John Laughland notes, "rules against hearsay, deeply entrenched in Common Law, are not observed and the Prosecutor's office has even suggested not calling witnesses to give evidence but only the tribunal's own 'war crimes investigators.'"

As noted, Arbour presumes guilt before trial; the concept of "innocent till convicted" is rejected, and she can declare that people linked with Arkan "will be tainted by their association with an indicted war criminal" (March 31). Arbour clearly does not believe in the basic rules of Western jurisprudence, and Laughland quotes her saying "The law, to me, should be creative and used to make things tight." And within a month of her elevation to the Canadian Supreme Court she was a member of a court majority that grafted onto Canadian law the dangerously unfair Tribunal practice of permitting a more liberal use of hearsay evidence in trials. The consequent corruption of the Canadian justice system, both by her appointment and her impact, mirrors that in the Canadian political system, whose leading members supported the NATO war without question.

NATO's Crimes

In bombing Yugoslavia from March 24 into June 1999, NATO was guilty of the serious crime of violating the UN Charter requirement that it not use force without UN Security Council sanction. It was also guilty of criminal aggression in attacking a sovereign state that was not going beyond its borders. In its defense, NATO claimed that "humanitarian" concerns demanded these actions and thus justified seemingly serious law violations. Apart from the fact that this reply sanctions law violations on the basis of self- serving judgments that contradict the rule of law, it is also called into question on its own grounds by counter-facts. First, the NATO bombing made "an internal humanitarian problem into a disaster" in the words of Rollie Keith, the returned Canadian OSCE human rights monitor in Kosovo. Second, the evidence is now clear that NATO refused to negotiate a settlement in Kosovo and insisted on a violent solution; that in the words of one State Department official, NATO deliberately "raised the bar" and precluded a compromise resolution because Serbia "needed to be bombed." These counter-facts suggest that the alleged humanitarian basis of the law violations was a cover for starkly political and geopolitical objectives.

NATO was also guilty of more traditional war crimes, including some that the Tribunal had found indictable when carried out by Serbs. Thus on March 8, 1996, the Serb leader Milan Martic was indicted for launching a rocket cluster-bomb attack on military targets in Zagreb in

May 1995, on the ground that the rocket was "not designed to hit military targets but to terrorize the civilians of Zagreb." The Tribunal report on the Croat Operation Storm in Krajina also provided solid evidence that a 48 hour Croat assault on the city of Knin was basically "shelling civilian targets," with fewer than 250 of 3,000 shells striking military targets. But no indictments followed from this evidence or for any other raid.

The same case for civilian targeting could be made for numerous NATO bombing raids, as in the cluster-bombing of Nis on May 7, 1999, in which a market and hospital far from any military target were hit in separate strikes--but no indictment has yet been handed down against NATO.

But NATO was also guilty of the bombing of non-military targets as systematic policy. On March 26, 1999, General Wesley Clark said that "We are going to very systematically and progressively work on his military forces...[to see] how much pain he is willing to suffer." But this focus on "military forces" wasn't effective, so NATO quickly turned to "taking down...the economic apparatus supporting" Serb military forces (Clinton's words), and NATO targets were gradually extended to factories of all kinds, electric power stations, water and sewage processing facilities, all transport, public buildings, and large numbers of schools and hospitals. In effect, it was NATO's strategy to bring Serbia to its knees by gradually escalating its attacks on the civil society.

But this policy was in clear violation of international law, one of whose fundamental elements is that civilian targets are off limits; international law prohibits the "wanton destruction of cities, towns or villages or devastation not justified by military necessity" (Sixth Principle of Nuremberg, formulated in 1950 by an international law commission at the behest of the UN). "Military necessity" clearly does not allow the destruction of a civil society to make it more difficult for the country to support its armed forces, any more than civilians can be killed directly on he ground that they pay taxes supporting the war machine or might some day become soldiers. The rendering of an entire population a hostage is a blatant violation of international law and acts carrying it out are war crimes.

On September 29, 1999, in response to a question on whether the Tribunal would investigate crimes committed in Kosovo after June 10, or those committed by NATO in Yugoslavia, prosecutor Carla del Ponte stated that "The primary focus of the Office of the Prosecutor must be on the investigation and prosecution of the five leaders of the FRY and Serbia who have already been indicted." Why this "must" be the focus, especially in light of all the evidence already assembled in preparing the favored indictments, was unexplained. In late December, it was finally reported that Del Ponte was reviewing the conduct of NATO, at the urging of Russia and several other "interested parties" ("U.N. Court Examines NATO's Yugoslavia War," NYT, Dec. 29, 1999). But the news report itself indicates that the focus is on the conduct of NATO pilots and their commanders, not the NATO decision-makers who made the ultimate decisions to target the civilian infrastructure. It also suggests the public relations nature of the inquiry, which would "go far in dispelling the belief...that the tribunal is a tool used by Western leaders to escape accountability." The report also indicates the delicate matter that the tribunal "depends on the military alliance to arrest and hand over suspects." It also quotes Del Ponte saying that "It's not my priority, because I have inquiries about genocide, about bodies in mass graves." We may rest assured that no indictments will result from this inquiry.

An impartial Tribunal would have gone to great pains to balance NATO's flood of documents by internal research and a welcoming of rival documentation. But although submissions have been made on NATO's crimes by Yugoslavia and a number of Western legal teams, the Tribunal didn't get around to these until this belated and surely nominal inquiry that is "not my priority," as the Tribunal "must" pursue the Serb villains, for reasons that are only too clear.

Beyond Orwell

NATO's leaders, frustrated in attacking the Serb military machine, quite openly turned to smashing the civil society of Serbia as their means of attaining the quick victory desired before the 50th Anniversary celebration of NATO's founding. Although this amounted to turning the civilian population of Serbia into hostages and attacking them and their means of sustenance--in gross violation of the laws of war--Arbour and her Tribunal not only failed to object to and prosecute NATO's leaders for war crimes, by indicting Milosevic on May 27 they gave NATO a moral cover permitting escalated attacks on the hostage population.

Arbour and the Tribunal thus present us with the amazing spectacle of an institution supposedly organized to contain, prevent, and prosecute for war crimes actually knowingly facilitating them. Furthermore, petitions submitted to the Tribunal during Arbour's tenure had called for prosecution of the leaders of NATO, including Canadian Prime Minister Jean Chretien, for the commission of war crimes. If she had been a prosecutor in Canada, Britain or the United States, she would have been subject to disbarment for considering and then accepting a job from a person she had been asked to charge. But Arbour was elevated to the Supreme Court of Canada by Chretien with hardly a mention of this conflict of interest and immorality.

In this post-Orwellian New World Order we are told that we live under the rule of law, but as Saint Augustine once said, "There are just laws and there are unjust laws, and an unjust law is no law at all."

February 13, 2000

Andre Vltchek – Christopher Black – Peter Koenig

2

AN IMPARTIAL TRIBUNAL, REALLY?

by Christopher Black

Private justice replacing public justice

The indictment of Slobodan Milosevic for alleged war crimes raises important questions about the impartiality and, ultimately, the purpose of the International Criminal Tribunal. For centuries, the independence of judicial bodies has been considered one of the fundamental precepts of the quest for justice. As Lord Hewart stated in 1924, it is "...of fundamental importance that justice should not only be done, but should manifestly and undoubtedly be seen to be done." It has also been said that there is nothing more important than the public administration of justice. But in the case of the International Criminal Tribunal a compelling argument can be made that private justice has replaced public justice, that even the appearance of fundamental justice has been replaced by an open contempt for justice.

It is clear that from the beginning, American, British, French and German interests were behind the creation of the Tribunal and worked ceaselessly behind the scenes in order to create it. They first considered doing so in regards to Iraq and Saddam Hussein, during the Gulf War. The idea apparently originated with the United States Department of the Army, which alone should tell you something about its true purpose. The rhetoric used to justify such a body to the general public was of course heavily seasoned with concerns for "human rights" the "dignity of the individual", "genocide" and "democracy".

However, they had a problem. It was generally agreed that no such tribunal could be created without the mechanism of a treaty which had to be ratified by all those affected by it. There was no time to create such a treaty with respect to Hussein so other methods were used to put pressure on the Iraqi government. But between 1991 and 1993, the use of an international criminal court as a means of effecting policy and to be created by the members of the Security Council, instead of by treaty, was pushed by those four countries.

A war crimes tribunal rather than a international court

A draft treaty to create a truly international criminal court, one which applied to all states, the last in a long list of attempts dating back to the 1890's, was put together. But its ratification has not taken place as several important powers, particularly the United States, refuse to sign it for fear of being caught in its web. For thirty years the United States has tried to block such a treaty. It opposes universal jurisdiction and it opposes an independent prosecutor. It wants any prosecutions to go through the Security Council subject to its right of veto. In fact, Jesse Helms, the conservative US senator said such a treaty, if presented to congress for ratification would be "dead on arrival". It would seem that the treaty is itself nothing more than window dressing to satisfy the public that the nations of the world really care about human rights and war crimes in order to complement their rhetoric about it. For without ratification by the major powers it is a dead letter. The United States remains stubborn in its opposition to this treaty but then it has a bit more to worry about than most countries.

The next opportunity to try this experiment was Yugoslavia. In order to accelerate the break up of that country into quasi-independent colonies, principally of Germany and the United States, it was necessary to discredit their leaderships. An effective propaganda weapon in such an exercise is of course a tribunal with an international character which the public will accept as a neutral instrument of justice but which is controlled for political ends.

The Tribunal was created by the Security Council in its Resolutions 808 and 827 of 1993. Both resolutions stated that the situation in Bosnia at that time, constituted a threat to international peace and security and that a tribunal to prosecute war criminals would help to restore peace. It all sounds very nice until one realizes that there was no basis for the characterization of the situation in Bosnia as a threat to international peace. It was a civil war (partly controlled by the very countries which wanted to create a tribunal). But the members of the Security Council had to characterize it that way otherwise the members of the Security Council had no jurisdiction to act. The setup for this characterization was Resolution 688 of 1991 in which the Security Council stated that disregard for human rights constitutes a threat to international security and can no longer be treated as an internal matter.

Undermining the UN Charter to make the Tribunal possible

This reinterpretation, this revision of the UN Charter, which in fact undermines the very basis of the Charter was forcefully advocated by the German foreign minister Mr. Genscher in speeches he gave to the German parliament and to the Canadian parliament in Ottawa and by British, French and of course American ministers in speeches and memorandums to each other.

Chapter VII of the UN Charter requires that there be a threat to the peace or an act of aggression before the Security Council can make use of its special powers set out in that Chapter. It has always been interpreted to mean and was meant to mean a threat to international peace not national peace. The members of the Security Council recognized this and so had to redefine a national problem as an international one. Yet in all those speeches and memoranda there is not one compelling reason given for doing this except vague references to the collapse of the socialist bloc, and the imperative to establish a new world order.

In fact, Mr. Genscher in his speech to the Canadian parliament stated unequivocally that no nation would any longer be allowed to ignore Security Council decisions. Even if this redefinition were a legitimate interpretation of the UN Charter, which it is not, the UN Charter only speaks of economic measures and then military measures, not judicial or criminal measures.

Chapter VII has to be read in context with Chapter I of the Charter which speaks of international cooperation in solving international problems of an economic, social, cultural or humanitarian character. It says nothing of humanitarian problems of a national character. It states that the UN is based on the principle of the sovereign equality of its members, a fundamental principle of international law, and the first guarantee of the right to self-determination of the world's peoples. If a people does not have the right of sovereignty, the right to self-determination is a sham. This principle is completely denied by the creation of the Tribunal. The Tribunal itself explicitly denies that this principle applies in its own statements as do its political supporters, but never, of course, in reference to themselves. Lastly, the

Charter states that nothing contained in the Charter shall authorize the UN to intervene in matters which are essentially within the domestic jurisdiction of any state. This fundamental principle, put in the Charter so that the UN could not be used by some members to bully others, has also been fatally undermined by the creation of the Tribunal. The members of the Security Council, more precisely, the permanent members, now hold the opposite position, and I submit, do so for reasons connected more with imperialism not humanitarianism.

In light of these facts the Security Council's authority to create such a tribunal is in my view more than questionable. That it was created is to be credited to Madeleine Albright, who used some effective persuasion with the Russian and Chinese members to vote for its creation in return for economic consideration and with a view to controlling smaller states within their own spheres of interest.

Yugoslavia could be used

Yugoslavia was the first experiment in using a quasi-judicial international body to attack the principle of sovereignty. And as the Americans have learned so well, the best way to get your domestic population behind you as you proceed to break another country, economically and militarily is to get them to hate those in power in that country. The Serb leadership was targeted, and transformed into caricatures of evil. There were comparisons to Adolf Hitler, a comparison used with surprising frequency by the United States against the long list of nations it has attacked in the last 50 years, though sometimes they are just labeled as common criminals, like

Manuel Noriega, or mad, like Ghadaffi, if the leader or the country is too small to make the Hitler comparison stick. I think Saddam Hussein was the first to be compared to Hitler, and declared a common criminal and a madman all at the same time.

The Tribunal from the outset was, as I have said, the creation of particular governments. Their motives are clear from the preliminary discussions in the Security Council on the creation of the court which focused almost entirely on crimes allegedly committed by Serbs and their leadership. Since its inception it has kept this focus. The majority of indictments have been directed at Serbs even though there is substantial evidence of the commission of serious war crimes by Croats and Bosnian Muslims.

Aggression and crimes against peace left out

The Tribunal has jurisdiction over war crimes and crimes against humanity, but crimes against peace, the worst crime under the Nuremberg principles, are not within the purview of the tribunal. The underlying reason for this is that the members of the Security Council preferred to reserve to themselves competence in the field of aggression and similar crimes against peace. The members of the Security Council have a very keen sense of humour or perhaps more accurately, self-preservation.

In a statement to the Secretary-General of the United Nation, Mr. Boutros-Boutros Ghali, on January 21, 1994, by Antonio Cassese the Tribunal's political character was made quite clear when he said in reference to the role of the Tribunal, "The political and diplomatic response (to the Balkans conflict) takes into account the exigencies and the tempo of the international community. The military response will come at the appropriate time." In other words, the Tribunal is considered a political response. He went on to state, "Our tribunal will not be simply "window dressing" but a decisive step in the construction of a new world order."

The governing statute is continuously violated: independence and financing

The governing statute of the Tribunal states in Article 16 that the Prosecutor shall act independently as a separate organ of the Tribunal and shall not seek or receive instruction from any government or any other source. Article 32 states that the expenses of the Tribunal shall be borne by the regular budget of the United Nations. Both of these provisions have been openly and continuously violated.

The Tribunal itself, through its senior officials openly brags about its particularly close ties to the American government. In her remarks to the United States Supreme Court in Washington,

D.C. on April 5th of this year, Judge Gabrielle Kirk Mcdonald, President of the Tribunal, and an American stated, "We benefited from the strong support of concerned governments and dedicated individuals such as Secretary Albright. As the permanent representative to the United Nations, she had worked with unceasing resolve to establish the Tribunal. Indeed, we often refer to her as the "mother of the Tribunal". If she is the mother then Bill Clinton is the father, as Louise Arbour confirmed by her action of reporting to the President of the United States the decision to indict Milosevic two days before she announced it to the rest of the world, in blatant violation of her duty to remain independent. Further, she and the current prosecutor have

made several public appearances with U.S officials, including Madeleine Albright, and both have openly stated that they rely on NATO governments for investigations, governments which have a great interest in the undermining of the Yugoslavian leadership.

NATO, not the UN, the gendarme of the Tribunal

In 1996, the prosecutor met with the Secretary-General of NATO and the Supreme Allied Commander in Europe to "establish contacts and begin discussing modalities of cooperation and Assistance". On May 9th, 1996 a memorandum of understanding between the

Office of the Prosecutor and Supreme Headquarters Allied Powers Europe (SHAPE) was signed by both parties. Further meetings have taken place since including that of the president of the Tribunal with General Wesley Clarke. The memorandum of May 9th spelled out the practical arrangements for support to the tribunal and the transfer of indicted persons to the Tribunal. In other words, NATO forces became the gendarmes of the Tribunal, not UN forces, and the Tribunal put itself at the disposal of NATO. This relationship has continued despite the Tribunal's requirement to be independent of any national government and, therefore, group of national governments.

Primarily US, not UN, funding

The Tribunal has received substantial funds from individual States, private foundations and corporations in violation of Article 32 of its Charter. Much of its money has come from the U.S. government directly in cash and donations of computer equipment. In the last year for which public figures are available, 1994/95, the United States provided $700,000 in cash and $2,300,000 worth of equipment. That same year the Open Society Institute, a foundation established by George Soros, the American billionaire financier, to bring "openness" to the former east bloc countries contributed $150,000 and the Rockefeller family, through the Rockefeller Foundation, contributed $50,000 and there have been donations from corporations such as Time-Warner, and Discovery Products, both US corporations. It also important to know that Mr. Soros' foundation not only funds the Tribunal it also funds the main KLA newspaper in Pristina, an obvious conflict of interest that has not been mentioned once in the western press.

The Tribunal also receives money from the United States Institute for Peace for its Outreach project, a public relations arm of the Tribunal set up to overcome opposition in the former Yugoslav republics to its work and the constant criticisms of selective prosecution and the application of double standards; objections which have obvious merit and which are never answered by anyone at the Tribunal or by any of its sponsors. The Institute for Peace is stated to be " an independent, non-partisan federal institution created and funded by Congress to strengthen the nation's capacity to promote the peaceful resolution of international conflict." Established in 1984 under Ronald Reagan, its Board of Directors is appointed by the President of the United States.

The Tribunal also receives support from the Coalition For International Justice whose purpose is also to enhance public opinion of the Tribunal. The CIJ was founded and is funded by, again, George Soros' Open Society Institute and something called CEELI, the Central and East European Law Institute, created by the American Bar Association and lawyers close to the U.S. government to promote the replacement of socialist legal systems with free market ones.

These groups also have supplied many of the legal staff of the Tribunal. In her speech to the Supreme Court, Judge Mcdonald said, "The Tribunal has been well served by the tremendous work of a number of lawyers who have come to the Tribunal through the CIJ and CEELI..." It is also interesting to note that the occasion of Judge McDonalds speech was her acceptance of an award from the American Bar Association and CEELI. In the same speech she also said that "We are now seeking funding from states and foundations to carry out this critical effort."

Not anybody's war crimes

The new prosecutor Carla Del Ponte, on September 30, 1999 at a press conference, thanked the director of the FBI for assisting the tribunal and stated "I am very appreciative of the important support that the U.S government has provided the tribunal. I look forward to their continued support." On September 29th, in response to a question as to whether the tribunal would be investigating crimes Committed in Kosovo after June 10, or crimes committed by others (meaning NATO) in the Yugoslav theatre of operations, "The primary focus of the Office of The Prosecutor must be on the investigation and prosecution of the five leaders of the FRY and Serbia who have already been indicted."

Why this "must" be is not explained. Why, if the Tribunal is impartial wouldn't it be just as focussed on NATO war crimes, the war crimes of Clinton, Schroeder, Chirac, Chretien etc? Why did it still need to investigate to support the indictments against the leaders of the government and military of Yugoslavia if there was already evidence to justify those indictments?

Well, we can speculate why when we consider that the last prosecutor, Louis Arbour, who was asked to investigate all NATO leaders for war crimes, instead accepted a job from one of them, the Prime Minister of Canada, Jean Chretien. She now sits in the scarlet robes of a judge of the

Supreme Court of Canada, a lifetime appointment, her reward for handing down the indictment against Mr. Milosevic, despite the lack of evidence and (if you believe the reports of the Spanish and RCMP forensic experts recently returned from Kosovo) the continuing lack of evidence of the systematic crimes he is accused of.

On April 19th Judge McDonald "expressed her deep appreciation to the U.S. Government for its pledge of $500,000 for the Outreach project which was announced on April 16 by Harold Koh, U.S. Assistant Secretary of State.

In her speech to the Council On Foreign Relations in New York on May 12 of this year Judge McDonald stated," The U.S. government has very generously agreed to provide $500,000 and to help to encourage other States to contribute. However, the moral imperative to end the violence in the region is shared by all, including the corporate sector. I am pleased, therefore, that a major corporation has recently donated computer equipment worth three million dollars, which will substantially enhance our operating capacity."

From the start, the Office of the Prosecutor has had meetings with NGO's that are eager to "cooperate with and assist the tribunal", many of them linked to George Soros through his Open Society Foundation. All this money flows through a special UN account which is financed by assessed contributions from member states and voluntary contributions from states and corporations again in violation of its statute.

As an aside it's interesting that its role as a propaganda tool was indirectly acknowledged by its own staff when they failed to provide for a courtroom or holding cells in their first budget of approximately $ 32 million dollars. The Security Council sent them back to redraft the budget to include those items. After all, this was supposed to be a criminal tribunal! They did so. The difference was an added expense of $500,000. It's also interesting to know that three of its first four rooms in the Peace Palace in the Hague were loaned to them by the Carnegie Foundation.

The Tribunal itself lays the charges

In order to give itself the appearance of a judicial body the Tribunal has persons appointed as judges, prosecutors, clerks, investigators, and has its own rules of procedure and evidence, its own prison system. It says it applies the presumption of innocence. However, unlike criminal courts, with which we are all familiar (or, perhaps not), the court itself is involved in the

laying of the charges. When a charge is to be laid the approval of one of the trial judges must be obtained. That approval is only given if a prima facie case is established. That is, a case which if not answered could result in a conviction. Yet, despite this close relationship between the prosecutor and the judges and the commitment to the charges the judges have made by signing the indictment, the rules insist on the presumption of innocence.

The presumption of innocence is compromised: automatic detention

This presumption is compromised in other ways. The most egregious is that upon arrest detention is automatic. There is no bail, no form of release pending trial, unless the prisoner proves "exceptional circumstances". Loss of job, loss of contact with friends, family, indeed country is not sufficient. Even ill health has not been sufficient to get bail. Prisoners are treated as if they had been convicted. They are kept in cells and have to obey prison rules, are subject to discipline if they do not, constant surveillance, censored mail, restricted family visits, communication with family at their own expense and there are restrictions on what they can see or hear on radio or television.

Prisoners have had to wait many months before a trial takes place, sometimes years. Yet, still they insist these men are presumed innocent. The question is by whom? By the judges, one of whom laid the charge in the first place?

No jury, sealed indictments, possibly secret trials and suspects can be detained for up to 90 days without charge!

Its rules of evidence are relaxed so that protections on the admission of hearsay evidence developed over centuries in all national courts are set aside and replaced by an anything is admissible if deemed relevant approach even if it is hearsay. There is no jury. Witnesses can testify anonymously, or not be shown in court. In its yearbook for 1994, this statement appears, "The tribunal does not need to shackle itself with restrictive rules which have developed out of the ancient trial-by-jury system." There are provisions in the rules for closed hearings, in circumstances which are vaguely defined, secret trials, the very essence of injustice and of political courts. It is now increasing its use of sealed indictments, so that no one knows if they have been charged until the military police swoop down on them on the street in any country. Suspects, persons not indicted, can be detained for up to ninety days without charge. We all know from experience what prisoners can undergo in a day or two at the mercy of most police forces. Ninety days. Anyone one of us, you and I, could be detained by the Tribunal for that length of time. All they have to say is they have some reason to suspect you. This is easily constructed.

Confessions free after custody in 90 days?

Perhaps its most dangerous rule is Rule 92 that states confessions shall be presumed to be free and voluntary unless the contrary is established (by the prisoner). Just think - presumed to be free and voluntary after 90 days at the mercy of military police and prosecutors. Almost every other court in the world presumes the opposite or, because of the notorious unreliability of confessions made in police custody are moving to prohibit their use entirely. This

Tribunal goes back to the days of Star Chamber and the justice of the 13th century. Finally, we have imprisonment of those sentenced in foreign countries so that not only are they imprisoned, they are at the same time exiled.

There is even a special provision for the obtaining of evidence from NGO's such as George Soros Open Society Foundation, whose conflict of interest has already been mentioned. Accused have the right to choose counsel on paper but in reality that right is infringed by the Registrar who can disqualify counsel for all sorts of reasons including being unfriendly to the Tribunal. Such a counsel will be supplied if the accuses insists strongly enough but it is not made easy. There are cases in which the Registrar has barred lawyers from particular countries because there are deemed to be too many of them already representing accused persons, and the use of its contempt powers is a powerful weapon to intimidate counsel. Lawyers have been subject to large fines for contempt.

Not a judicial body worthy of international respect

No citizen of any country in the world would consider themselves fairly tried before a court that was paid for, staffed and assisted by private citizens or corporations which had a direct stake in the outcome of the trial and who were, themselves, in practical terms, immune from that court. It is a well established principle of law that a party in a legal action, whether civil or criminal, is entitled to ask for the removal of any judge sitting on the case when there exists a reasonable apprehension of bias.

In this instance, a compelling argument can be made that the bias is not only apprehended, it is real, that it is not of one judge but of the entire tribunal, that this is not a judicial body worthy of international respect but a kangaroo court, a bogus court, with a political purpose serving very powerful and identifiable masters.

A crime against peace under the Nuremberg Principles?

To be consistent with my thesis, I will go further and say that as a political instrument designed to violate, to destroy, the integrity and sovereignty of a country, its creation is a crime against peace under the Nuremberg Principles. Instead of resolving conflict as it claims, it is used to justify conflict, instead of creating peace, it is used to justify war and therefore is an instrument of war.

Will Slobodan Milosevic receive a fair trial if they take him? Will the leaders of NATO, even be investigated let alone indicted for war crimes committed in the brutal attack on the civilian population of Yugoslavia, as my colleagues in Canada, South and Central America, Spain, Norway, Greece, Britain, and the United States have requested?

As the English say, the proof is in the pudding. Our requests have met with empty words and no action. We made the requests in order to bring to the attention of the world the crimes that were being committed by NATO. We believe we have succeeded in that. If we have not succeeded in bringing to justice the war criminals of NATO, it is because we have exposed the political nature of this Tribunal instead. It is up to all of us to act on this knowledge.

June 15, 2000

3

INTERNATIONAL JUSTICE NOW INTERNATIONAL OPPRESSION

by Christopher Black

"The Nuremberg Trials of 1946 advanced international law in a fundamental way. For the first time in history the victims of aggressive war brought their attackers to justice and aggression was defined as the ultimate war crime from which all others flow. Today, international war crimes trials are used by the aggressor to persecute the victims of their aggression. International law has turned full circle from justice to oppression, from justice to revenge."

What can better illustrate this than the one-sided justice at the ad hoc tribunals, the ICTY and ICTR, where the victims of western aggression are accused of the grossest slanders and crimes in order to obscure the real facts of those wars under a cloud of darkness and confusion. What can better illustrate this than the statement by the judges of the ICTR in the case of General Ndindiliyimana, in its judgement in the Military II case, just released, at paragraph 2191, that "The Defence submits that the indictment and arrest 'were motivated by political reasons'. The Chamber recalls that before this Chamber, the Defence stated that the prosecution made every effort to encourage Ndindiliyimana to testify against Colonel Bagasora, but Ndindiliyimana refused. The Prosecution did not deny this. Following his initial refusal, the Prosecution produced a far-reaching indictment charging Ndindiliyimana with a number of crimes....Most of those charges were eventually dropped."

Political reasons

As the judges of the ICTR revealed that the court's prosecutor indicted people for political reasons, the ICTY demanded that Serbia hand over General Mladic for allegedly engaging in a "joint criminal enterprise" to kill Croats and Bosnian Moslems. General Mladic maintains that he defended Serbs from the criminal actions of the Croat and Bosnian Moslem forces attacking his peoples, for which there is abundant evidence. Yet the victim once again is the accused and the witnesses brought against him are from the party of the aggressor.

Now we have the absurdity of the International Criminal Court issuing criminal indictments against various Africans whose common connection is to be in the way of western interests in Africa. The latest indictment against Colonel Ghaddafi, made because his country resists the aggression and war crimes of the USA and its satellites in Europe and Canada shows, even to the blind, that control of the ICC has been seized by the USA, even as that country refuses to be subject to its jurisdiction.

Shocking aspect

Never in history has "criminal justice" been perverted to such criminal ends. The most shocking aspect is the complete acquiescence of the nations of the world in this charade. Members of the Security Council, apart from the United States, have the power to annul the ad hoc tribunals but they do not. They have the power to refuse to refer clearly political accusations to the ICC. But they do not. It is they who are in charge and who are responsible, just as much as the USA.

General Mladic would have good reason to tell the ICTY judges that since they are a proxy for the Security Council, he wants to be tried by the Security Council itself, and then he could see who he was really up against and why. Colonel Gaddafi would have the same right to demand to be brought face to face with his real accusers in the Security Council so he could reveal to the world their true interests. But this right to face one's accuser, this right to honesty, will not be allowed. Instead they are faced with a theatre troop acting out a macabre play, a show for the public.

So corrupted

Indeed, the entire structure of "international justice" since 1946 has become so corrupted that it is difficult to see how it can be transformed into a vehicle to stop aggression as it was intended, instead of a propaganda tool justifying it. The rot has spread everywhere.

The nations of the world must once again stand up and demand that the principles of the United Nations Charter be adhered to. They were thought important once. They are important now. They must demand that this architecture be dismantled, that international justice be restored in the true sense of the phrase, and that the sovereignty of nations and self-determination of peoples be inviolate principles once again. But this architecture cannot be dismantled until the Security Council is abolished and the United Nations General Assembly represents the true interests of the peoples of the world in complete equality.

July 20, 2011

4

THE CRIMINALISATION OF INTERNATIONAL JUSTICE ANATOMY OF A WAR CRIMES TRIAL

by Christopher Black

The NATO ordered indictment of Muammar Gadaffi by the prosecutor of the International Criminal Court (ICC) during the NATO attack on Libya in 2011 echoed the indictment of President Milosevic by the prosecutor of the ad hoc International Criminal Tribunal For Yugoslavia, during the NATO attack on Yugoslavia in 1999. Both men ended up dead as a direct consequence, Gaddafi brutally murdered by NATO supported forces in Libya, Milosevic dead in his cell at Scheveningen in circumstances indicating criminal negligence or murder by the hands of the same forces. The indictments of these two men, whose only crime was to resist the diktats and imperial ambitions of the United States and its allies, had only one purpose, to serve as propaganda to justify NATO's aggression and the elimination of governments that refused to bend the knee. Consequently, those that issued the indictments are co-conspirators in the planning and execution of those wars. The international criminal justice machine has become a weapon of total war, used not to prosecute the criminals who conduct these wars, but to persecute the leaders of the countries who resist.

Milosevic and Gaddafi are not the only victims of this criminalised international legal structure. The list is long. The judicial murder of Saddam Hussein by the Americans and British and their Iraqi collaborators was also based on a clearly political sham indictment and though portrayed as an Iraqi affair was another show trial arranged by the imperial power. In fact American officers were in charge of the entire proceedings. Other national leaders who have become helpless victims of these tribunals include President Charles Taylor of Liberia, convicted despite a lack evidence of any criminal wrongdoing by the ad hoc Sierra Leone tribunal, Prime Minister Jean Kambanda of Rwanda, sentenced to life without a trial he vehemently demanded to have by the ad hoc Rwanda tribunal and most recently President Laurent Gbagbo of Ivory Coast, politically assassinated by his arrest, by French forces and his detention for 3 years at the ICC without any prima facie case being made out against him even up to today. Indictments have been issued against other national leaders who are in the way of the west, such as the President Bashir of Sudan and President Uhuru Kenyatta of Kenya, whose case is now suspended, since the ICC now admits that they have no evidence against him. Just recently there was talk in the western press of charges against President Putin. We all see how absurd and surreal the game has become.

The structural role these tribunals have played in the attempt by NATO to create its New World Order has been analysed and described by distinguished jurists and writers around the world. Since I am not a theorist nor a philosopher, but a trial lawyer, I wish to contribute to your understanding of the criminal nature of this international justice machine by relating to you my experience of defending a particular political prisoner held by it. I could tell you about the scandalous practices of the ICTY in the Milosevic trial in which I was involved through his international defence committee but these are well known and have been recounted by a number of eminent persons and writers. There are many victims of these tribunals but I will focus on this one particular case because it stands as an exemplar of the many.

On January 28, 2000, General Augustin Ndidiliyimana, the former Chief of Staff of the Rwanda gendarmerie and most senior ranking Rwandan military officer in 1994, was arrested in Belgium based on an indictment issued by Carla Del Ponte, then prosecutor of the International Criminal Tribunal For Rwanda, the ICTR. He fled to Belgium in June 1994 after receiving threats on his life. His entry into Belgium was authorised by the then Belgian Foreign Minister, Willy Claeys, later Secretary-General of NATO, who stated at the time that he had saved the lives of many Rwandans.

It is with the arrest that the criminality begins to appear. It was speculated in the Belgian press at the time that it was for political reasons and indeed, 11 years later, this speculation was confirmed when the trial judges delivered their judgement.

They stated, in the judgement dated May 17, 2011 the following:[1]

---

[1] This is the original paragraph number as issued on the date of judgement and as used in the appeal documents. It now appears on the ICTR website in the trial judgement of Case 00-56-T as paragraph 2190.

2191. The Defence submits that Ndindiliyimana's indictment and arrest "were motivated by political reasons".[3862] The Chamber recalls that before this Chamber, the Defence stated that the Prosecution made every effort to encourage Ndindiliyimana to testify against Colonel Bagosora, but Ndindiliyimana refused.[3863] The Prosecution did not deny this. Following his initial refusal to testify, the Prosecution produced a far-reaching Indictment charging Ndindiliyimana with a number of crimes pursuant to Article 6(1) of the Statute. Most of those charges were eventually dropped. The Defence further alleges that the Prosecution made repeated offers during the trial to drop the charges against Ndindiliyimana if he would agree to testify against Bagosora, but Ndindiliyimana repeatedly refused.[3864]

General Ndindiliyimana was considered a political "moderate" during the Rwanda War of 1990-94, a Hutu respected by Tutsis and Hutus alike and, as attested to by many witnesses including witnesses for the prosecution, his gendarmes did not commit crimes against civilians but tried to protect them where they could. So why was he arrested?

Because he was a potential leader of the country, because he refused to cooperate with the RPF regime installed by the United States after the war, because he knew too much about what really happened in Rwanda and who was really responsible for the violence, because he knew that UN and American forces, despite Clinton's denials, were directly involved in the final RPF offensive of 1994 and the murder of President Habyarimana. All these reasons were no doubt involved in his arrest but it quickly became clear that the prosecutor used his arrest to pressure him to give false evidence against Colonel Theoneste Bagosora, the former deputy minister of defence in Rwanda who was their primary target, the "big fish" of the prosecution.

The criminal methods used against him began immediately on his arrest. He and his counsel in Brussles met with two ICTR prosecution staffers who informed him that the indictment was just a formality to give the ICTR jurisdiction over him and that the real reason for his arrest was to accompany them to Arusha, Tanzania, the home of the ICTR, to meet with the prosecutor to be interviewed regarding events in Rwanda. Why this could not be done in Belgium without an indictment was not explained but based on these assurances neither he nor his counsel attempted to use the legal avenues available in Belgium to contest the arrest and extradition. They believed that he faced no jeopardy. The Rules of Procedure require that an accused be shown the indictment on arrest. He was shown nothing. Yet he voluntarily accompanied the ICTR staffers to Tanzania, and, to his surprise was immediately thrown in prison. Similar tricks were used to kidnap President Milosevic as we all remember when the Constitutional Court in Serbia held it was illegal to extradite him to The Hague. Even as they handed down their decision he was being forced onto an RAF plane in chains and dragged before the NATO tribunal, never to see his country again.

In June 2000 Ndindiliyamana contacted me by letter and asked me to be his counsel. I agreed and he submitted my name to the registrar to have me assigned. But their immediate reaction was to try to dissuade him from engaging me, stating that I had no experience, that I could not speak French, (he spoke no English) and attempted to persuade him to take counsel they preferred. This was a frequent occurrence at the ICTY and R and is now the norm at the ICC. Defence counsel who are seen to be too effective and willing to bring out the all the facts and let justice be done though the sky may fall, or, as Kant phrased, it "to let justice reign even if all the rascals in the world should perish from it", are prevented from representing accused by various means in favour of counsel who are either active agents of the western powers or who will only put up token defences The few strong ones who are able appear are hampered in every way possible and even thrown in prison as we recently saw in the Bemba case at the ICC. Nevertheless Ndindiliyimana persisted and finally I was allowed to represent him and to meet him later that summer.

The first thing to do obviously was to get hold of the

indictment and see what the charges were. But that proved to be very difficult. The indictment was not a simple statement that X is accused of committing crime Y at a certain place and a certain date. It was, instead, a 65 page propaganda tract, signed by Carla Del Ponte, setting out the Rwanda Patriotic Front-American, mass media version of the war, all of it false, all of it meant to prejudice the accused in the eyes of the judges but, more especially, meant for public consumption and prosecution press releases. In other words it was pure propaganda, and written as such. The other surprise was that entire lines, sections and even entire pages of the indictment were blacked out, including the names of co-accused. It was so bad that it was impossible to understand if any charges were actually contained in the document or what they were and from what we could read it appeared to offer a complete defence of his actions.

On his arrival in Arusha the general was not taken immediately before a judge for an initial appearance as required by the ICTR Rules of Procedure. Instead he was held for almost 4 months and did not make his first appearance before the judges of the tribunal until April 28th of that year. The delay was a deliberate tactic meant to soften him up psychologically. The same tactic was used against other prisoners, one example being Prime Minister Jean Kambanda, who instead of being brought before a judge on arrest was taken to a location hundreds of kilometres from the tribunal, held incommunicado for nine months and threatened by two Canadian police officers every day to make him confess to crimes he had not committed. These same Canadians were later implicated in the murder in 2005 of a member of his cabinet, which I will describe later.

When Ndindiliyimana was finally brought before a judge the lack of a proper indictment was raised by the duty counsel who stated the accused was being asked to plead to a document that was half blank. In response, the sitting judge simply said that was a defect in the form of the indictment and could be rectified later, instead of dismissing the case for lack of an indictment, as he should have done.

Upon my arrival at the tribunal, in July 2000, an American woman approached me in a hallway of the tribunal offices and informed me that she was in charge of the prosecution staff and wanted to talk with me. She informed me that she was not only a lawyer. She was also a Colonel in the US Air Force Reserves. I later learned she was also an agent in the CIA. She asked to meet me the next day to discuss a deal which was strange considering the charges they had made against my client of genocide. The next day, about 20 people walked into the meeting room where I was sitting alone. The attempt to intimidate me was clear. The American colonel made various proposals for a deal if we agreed to cooperate and testify against Colonel Bagosora, the former deputy minister of Defence. Our response was that the charges, so far as we could make them out, were false, that we could not accept his arrest and detention as a means of forcing him to give false testimony and demanded to have a trial. As an aside, I heard a number of times in private meeting with UN staffers, some at high levels, that everyone at the tribunal knew the general was a good man and not guilty of any thing but, as one insider told me, that's the way the Americans "are playing things here", and to watch my back.

On my next trip to Arusha, a couple of months later, to argue a motion for his release, I learned that their pressure had increased when I went to the UN Detention unit to meet with him and found that he had "disappeared" from the prison. The UN and Tanzanian guards refused to tell me where he was. It took a day of angry arguing with obstructive officials to find out that he had been transferred to a UN safe house in the town of Arusha. The excuse given to me was that he was in danger from other prisoners but in reality it was to keep him isolated psychologically, to weaken him, to soften him up, and to discredit him with the other prisoners by making it look like he was "making a deal."

We demanded that he be taken back to the UN Detention Unit but all our legal efforts to effect that were useless until I raised the issue in the press and to avoid further scandal, two days after the press raised the issue, he was returned to the UN prison, where, soon after, he was elected head of the prisoners' committee.

Over the next 4 years we faced constant obstructions in trying to find out what was going on, what charges he actually faced, what they were going to do and when he was going to have a trial. During this period, repeated offers were made by the prosecutors but all were refused; our position being simply that his arrest and detention to pressure him to testify were illegal and immoral and that he would only cooperate as a free man.

Demands for a speedy trial were met with shrugs of indifference. We were not given any relevant disclosure. Instead the prosecution buried us under thousands of irrelevant documents which the Registrar refused to pay me to read. I demanded that the prosecutor disclose all UN and other relevant documents of all the parties to the war and in 2003 I finally received several cd-roms with 100,000 documents contained on them. But there was no index or order to these documents and so we had to read every single one hoping to find something useful and, once again they refused to pay any fees for this work. They didn't want us to read them and thought that we never would. But we did and then I began to learn the truth about what had really happened in Rwanda, a truth that was completely opposite to what I had read in the mass media. So, in effect we never got any disclosure and had to create a defence for what we thought the general charges to be. To compound the problems, we were also refused sufficient investigative missions to locate and meet with witnesses to build our defence.

We became aware of other methods used to harass and interfere with the defence. Two Irish lawyers found out through sympathetic contacts in the UN security office that our office phone and fax lines were tapped. We learned that at least one defence lawyer was an agent of the prosecutor. Lawyers noticed they were followed and hotel rooms were broken into including the same Irish lawyers and mine. This happened to me in both Brussles and Arusha.

In 2003, a Scottish lawyer, Andrew McCarten, representing another accused at the ICTR, came to see me in Toronto stating he knew all about how the US and CIA controlled the tribunal at every level and that he feared for his life. He was very agitated. He had just arrived from New York where had tried to meet with Bill Clinton, and had been thrown out of his office. He told me details of the US military and CIA penetration of the tribunal and said he was going to send me documents of even darker things. The tribunal accused him of financial irregularities and kicked him out. Two weeks late he was dead. The police could find no cause for his car going off a cliff in Scotland. He was Scotland's foremost military lawyer.

On a visit to Arusha just after that I was visited by a major in American army intelligence, accompanied by an intelligence officer from the American State Department Research Intelligence Bureau who wanted to know what our trial strategy was and what my client's views were of African politics.

But the defence lawyers were not the only ones who faced problems. In 1997, Louise Arbour ordered an investigation into the shoot-down of the presidential plane, which resulted in the massacre of all on board, including the Hutu President of Rwanda, Habyarimana and the Hutu president of Burundi, Ntaryamira and the Army Chief of Staff. The invading Ugandan-RPF forces and Americans claimed that Hutu "extremists" shot down the plane.

An Australian lawyer, Michael Hourigan, was assigned to lead the investigation and in due course he reported to Arbour that his team had determined that it was in fact the RPF that had shot down the plane with the help of a foreign power and the CIA was implicated. Arbour, he stated in affidavit, seemed enthusiastic when he first informed her by telephone but when he was summoned to The Hague to meet with her, her attitude had totally changed to open hostility. He was ordered to hand over his evidence and ordered off the case.

To this day that file has been kept secret and no one named in his report has been charged. Fortunately Hourigan filed a report to the UN oversight office and that report detailing the evidence he had became available to us and was filed as evidence in the military trials. In his affidavit of November 27th, 2006, regarding his meeting with Louise Arbour, he stated at paragraph 36, "I feel that unknown persons from within the UN leadership and possibly elsewhere pressured Judge Arbour to end the National Teams investigations into the shooting down of President Habyarimana.", and at paragraph 38, referring to the reason he resigned, "…. I felt I could not work for Judge Arbour when, in my view, she acted for personal reasons against the interests of the ICTR, the UN and the world community which we served."

So, here we have not only proof of selective prosecution on the part of the prosecutor (only Hutus have been charged when evidence revealed in the trials these past 15 years shows the RPF forces are responsible for most of the killings) but the active aiding and abetting of a war crime, and obstruction of justice by Louise Arbour herself and those who successfully influenced her into dropping the investigation. Of course, once she had proved her value as an asset to Washington in this matter, they used her, two years later, to lay false charges against Slobodan Milosevic. Her reward was a series of lucrative moves to the Supreme Court of Canada, then the UN Human Rights Commission, and now sits as head of the CIA linked International Crisis Group.

In January 2004 the situation for the defence and the prisoners became so desperate that the defence lawyers organised a strike to protest the political nature of the charges and trials, the selective prosecutions, which gave the Kagame regime complete immunity and a green light to massacre millions of people in Congo, the poor working conditions for the defence, searches of defence counsel when they went to meet with their clients, and the isolation and conditions for the prisoners. The leader of that strike was Jean Degli, a Congolese lawyer based in Paris; an excellent advocate and a strong leader of the defence lawyers' association. Within a few months of the end of the strike he was also implicated in a financial scandal and forced out from the defence of a senior military officer. He had to go and he was gone. Once he left the tribunal the defence lawyers' association fell apart and never took any effective action again.

British and American lawyers would sometimes appear in the prison and announce to several accused that they had been appointed their lawyers. But the prisoners had not asked for them, did not know them, did not want them and became convinced that they were sent in by western intelligence agencies to control the outcome of the cases. The prisoners themselves created a list of defence lawyers they believed to work for western intelligence agencies. Those prisoners unlucky enough to fall prey to these people would always plead guilty to genocide in hope of a low sentence when there was no credible case against them. They were told they had no choice; that the cases could not be won. Too many fell for that. For those cases the tribunal could not control through friendly counsel the prosecution tried to insert someone inside the defence team to pass on information and to influence defence tactics and strategy. This was done in our team. We detected several people who were working for the prosecution as spies. It was difficult to trust anyone

They also sabotaged our team by trying to trap and arrest our lead investigator, a former Rwandan police major, and a very useful man to us in locating witnesses. On the very day that he arrived in Arusha, I was informed by a sympathetic official that they intended to arrest him on genocide charges, that his work programme had been suspended and that I better get him out of the country. So we had to quickly smuggle him out of Tanzania, at considerable cost, to avoid his arrest or worse. The charges were patently false, as he had been cleared by UN security and Rwanda well before he was engaged as our investigator. But the prosecution tactic effectively crippled our defence for over a year and we were never able to locate an investigator again with his experience and contacts. To this date, our demands to know why he was charged have been met by silence but it is worth noting that after this episode he was accepted into the Dutch police force which did a complete security check on him and determined that he had no involvement in the events of 1994.

The pressure increased when the prosecution circulated rumours that indicated they were intending to charge the general's wife as well. We all remember how President Milosevic was kept apart from his wife, Mira Markovic, for the same purpose.

Finally, almost 5 years after the general's arrest, the trial began, in September, 2004. To our complete surprise, at the very start of the trial the prosecutor stood up and filed a brand new indictment containing dozens of new charges including allegations of massacres we had never heard of and personal murders allegedly committed by the general himself. The accusations were of the worst and most sensational kind. It was clear they were meant to prejudice the accused in the eyes of the judges before the trial got going and in fact, as we saw in their judgement many of those were dropped without any evidence ever being presented. It was all a sham. We protested and demanded a delay to prepare a defence. We were denied and forced on and so had to prepare a defence on the run. At that point I was alone without co-counsel as the registrar refused to allow us to have counsel we wanted. The judges' attitude from the first day was openly hostile and they refused to allow us to discuss certain issues, or to cross-examine witnesses as we wanted. They openly sided with the prosecutors and sat back and did nothing as, each day, the prosecutors launched into vicious personal attacks on defence counsel and the accused.

The prosecution witnesses were all Hutu prisoners of the RPF, held without charge for ten years or more, in terrible conditions, many tortured, none of their testimony agreeing with the statements they had made prior to trial, much of it, double and triple hearsay. The prosecution never produced any forensic evidence of killings, no photos, videos, no names of victims, no DNA, no documents or orders, radio intercepts. No RPF officers were called to testify. The only evidence they had came out of the mouths of these Hutu prisoners. Their testimonies were a farce. The judges openly tried to help the prosecution when the witnesses were exposed under cross-examination as totally scripted. The prosecution used every dirty trick in the book to obstruct our cross-examinations and to rescue the witnesses as they fell apart in the witness box. Nevertheless, a number of them, once on the stand, had the courage to state that they had been forced to sign statements and testify falsely in return for release, favours or to avoid execution. We learned from these witnesses that the regime had set up schools in the prisons to recruit and train false witnesses, and the judges heard detailed accounts of how witnesses were recruited in these prisons, and that prosecution staff at the tribunal were involved in this scandal. What the fate of these prisoners was when they returned to Rwanda we do not know but the fate of those that cross the Rwanda regime is always unpleasant and permanent.

Even the judges, selected and groomed to be hostile to the defence began slowly to become uncomfortable with what they were hearing and disturbed on learning that all the witness statements disclosed to us post-dated the general's arrest.

We leaned that the judges were given documents to read that were not disclosed to the defence so we did not know what they were basing decisions on. The judges threatened my self and other counsel with arrest if we continued lines of questions they didn't want us to pursue, and there were daily angry confrontations in court between the judges and defence counsel when we tried to protect the rights of the accused and insisted on a fair trial. Throughout the trial, evidence came out that the enemy forces had committed mass atrocities against civilians but instead of the judges asking the prosecution why these forces were not charged they tried to silence us.

In 2005, during my cross-examination of a Belgian Army colonel concerning what is known as the Dallaire genocide fax, we learned that the translators were reading from scripts prepared by the prosecution instead of translating actual testimony of the witness. We were shocked and demanded an investigation as to how long this practice had been going on and demanded the prosecutors be charged. The judges again sat there stone-faced and despite our demands, nothing happened.

It was during this cross-examination that the Dallaire fax was proved to be a forgery and placed in UN files by a colonel in the British Army. But of course the media covering the trial never reported this crucial fact and to this day keep referring to the Dallaire fax as an essential document proving there was a planned genocide. But the prosecution was so embarrassed by this revelation that the fax was never again mentioned in any of the trials at the ICTR and though it was claimed to be the most important prosecution document in our trial, the prosecution never again raised it.

In 2006, the prosecution arranged to have the Appeal Chamber make the astounding declaration that the "genocide" was a judicially noticed fact despite the clear denial by the defence, despite the contrary evidence in the trials and despite the fact that the primary charge all the accused faced was genocide. In effect the tribunal stated the defence could not deny the principal charge against them.

But it didn't succeed in silencing the defence. We persisted in presenting our defence in spite of this decision and in our case, at least, the judges gave up fighting with us day after day and we continued to present the facts.

In September 2006 the well-known prosecution expert, Dr Alison Des Forges, testified in our trial and prepared an expert report for that purpose. The problem was that she removed from that report statements she had made in an earlier report that Ndindiliyimana was a man opposed to genocide and had tried to protect civilians. When she was confronted in cross-examination as to why she had attempted to mislead the judges she refused to answer the questions but it was clear from the reaction of the prosecutors that she had removed those exculpatory statements in an attempt to obstruct justice and did so on the orders of the prosecution. The trial judges took the rare step of censuring Dr. Des Forges for this deceit in the trial judgement.

In 2007 we witnessed another bizarre scene in which the Judges and prosecutors held a secret meeting on how to eliminate the unwanted testimony of a Tutsi prince, son of the last Tutsi king, and well known personality in Rwanda, named Antoine Nyetera, who testified that the RPF had done all the killing not the government and that he was a witness to it. Not liking the fact a prominent Tutsi was stating that the mass media version of events was false and that the RPF forces the prosecution refused to charge were responsible for most of the killings, they decided, in a secret meeting with the prosecutors, to announce in court that they were going to eliminate his testimony from the record. When all the defence counsel objected, we were met by a stone wall. To cover up what they did the daily minutes for that day were doctored as well.

We also began to see that transcripts were doctored. We were given draft transcripts each day in the morning but when we received the final version, certain words or key phrases were changed to the benefit of the prosecution, Again, complaints went nowhere. We noticed that we were being surveilled by UN security officers when meeting with witnesses in hotels. This was done quote openly and the effect was clearly to intimidate us. It was about this time that 35 of the prisoners wrote to the Security Council stating that they considered themselves to be political prisoners of the United Nations. There was no response to their letter.

In July 2008, a senior American ICTR official approached me in a café in Arusha, and told me he was a CIA officer, that they had murdered others who went to far at the tribunal, and that if I did not stop my defence work that they were going to kill me too. I reported this bizarre conversation to the President of the Tribunal the Norwegian judge, Mose, but again I was met with complete indifference. My client tried to reassure me that they would not actually touch me and were just trying to scare me. This was not the first time such a threat had been made. A member of the Rwandan government approached me at the beginning of the trial after watching me cross-examine their witnesses and told me that if I continued I did not have long to live. Complaints to the judges and UN security led nowhere. Tanzanian secret police approached me several times over the years and made similar remarks and it has not stopped even now. In July of this year Canadian intelligence officers came to see me in Toronto to tell me I was on a Rwandan hit list and asked me if I was going to stay active in the Rwandan file. It seemed to me they used the device of warning me of a threat to convey one.

In November 2005 Juvenal Uwilingiyimana, a former cabinet minister in Rwanda, who was being interviewed by two Canadian investigators working for Stephen Rapp, then chief of prosecutions at the ICTR, disappeared when he went to meet these investigators in Lille, France. These were the same Canadians who had kept Prime Minister Kambanda incommunicado for 9 months to extract a false confession from him. Weeks later, Uwilingiyimana's body was found in a canal in Brussles, naked, with its hands cut off. Just before he disappeared he wrote a letter to the tribunal stating that Rapp and his men were pressuring him to give false testimony and that they had threatened to kill him and cut his body into pieces unless he cooperated.

I and other counsel raised this letter and the murder in court and demanded that the prime suspects in the murder, Stephen Rapp and the two Canadians, be suspended and detained pending an investigation. Nothing was done. The Belgian police did no investigation and Rapp was promoted to the position of US roving ambassador for war crimes.

In 2008, a prosecution witness in our trial recanted stating that he was forced, under threat of death, to give false testimony. The defence succeeded in getting the judges to order his recall to be questioned about it and he was brought from Rwanda to a UN safe house in Arusha, The day before he was to testify he disappeared from that safe house and has never been seen since. The UN could not explain how he could disappear from one of their safe houses. Another prosecution witness recanted stating the same thing but in this case the prosecution accused me of bribing him. Two investigations concluded he was telling the truth, which included the fact that a prosecution counsel was involved in suborning perjury.

At about the same time an RPF military intelligence officer who had fled the regime testified that all the sections of the tribunal were penetrated by western and RPF intelligence officers and that the translators all worked for Rwandan intelligence and that the judges were seen as useful puppets.

In fact we noticed the presence several times during the trial of American army officers and senior members of the American Department of Justice sitting with the prosecutors. When we found out who they were we demanded that they be ejected and the judges were forced to order them removed from the courtroom. During the short cross-examination we were permitted of General Dallaire, by video link from Canadian Defence Headquarters in Ottawa, the cameraman made the mistake of pulling back from the close-up shot of the General's face and torso to a wide angle shot and we were shocked to see 5 senior Canadian Army officers sitting next to him when we had been told he was alone in the room with the technician and a court official. When we demanded to know who they were and who had given them orders to be there they refused to answer and the judges refused to order their removal. It was clear that the Canadian government was afraid of Dalllaire revealing Canada's role in the breakdown of the peace, the assassination of President Habyarimana and others and the mass killings that followed.

In 2008, I found hidden in prosecution files a letter from Paul Kagame, dated August, 1994, in which he refers to his and President Museveni's "plan for Zaire," in which he stated that the Hutus are in the way of that plan but that, with the help of the Americans, British and Belgians, the plan would go ahead. I raised this letter in court the next day as it indicated that the war in Rwanda was just the first phase for the greater war in the Congo that was planned probably as far back as 1990. The prosecution immediately accused me of forging this document, even though it came from their files, and that night I was openly followed by a Tanzanian police detective. I was forced to ask the judges for protection the next day who insisted that I be left alone. It is worth noting that attached to that letter was a report by USAID official Robert Gersony to the UN High Commission For Refugees stating that the RPF forces had committed widespread and systematic massacres of Hutu civilians starting in April 1994 and continuing to the date of the report of October 1994. It is also worth noting that stamped on the report was a note from one UNHCR official to another stating that this report must be kept confidential. This exculpatory evidence, shamefully hidden by the UN, had been in the hands of the prosecution for years, but illegally kept from us.

In 2011, despite the overwhelming evidence that Ndindiliiyimana had done all he could to save lives and to restore peace to Rwanda and that he was innocent of all the charges, the judges convicted him for failing to punish subordinates for two alleged crimes though they acquitted him on all the substantive charges and ordered his release.

The convictions were absurd on their face as one of the alleged incidents had never occurred and in the other his men were not involved.

When the Appeal Chamber threw out those convictions on February 7 2014, I learned from an inside source that the senior judge told him that the judges felt they had to convict him of something despite his clear innocence because they were afraid of the consequences from the Americans if they acquitted. It was also speculated by a number commentators that they had to justify his long illegal detention. As an aside, the day after the conviction was announced, I was surprised to receive an email from the American woman, the colonel, who had first dealt with the case in 2000 and offered us a deal. She is now a high official in the US State Department. She stated that she was angry that Ndindiliyimana had been convicted, that things were never meant to go that far and that, if ever I was in Washington, she would tell me what was really behind everything. But I have not gone to Washington and we have never met.

I have tried to give you a window into how these show trials are run, how it actually works at these tribunals. Each trial has its own stories to tell. It is a very depressing and dark picture. It was a very bitter experience. There is not much more I can say except that it seems to me that international justice worthy of the name cannot exist without an international order that is democratic; a world order in which the sovereignty and equality of nations is fundamental. Law and its legal structures reflect the social, economic and political relations of a society. To rebuild the legal architecture of international justice so that it is fair, impartial and universal we first have to change the fundamental economic, social and power relations that are its foundation. Without this mankind will continue down the path of reaction and war and the list of victims of these truly criminal tribunals will be long and the victims of a world war will include all of us. How is this to be done? I leave that to you.

September 26, 2014

5

WHY IS CANADA BOMBING IRAQ?

By Christopher Black

Canadians are bombing Iraqis and no one outside the deeply unpopular government of Stephen Harper really knows why. The propaganda system that controls the Canadian media succeeds in sowing confusion upon mystery and all we are allowed to understand is that Canada has once again revealed itself as a country without any existential existence. It is a regional backwater of the United States of America, the remaining vestiges of sovereignty and independence submerged in the swamp of American imperialism and culture.

Long gone are the glory days when a Canadian actually felt distinct in North America, when Canada tried to maintain an independent foreign policy and a national culture born out of the richness of the three founding peoples, the First Nations, the French and the English. Too many have forgotten that the Canadian provinces of the

British Empire in North America refused to join the rebellion of the rising bourgeoisie in the 13 colonies along the Atlantic coast. Many Americans who were persecuted by the rebels for staying loyal to the British Crown fled to Canada in the aftermath and never returned. They had a name, the United Empire Loyalists, and the Americans never forgave them or the Canadians for refusing to join in their grand project of the conquest of North America and, consequently, the first of the American wars of conquest was the invasion of Canada in the War of 1812, the primary objective of which was the takeover of all the remaining British territories on the continent.

The American propaganda then was the same as it is now. The invading American forces posted notices in towns and villages announcing that they were bringing the people of Canada "democracy and liberty." But no one wanted what they were offering and after many battles fought by British regulars, native forces and local militias the Americans were kicked out and put that objective on the back burner while they plundered the lands of the peoples of the interior and then turned on Mexico. They didn't attempt it again until President Grant contemplated using the Union Armies to invade just after the American Civil War but the idea was abandoned aside from support for Irish Fenian guerrilla raids into Canada in the late 1860s. After that a physical invasion was not necessary since the invasion of finance capital got them all they wanted without a shot fired.

Canada remained a formal colony of British capital until 1867 when it was finally organised as a self governing state within the British empire after a series of internal struggles for more self rule by the growing mercantile and industrial elites but it only achieved any real independence as a country in the 1930's as Britain's power rapidly declined after its huge losses of the First World War. But the establishment of a country more independent of Britain did not result in an independent nation. Canada relied on foreign capital to build its infrastructure, its continental railway systems, its hydro-electric projects, its factories, its cities and where British capital could not supply the need it was quickly replaced by American capital.

The domination of the country by the Americans accelerated after the Second World War but it was countered by a rising nationalist feeling generated in part by Canada's disproportionately large contribution to fighting the fascists in Europe. A nation of eleven million people fielded military forces of almost a million and in 1945 Canada had the third largest navy in the world. After the war the working classes, many of whom viewed the Soviet Union as the most progressive nation in the world, despite the elites' anti-Russian and anti-socialist propaganda, supported socialist ideals that resulted in the establishment of free national health care and low cost education, affordable housing and were enthusiastic about Canadian artists and writers. They saw how a nation like Russia had rapidly developed its industrial and societal resources in a landmass that was very similar to Canada and realised that they could do the same. But it was not to be. Soon the American dominance began to be felt, with the forced dumping of Hollywood films in Canadian theatres, the take over of oil and gas exploration and pipeline construction, the stifling of any really independent steps to national development and of course the fateful decision under US pressure to join the NATO alliance.

The years of the late 50's and 60's saw Canadian leaders trying to act independently of the American power. In one famous episode, Prime Minister Lester Pearson declined U.S. requests to send Canadian combat troops into the Vietnam War. Pearson spoke at Temple University in Philadelphia on 2 April 1965 and called for a pause in the American bombing of North Vietnam, so that a diplomatic solution to the war could be found. President Johnson, who rose to power through the coup d'état against President Kennedy in 1963, saw this criticism of American foreign policy on American soil as an intolerable sin. Before Pearson had finished his speech, he was summoned to Camp David, Maryland, to meet with Johnson the next day. Johnson, a very large man, who was a notorious thug, reportedly picked up Pearson, a very small man, by the lapels and shouted, "Don't you come into my living room and piss on my rug."

The last gasp of Canadian attempts at real independence took place under Prime Minister Pierre Trudeau who, though not withdrawing from NATO, tried to create a foreign policy in Canadian interests and was one of the first western leaders to open the door to China, long before Nixon, and remained friends with Fidel Castro all his life. It was Trudeau that finally negotiated with the British for the repatriation of the Canadian Constitution in 1982, finally severing the last legal ties to British rule. He called for the creation of a "Just Society" with real participatory democracy and concern for the collective good and for Canada to become more engaged with the rest of the world instead of just being fixated on the United States. But the fall of Trudeau and the rise of the right wing in Canada in the late 80's led to the rise of the continentalists, that is those Canadians financiers and industrialists who saw their interests lying in New York instead of Toronto. The counter-revolution in the USSR accelerated this process as neo-liberalism and free trade became the dominant doctrine and, in a series of free trade and security agreements, starting in 1993, Canada quickly surrendered its hard won sovereignty almost overnight to the interests of American capital.

As a result, in rapid succession, Canadian military forces were assigned the role of auxiliaries to American forces and helped the Americans overthrow the government of Rwanda in 1993, participated in the criminal aggression against Yugoslavia in 1999, the invasion and occupation of Afghanistan in 2001, participated in the overthrow of President Aristide of Haiti in 2004, assisted US forces in Iraq during the American invasion and occupation of Iraq, supplied forces in the Gulf of Aden to threaten Iran, played a major role in the bombing and destruction of Libya in 2011, supplied military supplies to the Kiev regime during the attacks on the peoples of the Donbas this summer and now is bombing Falllujah, the very heart of the Iraqi resistance to the American occupation.

Canadian forces operating in Iraq are insignificant, amounting to just a few planes and 600 personnel. This token contribution to the continued American operations has no real military purpose. So when we want to understand the reason for Canada's actions, its clear pandering to the diktats and on behalf of the interests of the United States we just have to know the history of the development of the country to understand that the real purpose for these military theatrics is propaganda. Canada's role is simply to provide an international cover to what is clearly an American operation. One can see this by reading the Canadian Ministry of Defence website on the action which refers to US requests and orders and which then provides a link to US Command Headquarters.

The lesson to be drawn from all this is that any nation that surrenders its sovereignty to a dominant power becomes the tool of that power. The interests of its own people count for nothing. International law and peace count for nothing. Human life counts for nothing. Yet, to the south, in Latin America, the nations that were once, like Canada, under the thumb of the American empire, have become vibrant, confident nations whose governments act in the interests of the collective population instead of the narrow interests of finance capital. In the east we see the energy of the changes accelerate in China, India and Russia. The example is there. Nations like Canada can choose their own path, their own destiny in peaceful cooperation with the nations and peoples of the world. The problem is how the people of Canada, and, indeed, all nations, can escape this domination and survive it. Unfortunately, with the continentalists still in control in Washington and Ottawa, New York and Toronto, and with American control of the economic resources at an intolerable level, the situation looks bleak for the immediate future. Canadians are nothing more than servants in their own house, when, to use the phrase of the Quebec nationalists in their struggle for self determination, we should be "maître chez nous," masters of our own house. The Canadian people are watching what is going on in the rest of the world and they are learning from what they see. In that lies, perhaps, some hope.

November 7, 2014

6

THE MISTRAL AFFAIR: BREACH OF CONTRACT OR HOSTILE ACT?

By Christopher Black

On November 18th 2014 Sputnik news reported that the French government has denied access to the Russian training crew for the Mistral ship Vladivostok docked at St. Nazaire. The French Ministry of Defence denied knowledge of the action but their denial is in line with the French President's continual habit of saying one thing and meaning another. The alarming question now has to be asked whether this is just a commercial breach of contract or a hostile act, because the French government has not just "failed" to deliver the first of the two Mistral ships contracted and paid for as the press reports state, it has refused to deliver them and will not unless certain conditions are met, political conditions, which have strategic importance for Russia and conditions that can never be met unless Russia surrenders its strategic position and its defence of the Ukrainians of the Donbass.

The announcement of the Mistral deal by President Sarkozy was made on December 24th, 2010. Russian Deputy Prime Minister Igor Sechin and French Foreign Minister Alain Juppe signed the contracts, on January 25, 2011. In retrospect, alarms about the deal should have gone off even before the ink was dry, as the signing came not long after France re-joined NATO in March 2009. This major change in French foreign policy sent the clear message that France was now strategically aligned with the United States, abandoning over 40 years of French independence from US military command. France's re-entry into NATO was the logical culmination of a long history of French cooperation with NATO. Since France, as a member of NATO, has to act in the interests of its master, it should come as no surprise that the French have taken another hostile action against Russia by taking part in the illegal economic embargo instituted by the Americans. France has taken actions against Russian interests for years.

In 1999, France took part in the NATO aggression against and occupation of Yugoslavia that succeeded in placing American bases in the Balkans directly threatening Russia's southwest flank. Just a few months after announcing the Mistral deal, Sarkozy was one of the most rabid of the dogs of war who betrayed Russia's trust in a UN no-fly zone resolution by using it as a trick to attack, and destroy Libya and murder Muammar Gadhafi, eliminating a Russian ally in the Mediterranean and North Africa. Since then, France has assisted the financing and training of anti-Assad forces in order to overthrow the government of Syria and force Russia out of its base at Tartus and the Mediterranean Sea.

Yet it is during these events that the contract for the ships went forward despite criticism in Russia about the ability of the ships to cope with a cold climate because of fuel problems, the refusal by NATO to hand over necessary military and electronic technology so the ships could function effectively, concerns about its high vulnerability to anti-ship missile attack requiring the assistance of several escort vessels in order to operate in hostile waters, and criticism about becoming reliant on other nations for defence requirements.

The French support for the overthrow of the elected government in Ukraine, its support for the Kiev regime's attacks on the civilian population of the Donbass and French participation in the economic warfare against Russia being conducted by the NATO allies, taken in the historical context, means that the refusal to hand over the ships due under the contracts is meant to weaken Russia militarily and politically.

The military effects are several. One of the ships was to be stationed on the Pacific Coast for operations to protect the Kuril Islands in particular, and one of them was to be used as the flagship of the Russian navy in the Mediterranean. Their ability to move a reinforced battalion of troops along with the capacity to launch multiple helicopters, transport landing craft and act as a command and control centre had both strategic and tactical importance. Further, Russia hoped to obtain advanced technology and the ability to build other Mistrals in Russia.

Politically the French refusal is meant to humiliate Russia on the world stage in order to weaken its prestige and support in the world, a refusal compounded by the insulting cat and mouse game being played by the French, first promising to deliver the ships, then hesitating, then promising again, but in the end never delivering. A cynical person could even wonder whether Russia was tricked all along and paid almost 1.2 billion euros in advance in early 2011 for ships it was never intended to get and was lured into wasting three years that could have been spent on developing similar vessels to be built in Russia.

The simple fact is Russia has handed over the money but France now has the ships and the money. Even if the French repaid the money plus penalties Russia's interests will have been damaged but the idea that France will willingly give back the money already paid plus penalties is naïve. France wants to hurt Russia and France cannot hurt Russia and then cover Russia's losses and any talk of France honouring the penalty clauses in the contract for failure to deliver when it has refused to honour the contract in the first place is just whistling in the dark.

Already there is talk in the French press about relying on the force majeure clauses in the contracts to avoid any Russian legal action to recover the money. President Putin reacted by stating that the French cannot rely on force majeure, as the contracts are very specific and not in favour of France. The positions of the parties are already being drawn and long years of arguing before courts and trade tribunals will not change the situation.

It is not just Russia that will suffer a loss. The repercussions are very serious for both countries. In France the union that represents the workers at St. Nazaire where the ships are built expressed "shock and outrage" Le Figaro reported, after Paris delayed delivery due to pressure from the US and EU and stated that the decision risked the loss of 2500 jobs in a country on the verge of recession or worse. It has given the far right party ammunition to attack President Hollande. Marie LePen demanded the ships be delivered or else risk undermining French credibility, its reliability in arms sales and its national honour.

Hollande's response is to play the game of denying the contract has been rescinded or breached by stating that it is still in effect and delivery will be made but then contradicts himself and states that "I will take my decision without any pressure, wherever it may come from, and based on two criteria; the interests of France and the appreciation I have of the situation." He also stated that the delivery of the ships is contingent on two conditions being met: a ceasefire in Ukraine and a peace deal between the Kiev regime and Moscow.

He said this when he knew that the Kiev regime is deliberately breaking the ceasefire on a daily basis and has no intention of abiding by it and that Poroshenko and the Americans have no intention of allowing peace in Ukraine. The fact is that France is locked into the American war logic and Hollande's statement that he is subject to no pressure is as laughable as his popularity ratings in France. The statements by President Obama at the G20 meeting Australia that Russia will be economically "isolated" unless it bows to US diktats and the deliberately insulting behaviour towards the Russian head of state by NATO leaders at the meeting and the current oil price war are glaring evidence that NATO's hostile intentions against Russia are becoming more acute with every day.

The fact is that France has acted to wound Russia and is acting in accord with the United States and its other NATO allies and is willing to do so because it has greater interests in mind which pale beside the predictable job losses, lawsuits and loss of reputation. Those interests are the interests of the NATO alliance as a whole that is preparing for war against Russia.

Russia has stated it will respond to the French refusal to deliver the Russian ships at the end of November. The Russian Upper House has suggested cancelling the contract. But this also has serious implications and will not make Russia whole as the French are unlikely to pay back the money. Poroshenko has threatened all out war against the Donbas and the fact that Ukraine cannot obtain coal supplies for the winter from other sources at a price it can afford suggests that an offensive to seize the Donbas coal mines is being considered and this will once again bring NATO and Russia in direct confrontation.

The countries of NATO and its allies in Japan and Australia are suffering serious problems as their economies sink into recession and fade into the shadows of the BRIC economies that are shaking off US dollar hegemony. Their leaders are mediocrities who think like gangsters. Their democracies have ceased to function in any real sense. They have painted themselves into a corner and see war as the only way out. Russia's response to the Mistral Affair will be interesting to see but whatever the response is it will be made in a world context and in the search for a peaceful resolution of the war that threatens us all.

November 18, 2014

7

NORTH KOREA, THE UN, AND WAR PROPAGANDA

By Christopher Black

The western propaganda machine is being pushed to its limits and could burst under the pressure as the United States and its coalition of the criminal spew out one set of lies after another against the nations and peoples who refuse to kowtow. The US sponsored resolution to refer criminal action against the Democratic Peoples Republic of Korea (DPRK) to the International Criminal Court based on a report by a UN Human Rights Council Commission of Inquiry is another product of this machine and one more example of the use of the United Nations organisation as a crude instrument of the American attempt to manipulate and dominate the world.

The report itself is an amazing document, not only because it is entirely contrived, but also because the "crimes" which the Commissioners allege take place in the DRPK are exactly the conditions that exist inside the United States itself. The hypocrisy is stunning but no one can be surprised when we learn in paragraph 31 of the report that the "public hearings" held by the Commission were conducted with the help of the governments of the United States, Britain, Japan and South Korea, all enemies of the DPRK, who arranged, according to the Commission itself, all the logistics, venues, interpreters, technology, security, press services and, importantly, the "witnesses." Nor can we be surprised when we look at the three members of the Commission: the Australian, Michael Donald Kirby, the Serb, Sonja Biserko, and the Indonesian, Marzuki Darusman, each one of them linked to CIA front groups somewhere in their careers.

Darusman, who was the Special Rapporteur regarding the DPRK and whose initial report is the basis for the creation of the DPRK commission, is a well known friend of the US and opportunist who became a member of Suharto's Golkar party in Indonesia which, with CIA help, murdered, 500,000 communists and people linked to left or labour groups in 1965.

In the eighties and nineties he turned on Suharto for the Americans and is now listed as an advisor to the United States Indonesia Society (USINDO), a US government front group whose president is David Merrill, who was a senior official with the United States Agency For International Development (USAID), a well-known front of the CIA, in various Asian and eastern European countries, during the eighties and nineties, and was an American ambassador to Bangladesh.

Darusman is also a member of the Global Leadership Foundation, whose patrons include such unsavoury characters as George W. Bush, Helmut Schmidt, and Lech Walesa. The Foundation is a syndicate of former western leaders that states it gives advice to world leaders on how to run their countries but does so secretly, outside democratic processes, and the knowledge of the people. Their slogan is "Helping Leaders Govern." Of course the citizens of the countries concerned think that it is the job of the people through their representatives to help their leaders govern but apparently that's not how it works. Chief Executive Officer, Sir Robert Fulton, a former general in the British Army, and, former Commandant of the British Royal Marines, heads the Foundation, which is incorporated in Switzerland but has its headquarters in London. Not surprisingly, its financing comes from companies such as Chevron, Barclays Bank, Goldman Sachs, Alcatel, BAE Systems, Exxon Mobile, The Ford Foundation, and many others of the same stripe.

The second member of the Commission is Sonja Biserko, a detested figure in Serbia where she is regarded as a NATO Quisling of the worst type. She openly conspired with the US and NATO against President Milosevic in the nineties, advocated the bombing of her own country by NATO in 1999 and called for the kidnapping of Milosevic to the NATO tribunal at The Hague. She is a founder and Director of the USAID funded Helsinki Human Rights Group linked to Human Rights Watch, another CIA front group. She is also a senior fellow at the United States Institute of Peace, an official agency of the American government the Board of which is appointed by the President of the United States with Congressional approval. Present members of the Board of Directors include Chuck Hagel and John Kerry.

Michael D. Kirby is an Australian judge who is a former president of the International Commission of Jurists, an organisation created in West Berlin to investigate alleged human rights abuses in the German Soviet Zone which was funded by the CIA through the American Fund For Free Jurists and the Ford Foundation and its founders included the head of the CIA, Allen Dulles. The ICJ was created in opposition to the International Association of Democratic

Lawyers, the IADL, an organisation of leftist lawyers around the world of which the writer is a member. Kirby opposed the move to make Australia a republic in the nineties and was a founding member of Australians For A Constitutional Monarchy that advocated the retention of the British monarchy in Australia.

All three were appointed by Ban Ki Moon, who has caused dismay at the United Nations because of his obstruction of anticorruption policies and attacks on the independence of the Office of Internal Oversight, the UN watchdog bureau, and because of his biased call for action in the Security Council against the DPRK during the Cheonan crisis of May 2010. The Secretary-General is supposed to represent the views of the Security Council, but Ban tends to ignore Russia and China in favor of obedience to the US, Britain, and France which should come as no surprise when his candidacy for Secretary-General was championed by President Bush after years of senior diplomatic service in the US puppet governments in South Korea.

The absurdity of the document produced by the Commission becomes plain in the opening paragraphs. Paragraph 2 states:

"Among the violations to be investigated were those pertaining to the right to food, those associated with prison camps, torture and inhuman treatment, arbitrary detention, discrimination, freedom of expression, the right to life, freedom of movement, and enforced disappearances, including in the form of abductions of nationals of other states."

Reading that one would think that the Commission was making inquiries into the conditions existing within the United States of America where a fifth of the population is reliant on food stamps to avoid starvation, where prisoners are used as forced labour for private businesses, where torture and inhumane treatment of common prisoners and prisoners of war is routine, where habeas corpus has been suspended and arbitrary detentions along with forced disappearances, through the euphemistically termed "rendition" programmes, of people all over the world is a routine practice, where freedom of expression for those disagreeing with US policies is severely limited, where the freedom of movement is restricted to countries approved by the government, where racial discrimination is rampant and where the right to life for many minority groups especially blacks, natives, Hispanics and the poor does not exist as police murders of members of those groups increase daily.

But of course the commissioners could not care less about human rights crimes against the people of the United States by the American regimes. Instead they succeed in showing themselves to be a politically motivated team of US agents who held show hearings and produced a politically driven report.

In paragraph 12 of the document they state that the DPRK has not provided any substantive input yet the DPRK issued a report of 167 pages on the human rights situation in the DPRK, on September 13, 2014, produced by the DPRK Association For Human Rights that refutes every one of the allegations made. Not surprisingly the DPRK slammed the UN report and stated that witness testimony was fabricated, a charge that should be seriously considered in light of the experience of this writer and other defence lawyers at the NATO-controlled Yugoslav and Rwanda tribunals where the fabrication of witness testimony by the US controlled prosecutors has been the preferred method of operation.

The report also states that "fear of reprisals...has limited the willingness of many ... foreign visitors to the DPRK to share their knowledge and information with the Commission." This is a surprising statement since this writer was a member of a team of lawyers who, on behalf of the National Lawyers Guild of the United States, an organisation affiliated with the IADL, made a visit to the

DPRK in 2003. Our report on what we observed has been available on the NLG website.

And covers all aspects of Korean society. The allegations being made then by the west are the same as the allegations made now but the Commission never bothered to read that report nor did they try to contact us for our views. Nor have they spoken to the 5 American Army officers we met at our hotel in Pyongyang, the day we arrived, all members of a remains recovery team whose mission was to locate the bodies of American soldiers killed in the Korean war and who were able to freely move around the country.

Once we got over our surprise that the first people we met in our hotel in this supposedly "isolated" country were American Army officers, we asked them what they thought of the country and conditions, since we had just arrived and did not know what to expect. We were surprised to here an American Major say:

"Look, don't quote me or use my name, but when we left Hawaii to come here we were told it was hell on earth, but we've been here for two years and nothing they told us was true. It's nice here and they treat us well. Everything we had heard in the western media, everything our superiors told us was complete and total bullshit."

This echoed a conversation we had with two Congolese diplomats who we met on the way out of the country. We asked them to compare their experiences and they stated they were shocked, that everything they had head about North Korea, all the negative propaganda, was false. They added that it would be a dream for most Africans to have the life that people in North Korea have.

The conclusion to all this is that the Commission of Inquiry Report is just another exercise in US propaganda. This conclusion is reinforced by the Commission's call for the Security Council to refer the matter to the International Criminal Court when they know this cannot be done legally since a strict reading of the Statute of the ICC only permits the Security Council to refer matters concerning countries that are already parties to the Treaty of Rome and the DPRK is not a party to the Treaty. In the alternative they call for the creation of another one of the ad hoc tribunals whose role as propaganda tools for the US and its allies is now notorious. Since this can never happen as Russia and China will never allow it, the single purpose of the report is to prepare the people of the west for war against the people of the DPRK by portraying their government as criminals, the same propaganda strategy the US has used against Yugoslavia, Iraq, Afghanistan, Libya, Syria, and now, as Obama tried to do at the G20 meeting in Australia, regarding the attack on flight MH17, Russia.

Bitter experience shows that once the criminal label is attached the dogs of war are soon unleashed, so it was a welcome sign that, despite a heavy disinformation campaign, 55 nations rejected the resolution against the DPRK, including Russia and China, while 12 other nations abstained. But, for all that, we must be alarmed and we must stay alert, because the principal propaganda target of this campaign is the domestic population of the NATO allies themselves so that they will support, or, at least, not resist, the next planned war.

November 30, 2014

8

CLIMATE CHANGE: A PLANETARY EMERGENCY

By Christopher Black

The stock markets are sliding, America is shaken by CIA torture practices, and extrajudicial killings by police, NATO continues to threaten Russia, world currencies are reeling under the blows of dropping oil prices and yet, and yet, there is something much worse threatening mankind than all these problems combined; the rapid warming of the planet due to fossil fuel emissions over the past century and a half that has scientists warning of mankind's extinction, not in the distant future, but within decades or less.

The world's response to this rapidly developing catastrophe is the 2014 United Nations Climate Change Conference in Lima, Peru, that is taking place, according to the UN's World Meteorological Organisation, in the warmest year on record and, despite the cool weather in the centre of North America and Russia, with temperatures in the Arctic many degrees Celsius above normal for early December, and with oppressive heat waves hitting one region after another in the southern hemisphere from South America to New Zealand, in what should be cool spring weather.

The website of the conference states that this 20th yearly meeting of the Conference of Parties to the 1992 UN Framework Convention on Climate Change and the 10th session of the Meeting of Parties to the 1997 Kyoto Protocol "will continue the negotiations towards a global climate agreement." The stated goal of the conference is to reduce greenhouse gases to limit the global temperature to 2 degrees above baseline.

There are two problems with the stated objective. The first is that the EU seeks legally binding 40 per cent cuts in emissions by 2030 while the USA, hamstrung by the right-wing Republicans in Congress, wants only politically binding agreements that are not legally enforceable. The US-China agreement of November 2014 on voluntary cuts in emissions while encouraging are, according to many scientists, far too little and far too late.

The second and more serious problem is that 2 degrees is already a danger to civilization and yet, even the conservative Intergovernmental Panel on Climate Change (IPCC) itself is predicting a 4 degree rise in temperatures by the end of the century if not earlier. According to several climate scientists such temperatures will lead to the extinction of human beings in a very short time.

The US science magazine Scientific American stated that the IPCC has understated the rate and intensity of climate change for over two decades. The Arctic Methane Emergency Group (AMEG) composed of leading world climate and arctic ice experts, agrees and insists that the IPCC depends too much on climate models that are increasingly divorced from observable facts.

On December 4th, 2014, AMEG, led by Dr. John Nissen, called a press conference in Lima, and stated that the rapid Arctic ice meltdown is a catastrophic threat to our survival and urged action be taken to refreeze the Arctic failing which there will be a "blue ocean event" meaning that by September 2015 the Arctic Ocean will be open water for the first time and that quickly thereafter catastrophic climate changes will begin to accelerate, including the loss of the Greenland ice sheet resulting in fast rising sea levels and the severe disruption of the jet stream which will cause and is causing abrupt and disastrous climate change in the Northern Hemisphere.

The AMEG group is alarmed by the quickly escalating emissions of methane from the Arctic Ocean seabed, as well as permafrost and tundra in a feedback loop that could raise temperatures very quickly to levels that make human life on the planet unsustainable. Indeed, they cite the work of Russian scientists Shakova and Semelitov to support their statement that a 50 gigaton burst of methane "is possible at any time" resulting in a temperature rise of 5 to 8 degrees or more in less than a decade which would lead to the extinction of life on earth. Doctors Peter Waddams, John Nissen and Paul Beckwith stated that such a methane release is a "time bomb" that puts us into a planetary emergency and called for immediate measures to be taken to cool the planet, remove CO_2 from the atmosphere, and to stop the acidification of the oceans that, in the last ten years, has wiped out 40% of the phytoplankton, the base of the ocean food chain.

Dr. Guy McPherson, of the University of Arizona, another leading climatologist, believes that it is already too late to stop the exponential actions of the at least 40 feedback mechanisms that have already begun to operate causing a rapid rise in temperatures and extreme climate change, mechanisms which he states are now unstoppable no matter what we do. Based on all the data currently available, he and others think that the present trend will lead to conditions in which mankind's very life resources, food, water and habitable zones will be so degraded in the next 15 years that the human species will be destroyed by 2030 in the northern hemisphere and by 2050 in the southern hemisphere, give or take a decade or so. The AMEG group while agreeing that this is the likely outcome if nothing is done, believes that geo-engineering can be used to cool the planet, one method proposed being the spraying of salt crystals into the atmosphere from 200 ships in the Atlantic Ocean which would have the effect of cooling the Atlantic and the Gulf Stream which is pushing heated water into the Arctic Ocean.

A frustrated Dr. Nissen said, "governments are doing nothing" as we see the effects of abrupt climate change causing crop failures, rising food prices and civil unrest in region after region. He stated that unless something is done to stop a blue ocean event from happening, "all hell will break loose."

Yet what do we see being done by governments? Nothing. The participants at the UN conference in Peru discuss minor cuts to emissions by countries that may or may not act on their promises and talk of these minor cuts being achieved at a point in time at which scientists are telling us we won't be here. It's as bizarre as it can get. All the other world problems pale in comparison with what mankind is facing yet not one world leader has stood up and called for action. It is left to second and third tier officials to waste time in bargaining over carbon tariffs which Dr. Nissen compared to rearranging deck chairs on the Titanic.

AMEG called for the leaders of the major industrial powers, China, Russia, America and the EU to immediately form an international emergency task force, set up on a war footing, to put into effect the measures they propose to cool the planet and encouraged all citizens of the world and non governmental groups to heed the alarm and make the the public aware of the danger we all face and to demand that immediate and effective action be taken or we are all destroyed, not in some distant future, but within the lifetime of this generation.

December 15, 2014

.

9

CUBAN RESISTANCE: AN EXAMPLE FOR THE WORLD

By Christopher Black

The ink on the agreement to normalise diplomatic relations between the United Sates and Cuba announced on December 17th, 2014 is barely dry and already the objective of the United States has been made clear in the statement of President Obama made on that day and in the press conference he held on Friday, December 19th.

On the 17th, in announcing the new policy, Obama stated that the US imposed blockade of Cuba "has not advanced our interests" and that, "this is fundamentally about "freedom," a code word for the freedom to do as America orders. In his press conference of Friday the 19th Obama stated that normalisation of relations "gives us an opportunity to have influence" with the people of Cuba so that "liberty" and "democracy" can be restored. "There will be a carrot and stick approach that we can apply." He added that the trade embargo did not succeed in bringing down the regime and so he hopes this new approach will succeed. The usual catchwords were used once again to disguise the never changing objective of the US imperialist faction, regime change in Cuba.

The hubris of Obama's remarks reached the peak of absurdity when he said, "No Cuban should face harassment, or arrest, or beatings, simply because they're exercising their universal right to be heard." That not one American journalist laughed aloud at this statement after the repression of the people of the United States for its entire history is remarkable in itself. Those of us who are old enough can remember the American National Guard shooting dead students protesting the Vietnam War at Kent State University, in Ohio and Georgia Technical College, in 1970. We can remember the assassinations of President Kennedy in 1963, Malcolm X in 1965, Martin Luther King, and Senator Bobby Kennedy in 1968, all by state agents, the murder of the Black Panther leaders Fred Hampton and Mark Clark in their beds by the FBI in 1969, the massacre by New York state police of dozens of prisoners protesting harsh conditions at Attica State prison in 1971, the suppression and murder of members of the American Indian Movement at the Oglala Sioux (Lakota) Pine Ridge reservation in 1973, the bombing of black women and children of the Move movement in 1985 by the police who dropped bombs from a helicopter on a Philadelphia house, killing eleven people including five children, injuring dozens and burning down two hundred homes, the massacre of 76 men, women and children burned to death at Waco, Texas in 1993 by order of the Clinton regime, the brutality of the police beatings and arrests of protestors at the World Trade Organisation meeting in Seattle in 1999, of the Occupy movement last year, and most recently the continuing beatings and use of military methods against protestors in Ferguson and other towns and cities in America protesting the continued extrajudicial executions by police of Americans who dare to walk the streets in the wrong colour skin. The list is endless but the point is made.

Obama's hypocrisy is underlined by the passage just a few days before of the Ukraine Freedom Act that calls for further "sanctions" against Russia to effect the fall of the Russian government, followed on the 18th by the signing by Obama of legislation imposing more "sanctions" on Venezuela for the same purpose and, on the 20th of December, "sanctions" against "Crimea", that is, once again, against Russia. Since all these actions are a serious violation of the UN Charter, the improper use of the word "sanctions" is meant to give a legal veneer to what are essentially acts of war.

It was a busy week for the Americans, relaxing "sanctions" on one country one day and increasing them against another the next. It must make their heads spin. It would be comical if it did not have serious consequences for the countries affected. Indeed, the imposition of "sanctions" against a country by the Americans has become a badge of honour. If you are a leader of a country that has not faced their "sanctions" then ipso facto you are a vassal state, as Canadian Prime Minister Harper proved Canada to be by once again mimicking the American action and announcing further Canadian "sanctions" against Russia on the 20th of December just after the EU and Obama, not having the nerve, himself, to act first.

The people of Cuba have demanded the respect of the United States since they succeeded in throwing out the corrupt US supported Batista dictatorship and its US Mafia allies in the Revolution of 1959. But even now with the agreement to normalise diplomatic relations the trade embargo remains in place and the US Congress, on cue from the White House, plays the game of objecting to Obama's proposal. No doubt this is part of the "carrot and stick" approach.

The establishment of diplomatic relations is always a positive step and dialogue is better than war. The Cuban people have suffered terribly under the trade embargo imposed by the Americans and the possibility of relief is something to be hoped for but to have to suffer the removal of that duress under threats if Cuba does not obey American diktats, and to be lectured about issues of freedom and democracy which reflect not what is going in Cuba but what is going on in the heart of America itself, adds insult to injury.

Meanwhile in Ukraine the US supports the suppression of democracy as the puppet regime in Kiev tries to eliminate the communists and carries out the old Roman practice of proscription, the mass elimination of political enemies of the regime with its "lustration" law put into effect in October. Even the EU complained about the proscriptions taking place but democracy, the right of citizens to freely choose their party and representatives, is not a concept that the ruling faction in the United States believes in, except as a propaganda device to fool the innocent, and the EU was ignored.

The US wants from Cuba the complete servility that Poroshenko displayed when he visited Washington and addressed the US Congress asking for help. His speech called to mind the words of Brutus to Cicero about a letter he wrote to the aspiring emperor Octavian, "Read again your words and deny that they are the supplications of a slave to a despot."

The American ruling faction, called so because the two parties are really one and the ties among its members are those of money and influence, is pitiless, as we have seen with their involvement in the shooting down of the MH17 airliner. They are relentless in their drive to save themselves from oblivion as the American economy and power balances on the edge of a precipice. The change in policy towards Cuba must be understood in this light.

The lesson to be drawn from the new American policy towards Cuba is that if a country is resolute and resists, the Americans will be forced to change their strategy but the change does not remove the danger. It simply transforms its characteristics. The Cubans are very aware that any change in policy by the Americans will bring new dangers. They have endured many hardships and a long struggle for independence, sovereignty and, an old-fashioned word, honour. By enduring the war crimes and crimes against humanity of the Americans from the Bay of Pigs invasion, to constant terrorist attacks, multiple assassination attempts on its leaders, the use of germ warfare, and the trade embargo, Cuba has set an example to the world how an independent nation can act with integrity and stay true to itself and its people and overcome its adversary. From their long struggle the Russian and Venezuelan people will take their example and they too will endure, as have all the countries that have resolutely faced American aggression.

December 29, 2014

10

PARIS AND VOLNOVAKHA: THE BRUTAL FACE OF NATO TERRORISM

By Christopher Black

The insatiable monster of destruction that is NATO displayed its brutal face to the world once again in Paris and Ukraine, just a few short days after the people of the west were enjoined by church and state to live in peace and goodwill. Allowed just enough of a ration of those two rare commodities to keep them acquiescent, they were soon kicked in the face by new assaults on their humanity.

Not content with shooting down Malaysian flight MH17, the massacre without pity in Odessa, or the shelling of towns and cities in the Donbass for months last year, the war criminals that control the NATO countries have now started to murder their own citizens in staged terrorist incidents while their agents and dupes in Kiev recommence the heavy shelling of civilians, hospitals, schools, power plants and infrastructure in a renewed Donbass offensive made more cruel by the effects of winter. The objective in both circumstances is the same, to terrorise the people so that they will do what the war faction wants which means, in the NATO countries themselves, to support, or better, even call for war against the Islamic State bases that happen to be in Syria and Iraq; in the Ukraine, to drive the people out and, with the new offensive, to force Russia to defend two fronts at the same time; its own borders and the peoples of the Donbass and its important ally on the Mediterranean, Syria.

A western citizen who does not have time to believe anything except what he is fed by the western propaganda system believes that Islamic terrorists connected to Islamic State in Syria and Iraq and Al Qaeda in Yemen, carried out the terrible attacks on civilians at Charlie Hebdo and elsewhere. They believe the police acted bravely and pay no attention to the many questions about the true circumstances and who was really behind these actions; questions which provide an obvious answer that arises as smoke from a fire and blackens the name of every leader in the NATO alliance.

Their immediate calls for war against the Islamic State, their amazingly rapid but expertly handled photo op at the Paris rally, followed by successively sinister warnings of similar actions in the USA and UK, the open letter to the Tines of London, of Obama and Cameron, howling like wolves on the hunt, of the greatness of their nations, their united brotherhood, their crusade against "terrorism", their natural right to rule, their vicious vendetta against Russia, all confirm the answer.

On the 7th of January, 11 civilians were killed in the incident at Charlie Hebdo in Paris. A few days later, on the 13th of January 13 civilians were murdered when, according to the driver, a landmine detonated beneath a bus at a Kiev checkpoint at Volnovakha. The NATO governments and the controlled western media began a lightning campaign about the incident in Paris with wall to wall TV coverage of the events, saturated press coverage, statements by every NATO leader, and the Pope himself, condemning the criminals, and the "terrorist" groups that were behind it. A huge rally of millions of people, if the press are to be believed, marched in Paris and around the world, with dozens of world leaders taking part.

But, when state terrorists, from Kiev, murdered 13 civilians, there was no reaction. It hardly dented the western press. In the Ukraine there was the usual and very quick claim by Kiev that the local "rebel" militia had done it using Grad rockets. But this was quickly shown to be doubtful from the damage to the bus, the drivers' statement and the statement by OSCE observers that Grad rockets fired at the checkpoint at the same time came from the north and not from the east where the anti-fascist militia were located. The murders in Paris shook the world society. The murders in Ukraine drew only a careless yawn.

The official NATO version of all these events, including the "terrorist" incidents in Canada and Australia, as expedient as it is dishonest, is simple, consistent and suspect-a just war is being fought in defence of freedom and peace against a foreign enemy: a degenerate religion is striving to subvert the liberties of the western peoples, to subjugate them to the flag of Islam, Russian imperial ambition threatens to annex Europe.

But NATO is the aggressor, and since its victims have law on their side it is necessary to demonstrate that the next victims of the NATO war on the world are "morally" wrong and are "morally" the aggressor. The same phrases and propaganda are used in all wars whenever public opinion needs persuading or deceiving. But we are not deceived.

The terrorist actions in Paris are part of the same machine that carried out the terrorist action against the bus at Volnovakha and the continuing terrorist attacks against the peoples of the Donbass. The NATO version in all these incidents, and the Kiev regime, for all intents and purposes, is now a part of the NATO system, is palpably fraudulent, and so the necessity of the drama, the political and factual mythology. Created belief can make history and the western press has become an expertly controlled system of creating the unconscious beliefs that the ruling classes need to manipulate the minds of their peoples.

The increasing propaganda about the militant Islamic groups in Syria in particular, the sequential "terrorist" incidents scattered through NATO countries and allies such as Australia, the request by the US Congress to have 80,000 US soldiers sent to Iraq on the pretext of fighting the Islamic State, their own creation, but really to be used to invade Syria from the east, the posting of a squadron of Canadian fighter bombers in the middle east, the arrival of the French aircraft carrier to the region just the day before the event in Paris, the Israeli assassination of the Iranian Republican Guard general and Hezbollah fighters on the 18th of January, all point to a large operation against Syria building up. Even the resignation on the 16th January of Stephen Rapp, the American ambassador at large for war crimes, points to a coming war against Syria. Rapp stated that he resigned because legal technicalities got in the way of prosecuting Assad. This was a pretext. We can now expect a campaign by the usual Hollywood pawns dripping honeyed quotes of "justice for all" and "justice in our time" as they smile with menace and demand that, since Assad cannot be dealt with judicially, he must be dealt with militarily, which was what, in effect, Obama requested the authority to do in his address to Congress, made in his State of the Union speech on January 20th. The request was a declaration of war on Syria and its allies.

The danger is great for if a war against Syria is begun then Russia must defend its ally or suffer a strategic defeat. It must defend the Donbass and its Ukraine borders or suffer the same. Yet this appears to be NATO's intention, to force Russia to back down and admit defeat or to resist and defend its allies and itself. The danger is the greater, as the

NATO leaders do not appear to have any rational appreciation of the risks they taking. It is beyond doubt that Russia today is capable of defending its interests and is determined to do so.

Meanwhile the charade of peace talks continues following on the Minsk formula with new talks scheduled in Normandy on the 21st of January. But it is clear, with the mobilization of men up to age 60 by the Kiev regime, the insane statements by Yatsenyuk that the Red Army liberation of Ukraine and Europe from the Nazis was Russian aggression, the continued NATO shipments of arms and advisers to Kiev, and the arrest in Paris on the 20th of January of 5 Russians from Chechnya on suspicion of planning terrorist attacks in France, that the NATO fascists are engaging in a fight-and-talk strategy, pretending to negotiate to keep Russia off-balance while using the time to prepare their next attack and extending the source of terrorism to Russia itself.

The Russian deputy foreign minister Grigory Karasin stated on the 19th of January: "It's the biggest, even strategic mistake to bank on a military solution to the crisis in Ukrainian society and to all of southeast Ukraine's problems. This can lead to irreversible consequences for Ukrainian statehood." A similar statement would no doubt be made about Syria and Karasin's statement needs no interpretation.

January 22, 2015

11

NATO: 3 MINUTES TO MIDNIGHT

By Christopher Black

It is with astonishment that one reads the news today, February 2nd, that the Russian air defence forces are holding massive air defence drills in the Baltic and Siberia shooting down all targets, while radiation, chemical and biological defence troops are undertaking large drills in the south east and Crimea, drills that are occurring just a few days after the Russian Armed Forces Chief of the General Staff, General Gerasimov stated that Russia is preparing its defences so that it can never be overcome by the US and NATO.

Russia is stating to the world that that it will continue to resist the daily attacks on the people of Russia being carried out on every level by the NATO countries and that it is prepared for the worst. On the economic front, Prime Minister Medvedev announced the banning of imports of industrial equipment for state purposes on the same day as the drills were announced. The astonishment is on two levels, first because Gerasimov's statement is a welcome fist in the face of the Americans and, and second because the leaders of the most powerful nations on earth are talking openly of general war and are openly preparing for it.

It is perhaps less astonishing that after a century of generalised warfare across the globe the imperialist forces coalesced in the NATO alliance are still engaged in the robbery and pillaging of entire countries to enrich themselves, never having succeeded in rising higher than the level of the Hitlerite thugs they admire.

In the Ukraine, the NATO controlled Kiev regime uses indiscriminate shelling of the towns and cities of the Donbass republics to terrorise the people. There are daily reports of mortar teams roaming the streets in civilian vehicles firing bombs randomly and of white phosphorus being used against civilian targets, proof that the Kiev regime is engaging in collective punishment of the civilian population. In all this, the regime is assisted by the NATO countries that are increasing their supply of mercenaries, weapons, ammunition, money and "advisers" to use against the people of the Donbass. Angela Merkel and Barak Obama are to meet in Washington next week to discuss provision of direct and open military assistance to the Kiev junta and we can be sure that peace will not be on their agenda but a NATO war against Russia will be. Of course these war crimes and crimes against humanity and the conspiracy to commit them taking place in the NATO capitals have not provoked any reaction in the western media or governments except to call for war against Russia and the International Criminal Court sits blind, mute and spineless, once again proving its total irrelevance except as a NATO propaganda tool.

The Minsk talks on January 31st never got off the ground as Kiev showed its contempt for the process by sending low-level officials and continuing the shelling of Donetsk and other cities. The junta refused a ceasefire, preferring to talk and fight at the same time, aping the attitude of the American international bully that runs the show. But a ceasefire is essential for real talks to begin. No one likes to negotiate looking down the barrel of a gun but the Americans and their satraps like to make people squirm while they issue their diktats.

The actions of the Kiev regime, its new offensive, its order for the mobilisation of the population and civilian vehicles, the presence in Kiev of American and other NATO military officers and their financiers like George Soros, all point to increased and continued fighting on the Ukrainian front. Russian Foreign Minister Serge Lavrov expressed his frustration with his reference to Obama's confession on CNN on February 1st that the Americans had succeeded in changing the government in Kiev, in fact overthrowing the legitimate government of Ukraine to replace it with their hand picked people. It was also a confession by Obama that they are responsible for the crimes being committed and that they are going to continue to commit them, that the Americans have no intention of allowing peace in Ukraine. Indeed, it was was a confession of a crime against peace. One day he will find himself in the dock.

Obama's remarks were made a day before the anniversary of the surrender of the German 6th Army at Stalingrad, in 1943, an army that came to conquer Russia but was itself destroyed by the courage and determination of the Red Army, an army that existed because Russia, with the Bolshevik Revolution in 1917, had thrown off the economic and political yoke of the old regime, and released a flowering of Russian industrial, scientific, economic and social development unprecedented in world history: a development that provided Russia with the capacity and will to resist the fascist forces then and now.

Russia has allies but Russia and the people of Ukraine should not stand alone against enemies common to us all. The anti-war movement in the western countries is nowhere to be seen yet the European governments managed to mobilise millions in a few days to demonstrate about the killings in Paris but no popular movement exists to go on the streets and once again shout John Lennon's call "Give Peace A Chance," and aim that call at the governments who are behind most of the wars on the planet. Instead despair reins. The social media are full of this despair and anger but no one moves to act where it counts, on the streets. "But" say wiser heads, "it's all been tried before and it stopped nothing, what's the point?" I don't know the answer but I do know that if we do not try to do something then the world is at grave risk. A short while ago the Bulletin of the Atomic Scientists reset the Doomsday Clock, the clock that tells us how close were are to exterminating ourselves. It was set forward 2 minutes. It is now 3 minutes to midnight.

I think it's worth quoting the reasons for resetting the clock,

"Unchecked climate change, global nuclear weapons modernizations, and outsized nuclear weapons arsenals pose extraordinary and undeniable threats to the continued existence of humanity, and world leaders have failed to act with the speed or on the scale required to protect citizens from potential catastrophe. These failures of political leadership endanger every person on Earth. Despite some modestly positive developments in the climate change arena, current efforts are entirely insufficient to prevent a catastrophic warming of Earth. Meanwhile, the United States and Russia have embarked on massive programs to modernize their nuclear triads— thereby undermining existing nuclear weapons treaties. The clock ticks now at just three minutes to midnight because international leaders are failing to perform their most important duty—ensuring and preserving the health and vitality of human civilization."

There you have it, friends, 3 minutes to midnight, and counting with every shell, with every bullet that's fired. The risk of nuclear war is great, perhaps never greater. So what are we going to do about it?

February 9, 2015

12

NATO WAR PROPAGANDA: A DANGER TO WORLD PEACE

By Christopher Black

The reaction of the media in the Nato countries to the murder of Boris Nemtsov reveals the next phase of the war against Russia. Defeated at Debaltsevo, defied by Russia, lectured by China, the Nato warlords need something immediate and dramatic to guide the imaginations of their peoples towards war. The constant propaganda offensive aimed at Russia is accelerating and is increasingly designed to identify Russia and its people not with the Russian government, but with a single man and, with the murder of Nemtsov, that man is now labelled assassin.

Across the broad spectrum of the "western" media in the past days there has appeared one story after another designed to make the average citizen believe that President Putin was personally involved in the killing. The facts of the case do not matter. The NATO governments deny any involvement in a provocation but their immediate denunciations, the morning following the murder, of Russian democracy, of Russian government, and of President Putin, convict them all on the charge of exploiting the murder as surely as if the assassins' bullets were theirs.

The labelling of resisting leaders as criminals has been used frequently in the west since the days of the Roman Empire and once a foreign leader is so labelled a war soon follows. In recent history the Americans and their NATO lieutenants identified President Milosevic as a criminal for simply refusing NATO's diktats. They did the same with Saddam Hussein, with Muammar Gaddafi and murdered them all, one way or another.

Once a head of state is demeaned in this way and reduced to a common criminal the people of the aggressor country are easily persuaded that his elimination, and the elimination of the government that supports him, is a necessary task. The persuasion has been going on since Putin's speech in 2007, which drew a line in the sand against American imperial ambitions in Eurasia, and reached new levels of hysteria when Flight MH17 was shot down last year. Evidence that it was probably the Kiev forces that committed the crime, with American collusion, was completely supressed by the western media and when more evidence of their culpability was produced the shoot down was erased from history and now is rarely mentioned. Since the overthrow of the legitimate government of Ukraine a year ago the western media have been caught time and again repeating US propaganda about Russian threats to peace in Europe, about Russian territorial ambitions and Russian regular army units being involved in the Donbass. Denials by Russia, and even observers of the OSCE, are ignored and the lies are repeated day after day after day.

The use of propaganda to incite hatred towards another people or government, and to incite calls for aggressive war and all the war crimes that flow from aggressive war are crimes against humanity and prohibited under international and national laws. Journalists who prostitute themselves by telling their fellow citizens lies are not only betraying the trust put in them by the people, and treating them with contempt, they are also war criminals and should be judged as such. Their responsibility in preparing the way for war is as great as those who plan the war and carry out the military operations of the war.

We need only look at the case of Juluis Streicher at the Nuremberg Trials in 1946 to understand that propagandists can be hanged too. Streicher neither gave orders for the extermination of Jews nor was involved in any military operations. But that did not prevent him from being convicted of crimes against humanity for producing the anti-semitic journal Der Sturmer that put out a constant barrage of hate propaganda against Jews. His role in preparing the ground for the dehumanization of Jews in Germany was determined to be critical in creating the conditions for their extermination by the Nazis. The Nuremberg prosecutors argued that his articles and speeches were incendiary and that he was an accessory to murder and therefore as culpable as those who actually carried out the killings. The Allied judges agreed and he was convicted of crimes against humanity and hanged in October 1946. The judgement stated in part that "...he infected the German mind with the virus of anti-semitism and incited the German people to active persecution and..murder."

The role of propaganda in preparing a nation's people to call for and support an aggressive war was never put better than by another Nazi, Herman Goering during the same trial that convicted Streicher. In an interview with Gustave Gilbert published in in 1947, in Nuremberg Diary, he said:

- Göring: "Why, of course, the people don't

want war. Why would some poor slob on a farm want to risk his life in a war when the best that he can get out of it is to come back to his farm in one piece? Naturally, the common people don't want war; neither in Russia nor in England nor in America, nor for that matter in Germany. That is understood. But, after all, it is the leaders of the country who determine the policy and it is always a simple matter to drag the people along, whether it is a democracy or a fascist dictatorship or a Parliament or a Communist dictatorship.

• Gilbert: "There is one difference. In a democracy, the people have some say in the matter through their elected representatives, and in the United States only Congress can declare wars.

• Göring: "Oh, that is all well and good, but, voice or no voice, the people can always be brought to the bidding of the leaders. That is easy. All you have to do is tell them they are being attacked and denounce the pacifists for lack of patriotism and exposing the country to danger. It works the same way in any country."

The Nuremberg principle that propaganda inciting aggressive war is a crime was codified in the International Covenant on Civil and Political Rights adopted by the General Assembly of the United Nations in 1966.

Article 20 states,

"1. Any propaganda for war shall be prohibited by law.

2. Any advocacy of national, racial or religious hatred that constitutes incitement to discrimination, hostility or violence shall be prohibited by law."

It was also included in Article 15 of the American Convention on Human Rights of 1969 that uses similar language. It is telling that both Canada and the United States, two of the worst offenders in the use of war propaganda, have refused to ratify the Convention, but this should not surprise us.

Today we see the use of propaganda as an offensive weapon against Russia not only in the press and other news media, we also see it in film and television. The American television series House of Cards, has now descended deep into the sewer of anti-Russian propaganda with a Russian leader named Petrov standing in for Putin, while those rank opportunists, Pussy Riot, used to try to embarrass Petrov in one episode, succeed only in embarrassing themselves.

The prohibition on the use of war propaganda in international covenants is important because war threatens the existence and exercise of all of the other political and civil rights contained in those covenants and of the UN Charter itself, including the right to live in peace. And since wars of aggression are illegal under customary international law and since propaganda related to aggressive war is illegal, actions could be taken in national courts against governments, corporations and individuals who engage in it.

The question of the identification of war propaganda presents no more difficulty than identifying aggressive war. Distinguishing it from mere expression of opinion or supposed reporting of facts is also not difficult. Any communication to the public that has the sole purpose of inflaming emotions and feelings of hatred, hostility and calls for war would fall under the definition of war propaganda, whether by distortion of facts, suppression of facts or the invention of facts.

In 1966, at a seminar in the United States on the meaning of propaganda, the Soviet press attaché in Washington stated that propaganda "had rather a broad meaning, implying purposeful dissemination of certain information that is to produce upon its recipient a certain reaction which from the viewpoint of the disseminator is desirable", and defined war propaganda to be both an "incitement to war between states and a means for preparing for aggressive war." The United States, on the other hand, has generally opposed efforts to prohibit the use of war propaganda in international law citing concerns about freedom of expression. But this is a false argument, used to justify the unjustifiable, the constant use of propaganda by the United States to create in the minds of its citizens the necessary emotions and reactions to support wars fought for the benefit of a few against the interests of the many.

War propaganda is a danger to world peace. It is a danger to democracy itself. Since wars of aggression are criminal acts, incitements to engage in them are also criminal acts. It is high time for the peoples of the world, against whom this propaganda is directed, and who are the true victims of these crimes, to wake up, to get on their feet, to put their fists in the air and protest the constant manipulation of their minds towards hatred and violence and war and demand the full implementation of the international covenants that prohibit it and the arrest and trial of those that use it.

March 13, 2015

13

UN IN UKRAINE: PEACEKEEPERS OR NATO TROJAN HORSE?

By Christopher Black

The same day that the March 4th deadline was reached for political steps to be taken to ameliorate the situation in the Ukraine between the Kiev regime and the Donbass governments, the UN confirmed that it had received a request from President Poroshenko for a "peace-keeping" force to be sent into Ukraine. The Russia UN ambassador, Vitaly Churkin, correctly remarked that this called into question the Kiev regime's commitment to the Minsk ceasefire agreement. The Donbass governments also rejected the idea, calling it premature, and stated that if there was to be such a force it must be Russian. They are both right. Insertion of foreign military forces into Ukraine at the request of Kiev can only be for aggressive purposes against the citizens of the Donbass and against Russia. The history of UN interventions in the past has too often been a history of betrayal of the peoples whose peace was supposed to be enforced and a disguised means of helping one side in the conflict to defeat the other.

We need only remember the UN "police action" in Korea in 1950-53 used to attack north Korea and China, Rwanda in 1993-94, where UN forces actively helped to overthrow the interim government and install the present Kagame dictatorship, Yugoslavia, in the 90's, where UN forces operated against the government in various theatres of operation, Haiti, where they have been used to consolidate the US overthrow of President Aristide in 2004 and the Congo where UN forces have done nothing to reign in the massacres of Congolese and Hutu refugees by Ugandan and Rwandan proxy forces yet readily harass and attack the forces trying to protect them.

We need only to examine the case of Rwanda to see how the system really works. In 1993 the UNAMIR force, commanded by Canadian General Dallaire, actively aided and abetted the enemy who had invaded the country from Uganda. UN documents produced in evidence in the military trials at the Rwanda War Crimes Tribunal showed that Dallaires' military observers, stationed in the north of the country to monitor enemy movements, made continuous reports to Dallaire of violations of the ceasefire agreement, including infiltration into the country of heavy artillery systems, light and heavy machine guns, mortars, and all the ammunition necessary to support those weapons. Dallaire never reported these violations of the peace accords to the government side but put a lot of effort into enforcing a weapons embargo against the government forces.

There was also evidence in the trials that certain elements of Dallaire's force colluded with the enemy force by turning a blind eye to its infiltration into the capital of thousands of enemy fighters that were later used to overwhelm the government forces and massacre civilians when they launched their final offensive in April 1994. The

UN also covered up evidence pointing to their culpability for assassinations of government officials and various political leaders and did nothing to investigate and stop continuous terrorist attacks against civilians. All this was done on behalf of the American and British interests and we cannot expect anything different from a western controlled UN force in Ukraine.

The Kiev junta is, in effect, calling for a NATO force to come into Ukraine, but wearing blue helmets, since it is clear that Kiev will never permit any Russian forces to be part of the contingent, nor a Russian general to be in command. The request was transparent as soon as it was made and raises the question whether a UN force inserted into the Ukraine would act as a force for keeping the peace or would be a NATO Trojan Horse.

The duplicity of the junta and NATO is emphasized by the new law passed by the Kiev parliament with respect to the status of the Donbass governments. Instead of consulting with those governments about constitutional reform, elections and the commitment to provide them with more autonomy, the new law mocks the Minsk cease-fire agreement and treats the Donbass governments as if they do not exist. In response the republics have refused further cooperation until the Kiev law is abolished and Foreign Minister Lavrov stated on March 18th that the parliament's action, "...rewrites the agreements, and putting it simply, grossly violates them."

Also on the 18th, the Ukrainian Defense Minister announced that Kiev has concluded 100 new arms contracts and will sign 160 more. This follows President Poroshenko's order for the expansion of the Kiev forces to 250,000 soldiers, and the additional announcement on the 18th that the Kiev Prime Minister has inspected new weaponry to be dispatched to the eastern Ukraine that on the 17th was declared to be "temporarily occupied."

Violations of the Minks agreement continue on the front lines as well with daily incidents of attacks and provocations along the contact lines between the Kiev and

Donbass forces, and an increase of the economic blockade of the region. Although the junta has removed some of its heavy artillery it becomes daily clearer that it has done so in order to refit, refurbish and reorganise for another offensive some time later in the spring. This concern is heightened by America's announcement that it will send several hundred soldiers to Ukraine and will hold joint exercises with Ukraine forces in a few months. Britain quickly followed suit with its own announcement to send in forces and Canada has also announced a willingness to send its troops on top of advisers and "trainers" already there, all of which is a violation of the Minks agreement requiring the removal of any foreign forces in Ukraine.

The continued shipment of arms to Ukraine by NATO countries, proved by their presence on the battlefield, the promise to send more, the known presence of mercenaries, many of whom once were and probably still are, members of NATO armies, and the continued collective punishment of the civilians of the Donbass are all further violations of the ceasefire agreement as well as international law.

More alarming news comes almost every day of NATO forces conducting one military exercise after another, from the Baltic to the Black Sea, of the Americans quickly building up their armoured and air forces in eastern Europe and of the intention to establish NATO command centres close to the Russian borders. The result, a dizzying spiral of provocations by NATO, and strong defensive responses by Russia.

The Secretary General of the United Nation, Ban Ki Moon, has said nothing about the aggressive actions of the NATO powers nor their violations of the Minks agreement and UN Charter and nothing about the Kiev request for a peacekeeping force. It should have been simple for him to make a statement supporting the full implementation of the ceasefire and to remind Kiev that since only the Security Council can approve a peacekeeping mission, it will never happen without Russian participation. But he has said nothing and it is obvious that this idea came from the United States, which would like to make political points by supporting such a request in the Security Council, knowing that Russia must oppose it. The Americans can then claim that Russia is being "obstructive" and therefore a NATO force has to be introduced to protect Ukraine against Russian "aggression." There can be no other reason for the Kiev demand. Once such a force is introduced, Ukraine becomes a de facto NATO state, and a direct threat to Russia.

The Minsk ceasefire agreement has brought a reprieve for the citizens of the Donbass and some relief from their suffering. But it is too little and too fragile to provide real hope for peace in the region. The peoples of Ukraine, of Russia, and of the world, need a complete cessation of the constant threats of war by the NATO powers and an honest commitment by them and the Kiev regime to peace and security in order for the situation to stabilise and for the peoples of the Ukraine to rebuild lives shattered by a NATO provoked war. But this honesty and this commitment to peace are nowhere to be found in the NATO countries and so, once again, in support of the diplomatic efforts being made from Moscow to Beijing, it lies with the citizens of the NATO state themselves to take up their responsibilities as citizens and demand that their governments abandon their aggressive polices, dismantle the NATO war alliance, and call for a new international legal framework that once and for all provides real and effective mechanisms to prevent war.

March 27, 2015

Andre Vltchek – Christopher Black – Peter Koenig

14

THE DEATH OF MILOSEVIC AND NATO RESPONSIBILITY

By Christopher Black

On March 11, 2006, President Slobodan Milosevic died in a NATO prison. No one has been held accountable for his death.   In the 9 years since the end of his lonely struggle to defend himself and his country against the false charges invented by the NATO powers, the only country to demand a public inquiry into the circumstances of his death came from Russia when Foreign Minister, Serge Lavrov, stated that Russia did not accept the Hague tribunal's denial of responsibility and demanded that an impartial and international investigation be conducted. Instead, The NATO tribunal made its own investigation, known as the Parker Report, and as expected, exonerated itself from all blame.

But his death cannot lie unexamined, the many

questions unanswered, those responsible unpunished. The world cannot continue to accept the substitution of war and brutality for peace and diplomacy. It cannot continue to tolerate governments that have contempt for peace, for humanity, the sovereignty of nations, the self-determination of peoples, and the rule of law.

The death of Slobodan Milosevic was clearly the only way out of the dilemma the NATO powers had put themselves in by charging him before the Hague tribunal. The propaganda against him was of an unprecedented scale. The trial was played in the press as one of the world's great dramas, as world theatre in which an evil man would be made to answer for his crimes. But of course, there had been no crimes, except those of the NATO alliance, and the attempt to fabricate a case against him collapsed into farce.

The trial was necessary from NATO's point of view in order to justify the aggression against Yugoslavia and the putsch by the DOS forces in Belgrade supported by NATO, by which democracy in Yugoslavia was finally destroyed and Serbia reduced to a NATO protectorate under a Quisling regime. His illegal arrest, by NATO forces in Belgrade, his illegal detention in Belgrade Central Prison, his illegal rendition to the former Gestapo prison at Scheveningen, near The Hague, and the show trial that followed, were all part of the drama played out for the world public, and it could only have one of two endings, the conviction, or the death, of President Milosevic.

Since the conviction of President Milosevic was clearly not possible after all the evidence was heard, his death became the only way out for the NATO powers. His acquittal would have brought down the entire structure of the propaganda framework of the NATO war machine and the western interests that use it as their armed fist.

NATO clearly did not expect President Milosevic to defend himself, nor with such courage and determination. The media coverage of the beginning of the trial was constant and front page. It was promised that it would be the trial of the century. Yet soon after it began the media coverage stopped and the trial was buried in the back pages. Things had gone terribly wrong for Nato right at the start. The key to the problem is the following statement of President Milosevic made to the judges of the Tribunal during the trial:

"This is a political trial. What is at issue here is not at all whether I committed a crime. What is at issue is that certain intentions are ascribed to me from which consequences are later derived that are beyond the expertise of any conceivable lawyer. The point here is that the truth about the events in the former Yugoslavia has to be told here. It is that which is at issue, not the procedural questions, because I'm not sitting here because I was accused of a specific crime. I'm sitting here because I am accused of conducting a policy against the interests of this or another party."

The prosecution, that is the United States and its allies, had not expected a real defence of any kind. This is clear from the inept indictments, confused charges, and the complete failure to bring any evidence that could withstand even basic scrutiny. The prosecution case fell apart as soon as it began. But once started, it had to continue. Nato was locked into a box of its own making. If they dropped the charges, or if he was acquitted, the political and geostrategic ramifications were enormous. Nato would have to explain the real reasons for the aggression against Yugoslavia. Its leaders themselves would face war crimes charges. The loss of prestige cannot be calculated. President Milosevic would once again be a popular political figure in the Balkans. The only way out for NATO was to end the trial but without releasing Milosevic or admitting the truth about the war. This logic required his death in prison and the abandonment of the trial.

The Parker Report contains facts indicating that, at a minimum, the Nato Tribunal engaged in conduct that was criminal regarding his treatment and that conduct resulted in his death. The Tribunal was told time and again that he was gravely ill with heart problems that needed proper investigation, treatment and complete rest before engaging in a trial. However, the Tribunal continually ignored the advice of the doctors and pushed him to keep going with the trial, knowing full well that the stress of the trial would certainly kill him.

The Tribunal refused prescribed medical treatment in Russia seemingly for political reasons and once again put the Tribunal's interests, whatever they are, ahead of Milosevic's health. In other words they deliberately withheld necessary medical treatment that could have lead to his death. This is a form of homicide and is manslaughter in the common law jurisdictions.

However, there are several unexplained facts contained in the Parker Report that need further investigation before ruling out poison or drugs designed to harm his health: the presence of the drugs rifampicin and droperidol in his system being the two key ones. No proper investigation was conducted as to how these drugs could have been introduced into his body. No consideration was given to their effect. Their presence combined with the unexplained long delay in getting his body to a medical facility for tests raises serious questions that need to be answered but which until today remain unanswered.

The Parker Report, despite its illogical conclusions, exonerating the Nato tribunal from blame, provides the basis for a call for a public inquiry into the death of President Milosevic. This is reinforced by the fact that the Commandant of the UN prison where President Milosevic was held, a Mr. McFadden, was, according to documents exposed by Wikileaks, supplying information to the US authorities about Milosevic throughout his detention and trial, and is further reinforced by the fact that Milosevic wrote a letter to the Russian Embassy a few days before his death stating that he believed he was being poisoned. Unfortunately he died before the letter could be delivered in time for a response.

All these facts taken together demand that a public international inquiry be held into the entirety of the circumstances of the death of President Milosevic, not only for his sake and the sake of his widow Mira Markovic and his son, but for the sake of all of us who face the constant aggressive actions and propaganda of the NATO powers. Justice requires it. International peace and security demand it.

March 23, 2015

15

SPRING LAMENT

By Christopher Black

Spring has arrived in the north but the flowers poking their heads above the warming ground do not bring smiles to those who see them. The song of birds, so pleasant to the ear tired of the winter winds does not warm the heart. The rising sun that brightens each day more than the last brings no promise of a happy summer. Instead the world sinks into an abyss so dark that it seems no light can ever escape it, dragged down a black hole of despair by greed and ambition, barbarity and cruelty, criminality and ignorance.

We need reason and kindness applied to the problems that face us but instead violence and brutality are the norms of modern conduct. How low mankind has sunk since the Enlightenment promised to bring us the benefits of our intelligence and curiosity about life, nature, science, law, and government. Voltaire is dead. Marx slandered. Shelley, Zola, Hugo, Steinbeck, who carries their torch now?

The hopes that mankind expressed then have been smashed by the economic system that produces the misery of the many for the riches of the few. The golden tree of democracy that sprang from the seed of the sacrifice of the people who struggled to plant it has been hacked and cut down to its roots, and struggles to rise again.

The world over, the people, the common people, the people who have to work for their living call for peace, for the elimination of ignorance, of superstition, for a chance to have a say in how their lives unfold. In a few countries modest successes have been achieved and in a few, great ones. But in the countries that make up what is termed the west, Europe and North America, the successes of the social revolutions of the past have been overturned, reaction has replaced progress and brute force and gangsterism are applauded by the servile and their intellectual apologists alike.

The threat of nuclear annihilation is so immediate that we talk about it openly every day. The western leaders, drunk with their own hubris and arrogance, push the limits of tolerance and threaten the mass murder of millions, and yet their peoples sit by their computer screens, their television sets, their mobile phones and instead of going onto the streets to demand the overthrow of this system, yearn only for more popcorn to stuff their mouths or easier ways to send strangers "selfies", sad photos of themselves, the only way they have of confirming their own bleak existence. Instead of being involved outside themselves to find meaning in life they descend into the sterility and the vacuity of their own vanity. Citizens, with a responsibility to those around them to ensure the justness of their societies have become bored consumers, each one expendable once the money runs out, as it always does.

Law, once seen as a means to ensure fairness and the smooth interaction of all the components of a complex society has become a tool for the oppressor instead of a guarantor of the right of the individual to express their full humanity. Instead of being used to liberate, it is used to dominate and suppress, to manipulate and exploit, to obfuscate and mislead. International Law, once the hope of mankind for a secure peace and rational and respectful relations among nations, is cynically twisted into a rope to hang those who resist the new barbarians who control the gates and levers of power.

Religion and philosophy are at an impasse. The wise words of their teachings seem to have little effect on the behaviour of most of mankind. Every religion shares the golden rule that no one should do to others what they are not willing to have done to themselves, but who lives it? Today we have no saints. Instead the masses are for whoever gives them a living.

During the 60's and the years after, of the last century the liberation movements in the European colonial empires and the reaction of the people to the Second World War produced an energy and an optimism that is now a fond memory of youth. The world was different then. The poor of the world, the working people of the world, had the Soviet Union to look to as a example of what they could do, the remarkable rise of socialist China, the historic victory of Vietnam over America, the heroic resistance and example of what humanity was capable of in Cuba, that giant among nations. There was revolution in the air in London, in Paris, in America, in politics, in music, in film, in philosophy. But now everything in the west has become grey, banal and uniform. Where are The Clash now or The Beatles? Where are the Sartre's and Camus', the Ginsberg's and the New Wave?

International Law had some application and effect then. But let's admit it. The whole structure depended on force, and counter force. Remove the one and the other ran riot over the world, a gangster drunk on power, pawing and raping every country it could for whatever it could get. Now we are reduced to the law of the savage whose only rule is that there are none, preying on the small and vulnerable, recognizing nothing but the power to take. Their philosophy is "Law? We make our own laws and we take what we need." Only the old Arab proverb describes our condition; " The world is a carcass and those who seek it are dogs." The western armies feed on the carrion of the dead on every continent, their cruelty so deep that it brings to mind the words of Ovid,

"Though men in shape, they scarce deserve the name;

Their savagery doth put the wolves to shame."

And everywhere there is fear and anxiety.

The West is politically and morally bankrupt. The free market has reduced everything to the status of commodity, human beings to ciphers, the state to a universal spy. Yet, in the east, in China, in Russia, in Latin America, a new energy has shone its light on human possibilities, on sharing, cooperation, love of mankind instead of hatred, peaceful cooperation instead of conflict and death. We in the west need now to look to the east, to the south, to our own past, to find the strength and the will to regenerate ourselves, to save ourselves, and the planet we live on, from those in our midst who would reduce us to slavery and hopelessness,

The way forward is marked out. We just have to take it and soon for storm clouds and thunder threaten. The path is dangerous and long. The fascists are revealed and the knives are drawn. In May we celebrate the final victory of the Red Army over European fascism, the liberation of Europe from the black shirts and the brown. The armies of the west fought on the same side then. Now they are with the fascists. No doubt they always were. We need a new liberation, a liberation of the west that can come only from the peoples of the west who only have to look up at the sky instead of down at the mud. We have no Red Army to help us now. We have to help ourselves. And, so I end this Lament, for there is not much more I can say, but let me share with you the words of the great revolutionary poet, Shelley, for they speak as I wish I could,

"And these words shall then become
Like Oppression's thundered doom
Ringing through each heart and brain,
Heard again-again-again-

Rise like Lions after slumber,
In unvanquishable number-
Shake your chains to earth like dew
Ye are many-they are few."

April 9, 2015

Andre Vltchek –   Christopher Black – Peter Koenig

PETER KOENIG

1

WHAT WILL HAPPEN TO GLOBAL ECONOMY IF BRICS ANNOUNCE LAUNCH OF NEW CURRENCY – BRICSO? – PART 1

By Peter Koenig
in interviews with Valentin Mândrășescu

For several decades, we've been told by the mainstream media that the West has a firm grip on the word's economy and that America decides the future of the world. Peter Koenig, former World Bank economist and Voice of Russia regular, outlines one of the scenarios in which America's plans for a New World Order are broken. This is

the first part of the series about "How to dismantle the New World Order".

Imagine – it is **December 31, 2013**. The Presidents of the BRICS (Brazil, Russia, India, China and South Africa) plus Iran and Venezuela call an impromptu press conference – in Paris – to present a 'Sea of Change in Economics,' as they call it. The announcement was circulated throughout the international media and diplomatic offices and embassies just a day before – an indication of urgency. Despite it being the last day of the year with most people thinking of their year-end festivities, the event calls the attention of many – especially the world of finance – and of course the media. The press meeting is planned for 18:00 at the Dolce Chantilly, in Chantilly, just 40 minutes from the center of Paris.

The seven presidents, accompanied by their Ministers of Finance, are seated in a half-moon panel in front of about 500 journalists from all over the world. The Chinese President and General Secretary of the Communist Party, Mr. Xi Jinping, opens the conference without fanfare, introducing the subject as an event that may have worldwide repercussions. He elaborates, "We the BRICS and some other hydrocarbon producing countries, like Iran and Venezuela – others may join in the future – have decided as of tomorrow – **January 1, 2014** – to introduce two new economic measures. First, the BRICS and Iran and Venezuela will launch a new currency, called the *Bricso*. The *Bricso* will, at least initially, be a virtual currency; similar to what the *Euro* was in its initial years of existence and currently the *Sucre* in the South American trading community of ALBA. The backbone of the *Bricso* is a basket of moneys of the BRICS and those of Iran and Venezuela. The individual country currencies will be weighed according to their respective economic strength - similar to the Special Drawing Rights – SDR – of the IMF. The initial basket of Seven, does not impede that later other countries, trading partners of the BRICS, may join the *Bricso.* "

Reality Check comment: One has to wonder: why do it in a sudden almost theatrical manner? The reason is simple: such a move is a declaration of war, an economic war, but a war none the less. Maybe, calling this operation a "revolution" or an "insurrection" would be more appropriate, but the essence remains the same. The West has abused its economic power and used its financial institutions to the detriment of the rest of the world. It was time to turn the tables. When global domination is at stake, it is a good idea to fire the first shot.

"Initially, each country will continue to use its own currency. In the course of the coming years we may decide to also issue the Bricso as a paper currency for all member currencies, similarly to the euro. For now, we believe, each member country will have to adapt its economy to certain established parameters of economic viability – criteria that were not followed seriously enough by the Euro member countries."

Reality Check comment: This plan has an important technical requirement. The new currency requires a central bank. Actually, BRICS countries are already building an alternative financial system. While kick-starting it into action on short notice is quite hard, using the new mechanisms for clearing the trades done with the new currency is not impossible.

Mr. Jinping went on – "The recently created BRICS Development Bank will initially act as the BRICS Central Bank, issuing guidelines and norms of economic and financial viability, for each member country to adopt, so as to create coherence among them and facilitate trading within, as well as outside the *Bricso* domain. As our economies evolve, we may consider other steps to adjust to the new dynamics, like – as mentioned before – issuing common paper money. The BRICS Central Bank will also act as a bank of last resource for the member countries, lending to their respective national central banks at inter-bank rates."

"We have also decided on an initial exchange rate between the US dollar and the *Bricso* – one *Bricso* equals 10 US dollars. This is roughly the relation of the outstanding debt – or unmet obligations – in proportion of the respective GDPs – of the US and the combined BRICS."

Reality Check comment: It doesn't take a prophet to predict that the western media will describe such a move as an attack on the dollar. Probably, stronger terms like "financial terrorism" are likely to be used. However, it is clear that the mainstream media will always demonize the BRICS countries so there is no point in trying to be "the good guy". Anyone who disagrees with the NWO will be labeled as an evildoer, tyrant and terrorist. History is written by the winners and if BRICS win this financial war, the leaders of the anti-dollar movement will be hailed as heroes. Given the financial atrocities the West has committed against the world, it is safe to assume that any act aimed at dismantling the existing global financial system is actually an act of self-defense.

A murmur went through the room gaining increasing strength. But before the noise got out of control, President Jinping continued with a raised voice – "The second important step we are announcing – also as of **January 1, 2014**, the BRICS, Iran and Venezuela will sell their hydrocarbon – primarily oil and gas – in *Bricsos*, in a newly created *Shanghai Oil Bourse*. In fact, all countries, oil producers and otherwise, wishing to trade in other currencies than the US dollar may do so at the *Shanghai Oil Bourse*, or in short the SOB. The reason for abandoning the dollar as an oil trading currency is its volatility. In fact, the dollar has lost its value – and its trust – over the past decades; it is beset by enormous debt and has no real economic backing. Many oil producers see their hydrocarbon wealth at risk."

"That is all for tonight. I wish you a fun-filled transition into 2014 and a happy New Year."

Reality Check comment: There is nothing unrealistic

about this scenario. Everything could be ready quickly. The oil companies will easily "unwind" their dollar-based contracts and even if they do it gradually, the global oil price is set by the "marginal" (aka "free") production that is not sold in advance. The same structure can easily work with 3-4 delivery points across the globe in order to ensure a fair, transparent and adequate pricing mechanism for all global producers and consumers.

The presidents and ministers collected their papers and were about to step down from the panel – when the aula exploded in yelling and shouting.

One voice barely pierced the noise on the floor – "What will happen to the US dollar?" - Screamed CNN's José Perez – "When suddenly a third of the world's hydrocarbon is traded in – eh – I mean in *Bricsos?*" – BBC correspondent, Jim Dillen, was afraid that the world economy may collapse. France's Bernard Betancourt, exclaimed – "Finally a relief from the dollar. But where is the gold? You did not mention it as part of the basket."

A spokesman of the Nigerian Embassy, who attended the Press Conference, asked simply – "What are we going to do with the worthless dollars in our coffers?"

Mr. Vladimir Putin, Russia's President, tapped the mike with his pen, attempting to soften the anxiety in the room. As quiet was restored, he said – "These measures will certainly have an impact on the world economy. To predict exactly what will happen is impossible. Time will tell. But, yes, there will be some collateral damage, especially in those countries that have been relying heavily on the US dollar, on trading with the United States. But it will also affect us, the BRICS. A large proportion of our dollar denominated reserves will be wiped out, as the dollar will undoubtedly plummet – but again, it is difficult to speculate at this time to what extent it will lose its value."

Reality Check comment: In judo, this is called a sacrifice-throw. Such moves require the thrower to move into a potentially disadvantageous position in order for it to be executed, such as falling to the ground. The momentum of the falling body adds power to the throw and requires comparatively little strength, compared to the effect. Sacrificing a part of currency reserves in order to bring down the American empire is definitely a good strategic move.

Mr. Putin directed his next words at the representative of Nigeria – "And, Sir, yours too – and that of other countries that have large amounts of US Treasury bonds in their central banks. But, ladies and gentlemen, I predict that this is only a short-lived loss, as we will quickly recover the value of the lost dollars through a stronger and more stable *Bricso*. To be precise, the artificial and highly inflated value of the US dollar – which in fact, has for decades had no real backing, other than the world's belief in America's strength. But by now, most of the world realizes that the only strength that Washington can stand for is brute military force. Its economy depends on wars and conflicts around the world. The US economy is indeed based on destruction – not construction. Accounting for all associated industries and services, way more than 50% of the US GDP consists of the American military industrial and security complex. The rest is consumption of goods made abroad, many of them in the BRICS countries, and of values of services blown out of proportion."

Reality Check comment: The crucial aspect of this operation is the message sent to the people of the world. The message is about the change of core principles of the global economy. Any change in the global financial system is useless without a proper change of the underlying ideology. For the BRICS to prevail, the professionals working on spreading the right message have to perform brilliantly. The world must see that the whole struggle is not about hijacking the current economic system, but it is about creating an equitable economic system.

Mr. Putin paused into a moment of silence, but then

continued before the outbreak of the next barrage of questions – "If America has chosen this way of life – living on debt and high above their means, some 5% of the world's population is consuming almost 30% of the world's resources, they may consider that to be their privilege. But it is not, since it has become a burden for the rest of the world – and for our planet. This way of life is quickly depleting the Earth's resources and destroying the environment by a boundless pillage of unrenewable natural resources and wars."

And after a reflective pause, Mr. Putin added – "And mind you, not even military action by Washington – lest it be nuclear and suicidal – could stop this bloodless strive for financial and economic justice and equality."

After scanning the audience, he continued – "In addition, Washington imposes the dollar as the world's main reserve currency, and money of reference to be used in international trade. As you may know, we the BRICS, as well as some other countries, are already using our own currencies for commercial exchanges and for dealing with commodities. It would be unfair to expect the world to rely on a sheer paper currency that has no backing – and eventually is at the mercy of the United States, for example subject to inhuman sanctions, like the people of Iran is currently suffering – and Iraq in the 1990s. They can be sanctioned because their trading transactions are dollar denominated. We are seeking a fairer, freer world, in which sovereign countries can live peacefully together without the threat of subjugation for not following the dictate of a self-styled empire."

Reality Check comment: Iran, India, Pakistan and Vietnam are already moving in the right direction. Iran is negotiating with India to trade its hydrocarbons in rubles and yuan. Pakistan is moving towards dropping dollar-denominated trading with China. India and Vietnam are progressively moving towards a close cooperation with the Customs Union of Russia, Kazakhstan and Belarus in which all members are strongly encouraged to drop the dollar in bilateral trade.

Silence. Mr. Putin looked around the room – into wide-eyed and confused faces. – "And as far as gold is concerned, yes, you are right. Gold is not in our basket. The value of gold is subject to speculation and manipulation, mostly by Western nations. The highly fluctuating value of gold is the result of speculation, but foremost, the result of fear. When world leaders, mostly westerners, are afraid of their unchecked and wildly uncontrolled economies, they resort to gold, as if gold would be a savior. But the rising value of gold is but a thermometer for a sick economy. The intrinsic value of gold is nothing more than its industrial value. Putting gold into the basket would make the basket, the new *Bricso,* vulnerable to those who will undoubtedly try to speculate with gold, and maybe even revert to the gold standard to save the dollar. Those who are willing to follow the dollar, perhaps under a newly created gold standard are welcome to do so. The BRICS and its affiliated countries are not dependent on that market. Our combined GDP is at least the size of that of the US and much stronger, more solid – it's based on real, hard production – and what's more – our countries account for almost 50% of the world population – not a negligible market."

Reality Check comment: The current huge gold reserves of the West are a direct result of their colonial past and looting of poorer countries. Therefore the repartition of gold reserves has nothing to do with economic strength of the country, only with its proficiency in being a colonial powerhouse in the past. So, gold would be a bad global "currency".

"And let me add one more caveat – while the Western world sees hydrocarbons as the panacea for energy, their driver for world domination – we know that hydrocarbons, petrol and gas, are just a passing fashion. The future is in renewable sources of energy. For example, the sun is an endless source of energy. Through photo-synthesis it can potentially achieve up to 97% efficiency of solar radiation, for which we will invest in research and development. In the meantime, we also need to refine research into Thorium reactors as an alternative to traditional nuclear power - and investigate sources we are barely aware of that they exist – all around us. But we, the BRICS and those who will associate with us, will put our economic resources into alternative and renewable resources of energy. This will, at once, save the planet, and save humanity from the dependence on those who control the oil."

Mr. Putin paused – his eyes scanning the room – quiet, full of unasked questions and worried facial expressions. He was compelled to continue, to quench the thirst for more answers, more explanations, since a world that has been living off instant gratification can hardly imagine a long-term solution to saving humanity and the planet.

He continued – "The future is with viable alternative energy sources and we're working on creating radically cheap energy that will allow us a higher standard of living and a drastically more efficient industry. Our search for better and sustainable energy is a long term proposition. We mustn't think about the next financial quarter or election cycle, we must think about future generations and start working today for the long term benefits of our children, grandchildren – and their descendants, who have the same right to our planet earth as we do."

"Tomorrow – or better yet, on *January 2, 2014*, because tomorrow is a holiday in most of the Western world – we will see the first impact of this economic revolution."

With these words Mr. Putin stepped away – ignoring the ensuing volley of questions. His colleagues followed.

Reality Check comment: Such an announcement hits the American economy, breaks the morale of the US vassals around the world and it is likely to create a massive panic. The gist of the BRICS' message is clear: this is the end of the world as we know it.

October 9, 2013

2

WHAT WILL HAPPEN TO GLOBAL ECONOMY IF BRICS ANNOUNCE LAUNCH OF NEW CURRENCY – BRICSO?
– PART 2

By Peter Koenig
in interviews with Valentin Mândrăşescu

Next is a hypothetical unfolding of events. A dynamic system, as the move described above, would engender the possibility of a myriad of different developments. Here is a possible scenario.

In the **next 24 hours** the media runs amok. There was

not much of a New Year's celebration in the Western Hemisphere. People were afraid. They were speculating what may happen. Some planned a run on the banks to withdraw their money, though not knowing what to do with it in a system that may collapse. They couldn't even convert their cash dollars and euros into *Bricsos*, as the *Bricso* was to be only a virtual currency. Some planned to convert their bank accounts into BRICS currencies. They would be safe. Others continued to trust the dollar, the existing system, no matter how defunct it was. They figured Washington will again find a solution to save them.

When the banks opened, **48 hours after the announcement**, the western stock markets literally collapsed. They had to be closed for an indefinite period of time to salvage what hadn't been wiped out yet and to consolidate and control the damage.

*Reality Check comment: Surely, the **President's Working Group on Financial Markets** (aka "Plunge Protection Team") would intervene in the markets, but when everyone is trying to sell their holdings no intervention can keep the markets afloat. The size of the US financial markets (esp. financial derivatives markets) is in the hundreds of trillions of dollars dwarfing the US gross national product. There is no way to avert a collapse if the BRICS pull the rug from under the US market.*

At the same time, there was indeed a run on the banks. Some wanted to withdraw, others to convert their money. The resulting chaos made the authorities close the banks again. After ten days, people took to the streets. They had no cash left to buy food and other necessities. The banks opened again, first for a few hours per day with strict withdrawal limits.

Reality Check comment: There is nothing surreal or impossible in this scenario. Actually, we can speculate that the US and EU banking systems have been preparing for a crisis of similar magnitude. The European "bail in" banking regulations and the Cyprus banking collapse are two examples of the West preparing for a generalized banking crisis.

After *a month*, as lines behind the counters got longer instead of subsiding, some European governments considered, especially the weaker Eurozone countries, to exit the Euro, revert to their former currencies and to nationalize their banks. This move would allow them to print their own money, stimulate their local economy with a national banking system for local production and internal consumption, thereby creating jobs – restoring confidence in society.

Reality Check comment: In this highly plausible scenario the IMF, European Commission and World Trade Organization (WTO) would be powerless with their likely sanctions, such as capital controls, international trade blockade, or a 'financial marshal law' to stabilize the illusionary 'markets' – simply because the markets would indeed be illusionary, since those countries which decided to exit the Euro and progress to local production for local consumptions have decided to get rid of their corrupted leaders and chose their own way of recovery. See Argentina after the 2001 collapse.

The US indeed ordered the IMF to re-introduce the gold standard at an arbitrary rate of US$ 2,000 / oz. and with a 'debt-equity' ratio of 10:1, meaning that a country's outstanding debt or unmet obligations, as is the case in the US, could be ten time higher than the gold coverage of its circulating money mass.

To protect the interests of the dollar economy, the IMF in unison with the BIS – Bank for International Settlement, the *de facto* central bank of central banks, also the presumed largest gold depository of the Western economy, introduced strict rules for countries that decided to follow the new gold standard. For example, *Quantitative Easing* – QE – a euphemism for printing money – was strictly controlled for the US dollar as well as for the Euro. The 10:1 ratio was not to be exceeded. Banks were again divided between investment banks and the traditional commercial banking, effectively bringing back the *Glass–Steagall Act* – that Bill Clinton declared 'dead' in 1998.

Reality Check comment: Basically, in this scenario, the BRICS countries forced the US to swallow the bitter pill of tough economic measures. Washington would have never accepted a limit on their "printing rights" unless it was forced to. Somewhat paradoxically, a brutal financial attack from the outside world may be necessary to make the US go back to a saner form of economy.

The Gulf State oil producers rushed to convert their dollar reserves into *Bricsos* – some into euros, as they didn't trust the BRICS. Of course, by the time the banks opened, the dollar had already lost about two thirds of its value vis-à-vis the Euro and the British Pound. The current loss from conversion into *Bricsos* would be even higher, but who knows what will happen to the Euro. Will the Eurozone stick together? – Fall apart? – Chose different alliances – maybe migrating towards the BRICS system?

Six months down the road, Greece, Spain, Portugal, Italy and Ireland had chosen to exit the Eurozone and to restart their economy with their local currencies; some of them quietly seeking an alliance with the BRICS. The Eastern European and Central Asian countries which recently acquired Eurozone status were in a dilemma: they desperately wanted to belong to the Western monetary system, but in trade they were closer to Russia and China, key partners of the BRICS. Their state of limbo would create internal unrest – parts of the population still identified with the former Soviet Union, others tried to stubbornly adhere to the dollar system, no matter how defunct it was.

Reality Check comment: One important consequence of this scenario is that political leaders around the world will see that the change is possible. The mere sight of the

BRICS' actions should have a liberating effect on the mindset of national leaders who grew accustomed to the idea that American economic hegemony is eternal and invulnerable. In this scenario, the Eurozone breakup becomes almost inevitable because the mechanisms of economic coercion employed by the European Commission will be "jammed" by the ensuing crisis. Without firing a single shot, the BRICS and their allies can start a chain reaction of financial liberation in Europe and around the world.

Western stock markets had opened again a few months earlier, but were trading cautiously, with firm limitations. Speculative buying *long* or *short* was prohibited. Stock market listed companies and corporations were carefully analyzed as to the extent of their autonomy within the *'Western markets'* – vs. dealing with the BRICS market.

What was left of the globalized *Western 'market economy'* was limping along. Many were in doubt whether they should remain faithful to a system that has let them down. Some thought to diversify into the BRICS domain, as they saw the long-term gains in a sounder and more just economy.

On the other hand, the BRICS and its two associate members, Iran and Venezuela, recovered rapidly from the first shock, as their new strong currency gave them a boost vis-à-vis the other half of the world economy which was still teetering on the dollar with some backing of the Euro.

Reality Check comment: In this scenario the BRICS would work hard to develop their internal market(s) in order to compensate the reduction of demand from the decaying western economies. Internal market development coupled with efforts to satisfy the internal demand with internally produced goods has created a virtuous cycle of sustainable economic development.

Within the first year, Indonesia and Malaysia joined the BRICS alliance. The BRICS market grew almost exponentially, not only in production and consumption, but also in research, especially for alternative, renewable sources of energy – a policy promised by the BRICS Presidents at their Press Conference in Paris on New Year's Eve 2014. Freedom from fossil fuels meant also political autonomy and a path towards real democracy and well-being. Food self-sufficiency for the BRICS and their allies will be achieved from day one. The West won't be able to jack up the prices for food commodities (markets crashed, lack of speculative capital). This will reduce the price of food worldwide. At the same time, the people in the West won't be able to consume as much as they did before 2014, making the food available to the whole non-western world at bargain prices.

Reality Check comment: This scenario creates the perfect environment for a "BRICS Renaissance" or "reverse brain-drain". For decades, the West has bought off the smartest and the best educated from around the world. In this scenario, the process has been reversed. Within the first year scientists began flocking to the banners of BRICS research institutions.

The new BRICS system became increasingly attractive even for those still adhering to the traditional, gold revamped 'dollar-euro economy'. As more of the richer, more prestigious – and remaining – Euro countries, Germany, France, The Netherlands, Finland, Sweden, Denmark – saw the benefits of trading with the BRICS system, the Euro became gradually a *constant* in trading with the BRICS market.

By early 2015, negotiations began to make the Euro part of the **Bricso** basket.

Reality Check comment: Hard feelings between politicians can't cancel objective economic needs. Europeans needed to sell their exports to the BRICS countries and needed to buy the hydrocarbons – while waiting for viable renewable energies to become marketable. Eventually, they got used with the new system even if they didn't like it.

At the **beginning of 2015** the *Shanghai Oil Bourse* was in full bloom. It traded trillions of *Bricsos*, not only from BRICS and associate countries, but from all over the world. Hydrocarbon producers realized that the *Bricso* was a stable currency, offering more long-term security then dealing in dollars. Hydrocarbon trading in dollars gradually subsided.

In addition, the SOB member countries agreed on levying an energy tax – one per-mil (0.1%) of the daily volume of trade – to fund research and investments for alternative renewable energies.

Reality Check comment: Besides providing a steady stream of financing for energy related research, such a tax is a wonderful damper for excessive volatility. In the West, financial oligarchy has always blocked any attempt to introduce a "transaction tax" or a "Tobin tax" on financial transactions. BRICS countries have the luxury to introduce financial safety measures that are impossible in the countries controlled by financial parasites.

The exchange rate of the gold-backed dollar tended to fluctuate significantly. Gold as the backbone of the dollar based Western economy was vulnerable to speculation. Even though the exchange rate to the dollar and associated currencies was fixed, speculative fluctuations influenced the conversion rates of the gold-dependent currencies – demonstrating the psychological factor of instability. Nobody was really sure if and when the IMF would decide on another gold-dollar parity rate. This could happen any time, since the IMF was still a mere extension of the US Treasury.

Reality Check comment: This is a very important aspect that most of the "gold bugs" get wrong. The return of the gold standard doesn't mean that the existing financial oligarchy will lose its grip on the American and European financial systems. The method of control may require adjustment but nothing will change if the whole financial infrastructure (i.e. the banks, the clearing houses, the exchanges) remains under the control of the same old financial clique. The gold standard per se is not a "silver bullet" for the global economic problems. A deeper reform is a needed.

The artificially inflated speculative value of gold was gradually falling towards its real intrinsic value. It still may take a while until the value of gold – which cannot be eaten in times of crisis – would end up at its mere industrial value. Gold has had a long-lasting tradition and thousands of years of history as one of the most precious metals, measuring the wealth of kings and czars. It will take a new way of thinking, new generations, to realize that what really counts are not primarily material values but cooperation, solidarity and peace among people. Material values always tend to interfere with these sustainable human values.

On the other hand, the *Bricso* had by now, **early 2015**, the solid backing of 9 nations, the economies of the five BRICS, plus those of Iran, Venezuela, Indonesia and Malaysia. – Mongolia, with a fast growing economy – about 10% per year – was also envisaging coming closer to the BRICS.

Reality Check comment: In a contest between a gold standard and a properly managed fiat standard, the fiat monetary system will win because few people will agree to replace the banking clique with a clique of the world's biggest mining companies.

As more countries tended to trade in *Bricsos*, the currency gained in strength. It became a solid reserve and reference currency for many non-BRICS countries. The energy tax was popular and its use transparent. It was a trend-setter for a different way of thinking. **From 2015 / 2016 forward**, protection of the environment and a life more integrated into nature with more social justice, using what nature had to offer without destroying it, became increasingly ingrained in the minds of people. These concepts were also reflected in teachings and culture.

Reality Check comment: The main change achieved through this financial and economic maneuvering is a "paradigm switch". The world's economy must embrace the ideology of "innovation without financialization". The current economic structure has an unnatural tilt or bias towards financial markets that tend to dominate over the traditional industrial economy and agricultural economics. Boosting innovation and curbing financialization is the key to a stable, sustainable and equitable economy.

From about 2020 onwards a shift from material to human life values became noticeable. A healthy environment, protection of species and resources became progressively important. A solid education and health services for all became important. The value of economies was no longer just linear, material and measurable growth – the old GDP – but included also – and to an ever-growing degree – values of well-being, such as capability of conflict resolution and living in harmony with each other and the environment.

What the BRICS had started in 2014 was perhaps a utopia – a new monetary and economic system, detached from wars and conflicts for greed, striving for peace and equality. There was no way to predict its outcome – other than faith that with political will the utopia might succeed.

October 14, 2013

3

DOLLAR HEGEMONY AND THE IRAN NUCLEAR ISSUE – THE STORY BEHIND THE STORY

By Peter Koenig

"International treaties are being held hostage by the west. There has been a lot of interference inside Iran by Washington. The nuclear issue is just an excuse to undermine the Islamic Republic and has very little to do with anything else." - Interview with RT by Soraya Sepahpour-Ulrich, 6 April 2015.

This statement is right on the dot. The artificially created nuclear issue – is just an excuse for regime change... perhaps yes. But there is more to it. While the expressed views on what the recent "Lausanne deal" really brought for Iran and the 5+1 participants may differ widely, one must sense that there is another *story behind the story.*

A little detail, nobody talks about, and maybe most pundits – even honest ones – are not aware of. In 2007 Iran was about to launch the *Iranian Oil Bourse (IOB)* – an international hydrocarbon exchange, akin to a stock exchange, where all countries, hydrocarbon producers or not, could trade this (still) chief energy source in euros, as an alternative to the US dollar.

This, of course would have meant the demise of dollar hegemony – the liberation of the world from the dollar stranglehold. This was inadmissible for Washington. It would have meant the end of the dollar as the world's chief reserve currency, and giving up the instrument of coercing the world into accepting Washington's dictate, the tool that serves to dish out sanctions left and right – no way!

Hundreds of billions of dollars' worth of hydrocarbons are traded on a daily basis; huge amounts of dollars that find no justification in the US economy, but – they allow the FED to print money at will – and every new dollar is a dollar of international debt, filling the reserve coffers of nations around the world, thereby also gradually devaluing the US currency, but barely affecting the US economy.

As long as petrol and gas are traded in dollars – a 'negotiated' imposition on Saudi Arabia by Father Bush, friend of the House of Saud, in the early 70s under the Carter Administration, in return for military protection – and as long as the world needs hydrocarbons to fuel its industries, so long the world will need dollars, insane amounts of dollars. The so-called Quantitative Easing (QE) allowed the US to print hundreds of billions, if not trillions of dollars to finance wars and conflicts around the globe, and to fund the relentless Zionist-Anglo-Saxon lie and propaganda machine. No problem. It's just debt. Debt – paradoxically carried by the very countries that the empire eventually fights and lies to; countries which hold dollars in their reserves.

Hardly anybody knows that the real US debt, consisting of 'unmet obligations' has risen in the last 7 years from about 48 trillion to close to 130 trillion dollars in 2014 (GAO – General Accounting Office), about seven and a half times the US GDP. Comparatively speaking, a debt by a multiple higher than that of 'troika' (EU-IMF-ECB) badgered and shattered Greece.

Allowing a country like Iran destroying the US hegemon's power base by taking a sovereign decision to abandon the dollar for oil and gas trading – no way. A pretext had to be invented to surmise the country which according to George W. Bush became a link of the axis of evil. What better than the nuclear threat – with the full support of Israel, of course. Bolstered by worldwide media manipulation, Iran became a nuclear menace not only for Israel and the entire region, but also for the US of A. A threat for the empire, some 15,000 km away, when at that time the most powerful Iranian long-range missile had a range capacity of about 2,000 km.

This sounds almost like the latest (bad) Obama joke, accusing Venezuela to be an imminent threat to the United States. It would be laughable, if it wouldn't be so sad, so criminal actually. Because this lie is followed by economic warfare, akin to the one led against Russia – which – eventually backfired punishing the 'sanctioneers' themselves, especially the Europeans. When the real impact of the 'sanctions' became evident, the MSM were simply silent. People easily forget. Without opening their eyes, they remain gullible for the next lie.

The dollar is the ultimate pillar of the empire's world hegemony. Without it, it is doomed. Washington knows it. You don't have to look far to find similar examples to that of Iran. When Saddam Hussein announced in the late 1990's that he would sell Iraq's petrol in euros, as soon as the embargo would end in 2000, a reason had to be found to invade his country. The WMD menace that never existed was sold around the world, including at the UN Security Council, and – bingo – the western media killing machine had created a motive for invading Iraq and to murder Saddam. As if this wasn't enough, he was suddenly linked to 9/11 – and big miracle, Americans bought even this lie.

Muammar Gadhafi was another victim for asserting his country's sovereignty. He announced a new hard currency for Africa, the Gold Dinar, backed by Libyan gold. Libyan and African hydrocarbons could henceforth be traded in an alternative currency to the dollar, the Gold Dinar. Gadhafi also intended to free Africans from the western predatory telephone giants, by introducing a Libya sponsored low-price mobile network throughout Africa. Gadhafi was atrociously murdered by CIA handlers on 20 October 2011. Libya today is a hotbed of civil unrest and murder.

Iran's case is a bit more complicated. Iran has Russia and China backing. Nevertheless, with the propaganda machine painting a nuclear danger to the world, Iran could be brought to her knees, no problem. No matter what logic said and still says, no matter that the 15 US key intelligence agencies assured the then Bush Administration that Iran has no plans of manufacturing a nuclear bomb, that Iran was genuine in using its enriched uranium for power generation and for medical purposes.

No matter that Iran's enrichment process reached a mere 20% purity, enough for medical purposes, but far from the 97% required for a nuclear bomb, Iran had to be oppressed and under a web of lies made a pariah state, a risk for the world. That's what the average American and European today believes. It's a shame. Nobody openly dares talking about the only nuclear threat in the Middle East, Israel. That is another shame.

No matter what the Lausanne deal is today, or next June, after three more months of intense, but useless negotiations, no matter what a UN resolution would say about the deal, about the lifting of sanctions – Washington will always find a pretext to keep the stranglehold on Iran. As Soraya Sepahpour-Ulrich said, "*International treaties are being held hostage by the west*"- there is no international compact or law that prevents the only rogue state in the world, the atrociously criminal US empire from crushing its way to satisfy its abject greed.

Always – that is, as long as empire survives. And yes, the economic survival is only a question of time. Fifteen years ago some 90% of worldwide reserve holdings were kept in US dollars, or dollar denominated securities. In 2010 the ratio shrunk to about 60%; today it is approaching 50%. When it sinks below 50%, governments around the globe may gradually lose confidence in the greenback, seeing it as what it is and has been for the last 100 years, nothing else but a fraudulent Mickey-Mouse currency at the service of a Zionist dominated western financial system, not worth the paper it's printed on; a currency that has been abusing and impoverishing the 'non-aligned' world at will.

Iran knows it, Russia knows it – without direct confrontation, the empire's grip may not hold as long as the Iran deal is planned to last, some 20 to 30 years. Therefore, the large concessions that Iran had to make for 'peace' – to reduce its enrichment process to 3.37% just enough to fuel power plants, and to sell or transfer its stock of 20% enriched medical-grade uranium abroad – these concessions to reach this 'glorious' interim agreement, are unimportant. It is a winner for Iran, as announced by Iran's Foreign Minister, Mohammad Javad Zarif, as well as Russia's Sergei Lavrov. Even if Washington derails the agreement within the next three months, or at any time at will, as is likely, Iran has won a battle of credibility worldwide, as she is ready to adhere to a signed agreement, no matter how far its sets her back.

In fact, the rotten palaces of empire are crumbling as these lines are going to print. Two new international Asian based development and investment banks have been created within the last two years. The BRICS Development Bank was signed into existence in Brazil in July 2014 by the leaders of the 5 BRICS countries – Brazil, Russia, India, China and South Africa. Earlier this year sponsored by China and 20 other countries, the Asian Investment and Infrastructure Bank – AIIB, located in Shanghai, was created. Iran is a founding member of the AIIB.

Ecuador's Foreign Minister has also just announced that the Venezuela sponsored Banco del Sur – development bank for the Latin American hemisphere – will become operational in the course of 2015. These three banks are direct challenges to the Washington dominated IMF, World Bank and IDB (Inter-American Development Bank). Guess which ones are the most notorious 'allies' of Washington and which against the will of the White House, are joining AIIB's forty-some membership? – They include the epitome of neoliberal Europeans – UK, France, Germany, Italy and Switzerland.

Washington's seemingly blind and preposterous arrogance drives the closest allies into the 'adversary's camp. The FED (Federal Reserve Bank) announced on 2 April 2015 that it fined the German Commerzbank with 1.7 billion US dollars for dealing with Cuba, Sudan and Iran – Washington sanctioned countries.

This can only happen as long as all international banking transactions have to be channeled through US banks and controlled by the Rothschild dominated BIS – Bank for International Settlement. Russia, China and other SCO (Shanghai Cooperation Organization) aligned countries have already broken away from the dollar system for international contracts and money transfers, including hydrocarbon trading. They are about to launch an alternative to the western ruled privately owned SWIFT transfer systems. The new system could be joined by any country wanting to break loose from the predatory dollar claws.

When even the staunchest stooges of empire seek

alliances in the East, the writing is on the wall, that the economic winds are shifting, that a tectonic sea-change is in the offing and that the Iran nuclear deal, one way or another, doesn't really matter in the foreseeable future.

April 9, 2015

4

CUBA – BETWEEN A ROCK AND A HARD PLACE

By Peter Koenig

On 17 December 2014, President Obama declared that 55 years of embargo didn't work in bringing 'freedom' to Cuba. He proposed reestablishing diplomatic relations with the southern neighbor. An emotion of joy shook the world, especially Latin America. Raul Castro received wires and calls of congratulations. Cubans cheered "we won, we won!" – The US Congress right wing was not quite ready for this initiative and, indeed, there was no concrete mention of how and when the 'blockade' would be lifted.

Surely, Washington wants to impose its conditions. Washington conditions never serve an ally, let alone a foe. Washington conditions are always set to first serve the 'national interest'- i.e. the interest of the US corporate and financial elite. Most vassals simply accept. Their happiness to be recognized in the Washington camp compensates for all the pitfalls Washington hegemony imposes. Just look at Europe with the TTIP (Transatlantic Trade and Investment Pact) which – currently being negotiated in secret! – if approved by the neoliberal European Commission, spells not only disaster for European generations to come, but means the EU being literally colonized by the US; slavehood for EU citizens.

Cuba will not accept such conditions, for sure. Cuba has already set some of its own conditions, one of them being the return of Guantanamo, originally and under past Cuban puppet governments a 99-year concession that has expired years ago. Guantanamo today is pure theft. The criminal capture of a piece of another country's territory, so that no US law could be applied to the crimes committed there. Torture of so-called 'terrorists' and terrorist suspects in the US-stolen enclave of Guantanamo are well and alive. No US law can stop the crime. International laws are ignored by empire. Washington, the exceptional nation, is above all laws. If a judge, national or international, doesn't conform, he is simply removed or eliminated.

Two days after Obama's bold initiative, on 19 December 2015, he went to the Washington Press Club to tell a horde of puppet journalists, conservative politicians and onlookers that soft measures, like reestablishing diplomatic relations with Havana might be more successful in bringing the desired regime change to Cuba than more years of isolation. He couldn't have been more direct and more honest about his intention. The Cuban Government and whoever else listened didn't miss the point.

Isolation has been gradually fading over the past years. Russia and China and many 'amigos' in Latin America and Europe – Venezuela, Brazil, Argentina, Mexico, Spain, France, to name just a few – have established almost regular trading relations with Cuba. Despite the constant threat of 'sanctions' by empire. It is high time for the White House to change tactics if it doesn't want to lose out to its arch-enemies Russia and China.

—

Many Cubans have a sense of disillusion, that they simply welcome any possibility of change. When asked, almost all say, 'it's a good thing. We are looking forward to it'. However, they are discrete. Nobody openly complains and less so to curious foreigners. When prompted about how they think Washington will help them, they don't know. They just want change. Not regime change, to be sure, a better life. They want hope. They want a chance for future generations. Cubans are not hungry. But they see an enormous disparity between themselves and the rest of the world. Especially when they see plane loads of tourists arriving, spending multiples of their monthly incomes for one night in four or five star hotels.

They are not jealous per se, but they see the enormous difference between themselves and those who have access to foreign exchange, including some Cubans who receive money from their families in the US, Cubans able to travel abroad as artists or academics, or Cubans able to mount small businesses with the help of friends and families abroad. They see that something is not quite right. And this in a country where social and economic equality is one of the Government's priorities.

Cubans are not afraid of hard work. Cubans are creative; they have great ideas; they are highly educated; they know what is going on in the world, much better than the average European, or North American for that matter. Cubans are inventive. They have savvy for advancing their country and improving living conditions for themselves.

Cuba has large agricultural areas, fertile land, but according to local academics, more than 50% of suitable agricultural acreage lies idle. Cuban farmers lack incentives. Government controlled prices do not cover costs, or leave insufficient margin for the hard work of farming. Cuba, with its 11 million inhabitants could be more than food self-sufficient. However, Cuba imports about 80% of food which it rations to its people.

None of the Cubans want to lose the tremendous achievements of their Revolution – one of the world's best systems of health and education, a country of peace and tranquility – a country where crime is almost non-existent. What they want is a standard of living that corresponds to their capacities – physical, academic and entrepreneurial. When prompted, they also realize that Washington doesn't bring the solution. The solution has to be found from within.

They see what Washington is doing to their brothers in Venezuela – sanctions, embargoes, outright economic warfare. – And for what? – To subjugate the people and to control their resources; colonization of the Bolivarian nation, the first step in taking back Obama's 'backyard' – South America – the only part of the world, other than Russia and China, that has successfully detached itself from empire in the last couple of decades and so far resisted Washington's attempts in meddling in South America's sovereign affairs. They have created UNASUR and ALBA, solidifying their unity.

Cubans say we are strong. We have 56 years of revolution on our backs and in our hearts; we know how to defend ourselves. We have fought a civil war for more than 5 years and kicked the Yankees out. We have successfully defended ourselves against the empire's aggression by air and sea, led by President Kennedy in 1961. We will do it again, if we must. Indeed, Cubans are strong. They are tenacious. They have tremendous will power.

But Cubans also must be reminded of today's reality. Once Washington puts its heavy boots in a country, it's (almost) impossible to get rid of them. If the boots are insufficient, the three-branched war machine will follow – bombs, 'sanctions' by economic fascism (neoliberalism) – and relentless propaganda. Everywhere they put their foot, they sow disaster, leave behind rubble and death, countless refugees, desolation for generations to come. Cubans know that.

***

I talked to dozens of people in the street, in restaurants, shops, libraries – from workers, to taxi drivers, to medical doctors, to economists, to professors and other academics, to artists and even an Angola war veteran – their views are consistent: 'We can't continue like this'. These people are all brilliant in their own ways. And they are all desperate for a better life with a vision towards the future. – But to repeat, not regime change at all, especially not Washington style, but internal change for a better life and a brighter future.

A cab driver told me, Cuba is wonderful, a bit tranquilo – even boring. But your country is flooded with tourists like never before, I countered. There is hardly an empty bed in Havana; you have more tourists than your infrastructure can reasonably absorb. Yes, he said. But almost all of them are 'package tourists'. They come in prearranged, all inclusive tours. They are picked up in buses from the airport, brought to four or five star hotels, then driven around from one site seeing place to another; they eat in pre-arranged restaurants and then – hop, he flipped with his fingers – and off they are. None of them touches any local business; they don't take taxis, they hardly talk to Cubans; they don't see how we really live.

The money the international tourists pay for their tours is shared between the foreign travel agent and the Cuban government. None of it trickles down to us, the common people, who earn the equivalent of between 25 and 40 dollars a month, while a room in a 5 star hotel costs up to US\$ 300 a night, or 15 to 20 times the monthly wage of the average Cuban. He didn't sound jealous at all; just matter-of-factly.

***

Cuba's economy is beset by multi-layered distortions – distortions as results of accumulated 'corrections' over the past 50 years that led to an economic and financial complexity, today unreformable by traditional means.

After the collapse of the Soviet Union, when the pillars of the Cuban economy suddenly and for the Cubans apparently without warning imploded, corrections and counter-corrections multiplied Cuba's economic conundrum.

For the past twenty-five years, Cuba has known a two-tier economic system of sorts. The country uses two currencies, one for local use, the Cuban Peso (CUP) and the Cuban Convertible (CUC), mostly for foreigners and foreign trade. The CUC is closely linked to the US dollar, almost one-to-one. The conversion rate between the CUP and the CUC is 1 : 25. It takes 25 CUP for one CUC. The average Cuban monthly salary is between about 600 and 900 CUP, i.e. about 25 to 40 US dollars equivalent, the relation between the earnings is that of a worker versus a medical doctor. Of course, food, lodging, electricity, water and other services are state controlled and cheap; education, health and other social services are free. Nevertheless, this two-currency system creates an enormous gap between those with access to foreign exchange and those who simply live on their CUPs.

The Cuban GDP is said to be close to the equivalent of US$ 70 billion, although it is difficult to understand the arithmetic behind this indicator, given the monetary distortion. Total services, including tourism account for almost 75% of GDP, Industry, including nickel exports, for 20%, while agriculture contributes a mere 5% to Cuba's economic output. Similarly, GDP growth over the past 5 years has been unstable, fluctuating, between 1% and 4 %; today it stands at about 1.4%.

Debt is about 37% of GDP, less than that of the average Latin American country. Foreign reserves are said to be US$ 10 billion, about 15% of GDP, a healthy reserve for a country with 11 million people. However, the reserve is left untouched, like money in a safe, with the expectation that it might attract foreign investors – and serve as a rescue and recovery fund for hurricane disasters.

The currency distortion exacerbated by the lopsided

GDP composition and the unused reserve funds, one would think requires first and foremost an internal, perhaps radical restructuring of the economy. It could start with delinking the CUC from the dollar and devaluing the CUC to a level which would allow eliminating the local CUP, converting Cuba into a single currency system, a step taken by China, when they transformed their double currency system into a one-currency economy in 1984. This might mean starting from square one, so to speak – local production for local markets. Loosening at the same time Government control on local initiatives would bring the necessary incentives to restart the productive engine.

Argentina may serve as an example. When Argentina's economy collapsed in 2001, the Government broke the peso-dollar parity, devalued the peso by some 60% and started afresh – local production for local consumption. With its own currency, Argentina gained back its economic sovereignty, thus, the ability to negotiate its foreign debt at its own terms. Over the next decade, Argentina grew on average by 8% – a highly distributive DGP growth, helping to reduce poverty from close to 70% in 2001 to way below 10% in 2014.

The solutions for an internal problem never come from outside and less so from the United States. Foreign investments usually come with strings attached, some with steel chains. Following the US and European conditions for their investments, might imply accepting the dictate of the IMF, World Bank and IDB (Inter-American Development Bank) neoliberal economic disaster policies. What these policies of economic fascism have done and are still doing to the world – so-called 'structural adjustments' in Africa, Latin America, Asia – and lately the manufactured Eurozone crises starting in Greece, Spain, Portugal, Ireland and even Italy – speak for themselves.

The latest example of empire's destruction for dominance is Ukraine; first by a CIA / State Department / NATO inspired coup in February 2014, then by a civil war instigated by the newly US / EU-imposed Nazi-

Government of criminal thugs in Kiev – civil war against the eastern Ukraine brothers, led by CIA mercenaries with NATO 'advisors' – and finally by an illegal financial war, theft of resources driven by debt, imposed by the infamous 'troika' – IMF, European Central Bank (ECB) and EC (European Commission).

Cuba's sizable reserves might serve to initiate economic recovery in priority sectors like agriculture, telecommunication, tourism and rehabilitation of local infrastructure. The conditions and priorities for foreign investments should always be laid down by the host country. Foreign investors should be linked up with local enterprises as joint ventures, like China did, when it opened its borders to foreign investments in the 1980s. A foreign partner must never be allowed a majority holding. In the case of Cuba, priorities for foreign investors might include, among other sectors, cutting edge technologies in communication and computer sciences.

***

According to a Cuban economist, an academician, the multi-faceted complexity of economic distortions, combined with the need for investments and increased output efficiency, leads to fear of making the wrong decisions which leads to inertia which leads to a stagnant economy that lacks incentives for people's initiatives. This vicious circle of inaction must be broken, but certainly not by an outside 'change agent', but from within.

From within – always with the credo 'Hasta la Victoria Siempre!'

March 20, 2015

5

US EMBASSY IN HAVANA: WASHINGTON'S "CUBA GAMBIT"

By Peter Koenig

The lame duck, Obama, extending a conciliatory hand to Cuba by opening an embassy in Havana, by reopening, after 54 years of a criminal and crippling embargo, diplomatic relations? – At the same time Obama is making not a single concession in terms of lifting the blockade. This smells like a trap.

Imagine – a US Embassy in Havana – it would open the floodgates for US NED (National Endowment for Democracy) funded 'NGOs', for Washington's spies and anti-Castro propaganda machine; it would have free hand to destabilize the country. And what would Cuba gain? –

Zilch, zero, nothing. Not even a gradual lifting of the embargo had been announced. To the contrary, it would open Cuba's borders to the vultures of Florida Cubans, eventually to theirs and other foreign investments, subjugating the country's huge social gains over the last half a century – universal free education and health services, by far the best social system of the Americas – to the sledgehammer of neoliberal privatization.

Why would Cuba now need a US Embassy? After 54 years of struggling and surviving against Washington's nod? – In fact, nobody needs the empire – the empire's consent to financially and economically survive. Suffice it to look at the 'engineered' decay of the Russian ruble which eventually will leave Russia better off than before the downward slide of its currency and the likewise 'engineered' downward spin of the price of petrol. Everybody knows that the Middle Eastern oil producers, Obama's stooges, will not forever shoot themselves in the foot by flooding the petrol market and foregoing their oil revenues.

What Cuba needs is free access to international markets – outside and independent of the United States. Cuba needs to integrate into an independent financial and monetary system, detached from the corrupt casino dollar. Solidarity by the rest of the world which has already helped Cuba survive the illegal, inhuman US embargo is now more than ever of the order. The support of a unity of nations must now help stem the temptation to bend to Washington's offer of 'diplomacy'.

With the establishment of diplomatic relations, Cuba would be condemned to adopt the dollar as trading currency – no escaping the dollar, if ever Cuba wanted to hope for the good deeds of the empire – the lifting of the blockade.

Look what happened in Bolivia, Venezuela and Ecuador – once a US Embassy is established, all the nefarious destabilizing elements could sneak in, willy-nilly.

Plus, economic 'sanctions', would be nearer than ever, if Cuba doesn't behave. Both Bolivia and Venezuela have learned their lessons the hard way. After they closed the US Embassy and sent US organizations and NGOs home, they could breathe again. Though Venezuela is still suffering from Washington's diabolical arm of propaganda and direct interference in domestic affairs, she has no longer the burden of maintaining a 'diplomatic' tie with the northern aggressor.

Most importantly, however – the US is vying for Cuban hydrocarbons, estimated today at 20 billion barrels of offshore oil reserves. Cuba, like Venezuela, is close to US Mexican Gulf shores, where the major refineries are waiting for the crude. During his tour of South America in July 2014, President Putin in a meeting with Cuban President, Raul Castro, signed an agreement whereby the Russian oil company, Rosneft, will assist the Cuban oil producer, Cupet, exploring and exploiting the island's offshore petrol.

Is it coincidence or sheer self-interest, that just now, when Russia is digging for oil in Obama's backyard that he is offering diplomatic ties with the 54 years embargoed Caribbean island? – Your guess.

Venezuela has the world's largest remaining hydrocarbon reserves, about 300 billion barrels. They are close to the US shores and would be the best bet for US mega-oil. But the White House's destabilizing efforts in Venezuela seem to fail. These efforts and other State Department blunders have helped increase US isolation in Latin America.

Why not trying another approach? – A well disguised lie; insinuating with the opening of an embassy in Havana that the deadly embargo might ease in some undefined future between the brutal Goliath of the north and castigated David of the Caribbean. An embassy in Cuba may also earn some much needed kudos with other Latin American neighbors who have been upset for years about the criminal strangulation by the empire of one of their brothers.

In fact, first reactions from Latin America to Obama's diplomatic initiative were positive. But caution is in order. – The establishment of a US embassy in Havana might be more than just a floodgate for US secret service agents and anti-Cuba propaganda. A US Embassy in Havana might begin breaking down US isolation in South America, especially in Brazil and Argentina. It might become a backdoor for Washington to gain access to these countries huge natural resources.

Knowing about Washington's agenda of world dominance, it would be difficult to imagine that there is even a shred of goodwill behind Obama's move to 'normalize' relations with Cuba.

December 24, 2014

6

GREECE – SYRIZA – SUBSERVIENCE TO NEOLIBERALISM – THE KILLING PLAGUE THAT KNOWS NO MERCY?

By Peter Koenig

To begin with, let's be clear, neoliberalism is a criminal, murderous plague that knows no mercy. Neoliberalism is the root of (almost) all evil of the 21st Century. Neoliberalism is the cause for most current wars, conflicts and civil strife around the globe. Neoliberalism is the expression of abject greed for accumulation of resources by a few, for which tens of millions of people have to die. Neoliberalism and its feudal banking system, led by Wall Street and its intricate network of international finance, steals public infrastructure, public safety nets – public investments paid for by nations' citizens – robs nations of their resources (labor, physical resources above-and underground) – by avid schemes of privatization, justified under the pretext of 'structural reforms' to 'salvage' poor but often resources-rich countries from bankruptcy.

Rescue by structural reform or adjustment is synonymous with deceit. Even IMF chief, Christine Lagarde, admitted that the model failed in Greece, thereby admitting that the notion of 'austerity' for the poor as a means for economic recovery is not working. – No news to most of us.

The neoliberal concept is no innovation of today. It was born in the 1930s in Europe as a response (sic) to the US depression of the 1930s. It was initially thought of as a moderate form of giving the private sector more liberty for initiatives and investments, while limiting government control.

The concept was revamped after WWII in Washington rightwing think tanks (sic), such as the American Enterprise Institute, the Heritage Foundation, Political Economy Research Centre and the like. In the UK developing hard-core neoliberalism was mostly in the domain of the Institute of Economic Affairs. Prominent, mostly Zionist 'scholars' elaborated the idea through the sixties and seventies into a market fundamentalism which was launched in the 1980s in the United States under President Reagan and in Europe under UK's Prime Minister Thatcher. The concept culminated in the so-called Washington Consensus in 1989, depicting a series of *'everything-goes'* market reform policies, to be adopted by the Washington based financial institutions, World Bank, IDB, IMF, FED, US Treasury.

Since then, neoliberalism has engulfed the world like brushfire. It knows no boundaries. It is influencing world economies like no other economic concept did before. If not by physical weapons and bloodletting wars, neoliberalism is also devastating lives, causing misery, destroying entire nations, by its financial instruments, chiefly represented by the Bretton Woods institutions, World Bank and International Monetary Fund – and lately also the European Central Bank (ECB), the economic sledgehammer of the European Union's 19 Eurozone countries. The IMF, ECB and the European Commission (EC) have become known as the infamous 'troika', the cause for economic strangulation of the southern European nations – Greece, Portugal, Spain, Ireland – and even Italy.

Case in point is Greece. Last Friday, 20 February, Greece's newly elected Prime Minister, Alexis Tsipras, and his Finance Minister, Yanis Varoufakis, of Syriza, the alliance of so-called left-wing parties, went through a marathon session of attempted negotiations with Brussels over her € 240 billion plus debt, due at the end of February 2015. They asked for a 6-month extension without any strings attached, meaning – no more socially debilitating austerity programs. Perhaps they were dreaming, or simply not listening to the utter arrogant advance warnings of Brussels' elitist neoliberal talking heads, especially Germany's financial hawk, Minister of Finance, Wolfgang Schäuble, and the ultra-neoliberal chairman of the group of the 19 Eurozone finance chiefs, Jeroen Dijsselbloem.

The latter said that Athens had given its "unequivocal commitment to honour their financial obligations" to creditors, and he will hold her to the promise. This commitment refers to Mr.Tsipras' predecessor's, Mr. Alekos Alavanos, Letter of Agreement signed with the EU.

The result was predictable. Tsipras who campaigned under the radical but noble stand of 'no concessions' to the lords of Brussels, and his Finance Minister, caved in miserably. They did not get a six months extension, but only 4 months – under the condition that Greece submits a comprehensive list of reforms and reform mechanisms byMonday night, 23 February; basically the same list of austerity measures agreed upon by Tsipras' predecessor. Implementation of the reforms would be supervised by the troika. At the outset, Tsipras-Varoufakis meekly accepted the EU conditions.

As James Petras puts it in "*The Assassination of Greece*":

"Every major financial institution – the European Central Bank, the European Commission and the IMF – toes the line: no dissent or deviation is allowed. Greece must accept EU dictates or face major financial reprisals. "Economic strangulation or perpetual debt peonage" is the lesson which Brussels tends to all member states of the EU. While ostensibly speaking to Greece – it is a message directed to all states, opposition movements and trade unions who call into question the dictates of the Brussels oligarchy and its Berlin overlords."

During Friday, 20 February, while the financial marathon rambled on in Brussels, one billion euros were withdrawn from Geek banks, in anticipation of failed negotiations and possible expulsion of Greece from the Eurozone – the so-called *Grexit*.

It is unclear how Tsipras-Varoufakis are going to explain the hapless result brought back from Brussels to their electorate. It must remind those who can still remember how Andreas Papandreou, member of the Pan-Hellenic Socialist Party, elected as first PM after Greece was admitted in 1980 to the EU, betrayed his constituency. He promised them that Greece would exit NATO and the European Economic Community, that Greece would develop her own economy with economic growth at her pace. Soon after election he reneged on both promises. – Will the Greek people buy the Tsipras-Varoufakis 'explanations' for not honoring Syriza's pre-election commitments?

Greece has various options. Tsipras-Varoufakis must know them. Perhaps they keep them hidden away until "the last ditch" moment. To begin with, they could have imposed and still can impose strict capital transfer controls, to avoid the outflow of precious capital from Greek oligarchs, capital that eventually is missing for rebuilding Greece's economy and would need to be replaced by new debt. Although, this is basically against EU's rule of free transfer of capital, Greece as a sovereign country, can roll back its EU vassal status, take back its sovereignty and do what every reasonable central bank would do in Greece's situation – impose capital transfer restrictions. After all, the Euro is also – and still is – Greece's currency.

The EU might not like it – nor would the Greek oligarchs – but it would be a bold step in the right direction. And should it result in Jeroen Dijsselbloem's and Germany's Wolfgang Schäuble's boisterous threats of 'sanctions' – then so be it. – Why not call their bluff? – Submitting a letter on Monday that says just that – *we are happy to accept your extension of 4 months, but are morally, socially and economically unable to meet your conditions of austerity.* Period.

The EU has no interest whatsoever in a Greek exit. In fact, they are afraid of a *Grexit*, not only because of a potential default on the Greek debt, but it could open a floodgate for other southern European countries in distress to follow the Greek example. That would be the end of the Euro as we know it. It might be the final blow to the dollar-euro house of cards, house of casino money.

Tsipras–Varoufakis should stick to their promise – no more austerity programs. No more privatizations of public property, no more cuts in pensions and salaries; to the contrary, rolling back the cuts already administered, bringing back decent life conditions to the Greek people, gradually averting the illegal troika imposed misery.

Greece's debt today stands at 175 % of her economic output. The best – and only decent and socially as well as economically viable option – is exiting the Eurozone by her own decision. Greece would be declared bankrupt. The Anglo-Saxon rating agencies would be quick in down-grading Greece financially to 'junk'. The financial markets would shun her. No more money, but utmost pressure to repay what they can. Greece would be in the enviable position of negotiating debt repayment at *HER* own terms – à la Argentina in 2001.

No country can be left to starve, especially when the debt was contracted illegally or under coercion. International law allows renegotiation of such contracts – contracts signed under pressure or by corrupt governments.

Finally – or perhaps refreshingly – Greece could look east, to the Russia-China alliance. Their assistance under much more reasonable conditions is virtually assured. – Why insisting on following a defunct predatory system, when there are new promising development potentials looming on the horizon?

February 24, 2015

7

Open Letter to Mr. Alexis Tsipras, Prime Minister of Greece

GREECE'S DEBT OVERHANG. LOOTED BY WALL STREET AND THE EUROPEAN CENTRAL BANK

By Peter Koenig

Dear Mr. Tsipras,

Let me first congratulate you for winning the elections on 25 January 2015. And congratulations also for dismissing the troika as one of your first deeds. Well done!

It is encouraging to see that the majority of voting Greek dares to vote for a change from the relentless misery imposed by the infamous troika – ECB, EC and IMF. The Greek people have entrusted you with the delicate task of pulling Greece out of the morass, where she has been put – totally unjustified – by this notorious troika.

Mr. Tsipras, your Government has been tricked into believing that Greece's debt is insurmountable and could pull Europe into an abyss. Instead your country is being looted by Wall Street and their European allied too-big-to-fail banksters. Of course, with the connivance of your neoliberal predecessors, some of whom have been associated with one of the biggest Wall Street gangsters, Goldman Sachs. Indeed, the President of the European Central Bank has also been associated with this criminal financial institution. In other words, the EU financial system today is run by the extended arm of Goldman Sachs – and its Washington masters.

Neoliberalism is a murderous plague. It is invading at brushfire speed the entire western world. What makes it even more diabolical is that it controls almost all the western media. Ninety percent of the news we get in the West are controlled by six giant Anglo-Saxon media corporations. They dish out every day nefarious propaganda – lies after lies after ugly lies. They brainwash people into believing what is not.

They made Europe believe that Greece with a mere 2% of the Eurozone GDP and with about 109% debt to GDP in 2009 was a danger for Europe. If Europe was to survive economically, Greece had to be 'rescued' – and that with hundreds of billions of Euros in new debt!

The Greek debt would have been totally manageable without outside interference. Compare it with the US current debt of 105%, and with 'long-term unmet obligations' (5 years) of US$ 128 trillion, more than seven times its GDP; debt that will never be paid back, but is largely absorbed by foreign nations who hold dollar reserves – as long as the dollar remains the world's main reserve currency.

That's when the infamous troika struck – the extended arm of Washington. It decided that Greece would need about €300 billion in different packages over about 4 years. They imposed their usual draconian conditions. Your neoliberal predecessors played along. Greece had to punish its population with severe 'austerity' programs. In reality, 'austerity' is a mere euphemism for the misery they forced the Greek Government to impose on its people; privatizing public assets, reducing public services, health and education benefits, pensions, minimum wages, dismissing public servants – overall increasing unemployment from about 10% to close to 30%, and above 60% for young people, as you well know, Mr. Tsipras, causing outright famine and sometimes death from sheer destitution.

The ECB would not lend directly to Greece at favorable interbank rates as central banks normally would. The ECB was not created as a central bank, but as a watchdog and manipulator of the European economy, in the service of its North American masters. The ECB lent to giant too-big-to-fail mostly German and French banks at interbank rates of 1% or less. These banksters then on-lent the proceeds to Greece at horrendous 6% or 7%. They pocketed huge profits. They claimed the 'risk' justified the margins. They knew they would never lose. If Greece was unable to repay the debt, the money would come from the European tax-payers.

If this model worked, the troika could apply it elsewhere in Europe.

As you know, Mr. Tsipras, it did work. Solidarity among European nations, if it ever existed, was decimated by neoliberalism. Greece was followed by Portugal, Ireland, Spain and even Italy, who at that time was led by Mr. Monti, also a former Goldman-Sachs henchman.

Later the evil troika applied an even more drastic formula to Cyprus. Instead of 'bailing out', they insisted on 'bailing in', meaning that the banks had to take (steal) the money from their depositors. This new 'rescue model' has recently been approved in the US as the new norm, and soon thereafter it was also sanctioned by Brussels. Not surprisingly it got very little press coverage, lest it might have caused a run on the banks.

Hence, the artificial Greek crisis morphed into a manufactured European crisis. The media hype allowed it, as nobody asked, why? – Why a crisis when the European economy was so much stronger than that of the US; was then and still is today. It was and is backed by a solid economy.

The real purpose behind this fake European economic calamity was the weak dollar at the time. It risked to be replaced by the euro as chief reserve currency – which would have jeopardized the dollar's world hegemony.

The combined EU economy (28 member countries) was then and is still today the world's strongest economy – €14.303 trillion (US$18.451 trillion, est. 2014), as compared to that of the US with US$ 17.4 trillion. Hence, the euro had to be weakened – not destroyed, it was needed for trade and to subordinate Europe – but severely weakened, so that the dollar could regain its inflated strength. And – as an added benefit, the European mafia banksters and their transatlantic partners filled their pockets with the proceeds of Southern Europe's public and social services.

Thanks to the media propaganda and deceit machine, it worked again. Europe's debt increased from an average of about 70% in 2009 to close to 100% of GDP today. Greece's GDP declined from € 242 in 2008 to € 201 in 2014 (-17%) and her debt increased by 21% to 160% in the same period. The dollar is kept artificially strong and the euro weak.

Today, Mr. Tsipras, you were in Brussels and Mr. Varoufakis, your Minister of Finance, was in London and Frankfurt, seeking understanding for the Greek predicament, seeking forgiveness or postponement of debt. You will shake hands and even embrace with these cold, calculated leaders of Europe and European finance, but they will not budge. They will embarrass you; they will try to scare you with expulsion from the Eurozone.

There is only one way out for Greece, Mr. Tsipras: You take the first step; you exit the Eurozone at your own initiative, return to your solid currency the drachma, and start anew. You may look at the example of Argentina in 2001, when she decided to abandon the imposed peso-dollar parity, devaluing her currency and starting afresh – with the principle of local production for local markets. Forget globalization. It has killed many economies around the world and hundreds of thousands of people. You may then renegotiate the Greek debt under YOUR terms. Greece has the background for a solid economy with her biggest asset – a wonderful and well educated people.

Perhaps equally important, you will open a gate for other European countries in distress to follow your example. You may evoke a new solidarity among nations. That's what Brussels is most afraid of. If that happens their house of cards may collapse – and with it possibly the entire dollar dominated western casino scheme.

February 6, 2015

8

THE EUROZONE IN CRISIS: THE GREEK ELECTIONS, AN OPPORTUNITY OF THE CENTURY, A GATEWAY FOR EUROPE

By Peter Koenig

"Greece could be ousted from the Eurozone", warned deputy parliamentary leader of Angela Merkel's CDU Party, Michael Fuchs, on 31 December 2014. He added, the Eurozone was no longer obligated to rescue Greece from its current crisis. He was alluding to the coming Snap elections on 25 January 2015, in case Greece's opposition parties, SYRIZA (Coalition of the Radical Left), would win which at this point is a fair possibility, as they

currently hold a slim 3.5 point lead over the right wing ruling coalition, New Democracy (ND) and PASOK.

Similar remarks were made by the EU Commissioner, Jean-Claude Juncker. – What an affront to Greece's sovereignty!

Notwithstanding the horrendous arrogance of interfering in a country's internal affairs, Greece's exit from the Eurozone would be an outright blessing for the country, for its people, for its future economy and prosperity – period.

In 2008 Greece was chosen by the troika (IMF, European Central Bank- ECB – and European Commission – EC) for a malicious test to be allegedly 'rescued' from bankruptcy; but in reality for being robbed of her people's savings, social safety nets, pension funds, health care system, education – causing horrendous unemployment, poverty and suffocating debt. If the people of Europe would not react, then the model could be applied elsewhere in Europe.

Other than in Greece itself, protests were running low in Europe. Solidarity had been decimated by the US-led neoliberal privatization onslaught since the 1990's; as well as by the Washington-NED (National Endowment for Democracy) funded propaganda and 'NGO' interference in Europe's sovereign nations. Curiously, during the same time basically all European governments were replaced with neoliberal leaders (sic), who would become the new stooges of Brussels; as the EU, Brussels itself, would become a new colony of Washington. This de-democratization of Europe happened against the will of the majority of the European people.

The Greek 'experiment' therefore passed without much fanfare and was widely accepted throughout Europe and the rest of the world, as *'it serves them right'*. Capitalist propaganda had long since labeled Greece as corrupt and lazy; a country that with its high indebtedness would become a danger for the Euro-zone.

The 'successful' Greek test would open the doors for other mainly southern European countries – Spain, Portugal, Cyprus, Italy, Ireland – to fall into the merciless fangs of the FED, Wall Street and its transatlantic puppets, ECB and European TBTF (too-big-to-fail) mega banks.

From 2009 onwards the fabricated Euro-crisis would become a bonanza for the United States, whose ten-fold indebted (petro) dollar was rapidly losing in value. Its world supremacy was threatened by gradually being replaced as reserve currency around the globe by the much stronger euro. The euro was backed by a solid European economy. The combined EU economy (28 member countries) was then and is still today the world's strongest economy – €14.303 trillion (US$18.451 trillion, est. 2014), as compared to that of the US with US$ 17.4 trillion. Hence, the euro had to be weakened – not destroyed, it was needed for trde and to subordinate Europe – but severely weakened, so that the dollar could regain its inflated strength.

The public at large was being told and believed that Greek with barely 2% of the Eurozone's GDP was a threat to Europe. What nonsense! In 2008, when the troika adventure started, Greek's debt to GDP ratio was a mere 109.3%, totally manageable within the huge EU economy and without need of outside interference.

Today, Greece is much worse off than it was in 2008, when her GDP was at € 242 billion with a debt ratio of 109.3, as compared to today (2014) with a 17% lower GDP (€ 201 billion) and a 21% higher debt (debt – GDP ratio: 160%). Mega banks from Germany and France are the biggest lenders. They onlend to Greece cheap ECB money they receive for less than 1% – at between 5% and 7%. This is not only monetary abuse, it is outright theft of the last half century accumulated savings, social safety net and public services of the Greek population.

In Total, Greece has been 'bailed out' by private banksters with some € 240 billion, plus a Greek bond purchase of €50 billion by the ECB. New bailouts may be considered, according to German media, there is a possibility that the euro zone would have to support Greece with an extra 10 billion to 20 billion euros in 2015 / 2016. This, of course, would be against another package of more austerity programs.

Ironically, according to IMF's recent own *mea culpa*, serious mistakes were made in dealing with the 'Greek crisis. Yet the game goes on.

These cold, linear figures disguise an ever harder reality; the social destruction, misery and outright death – death by lacking health services and from complications due to starvation – the austerity programs brought with them. Overall unemployment is hovering above 25% and around 65% for young people (15-24 yrs.). Further annihilation of Greece's social fabric includes cuts in pensions (20%), minimum wages (22%), 5%reduction in social security – and, of course, the neoliberal one-fits-all solution of privatization – land, public utilities, mining rights (with no environmental safeguards) and other state assets.

If SYRIZA, the coalition of the Radical Left, wins on January 25, **Alexis Tsipras, Syriza's leader, said already, 'Greece will stay in the Eurozone, but Europe should erase a big part of the debt'.** Greece has several non-orthodox options to get out of her quagmire. Although Zyriza is composed of large sections of middle-class Greeks (to the extent that the middle class still exists in Greece), who may after all still like the expected benefits of the euro, pressure of working class support may require other alternatives from Zyriza.

The most radical option, but the economically most sustainable one of all, would be for Greece to exit the Eurozone on her own, return to her old, devalued currency, the Drachma, and begin renegotiating her debt with her creditors, the 'troika' – akin to what Argentina did in 2001, when they abandoned the US dollar-peso parity and renegotiated their foreign debt with a heftily devalued peso (never mind the recent vulture funds' pressure on Argentina; it will not succeed).

The idea is for Greece to start afresh from a new slate, following the principle of local production for local markets, building up a solid economy as a sovereign country, independent of outside interference. The potential is there. The bankrupt banking system could be nationalized and the Greek central bank would lend to the nationalized local banks for onlending at favorable terms to stimulate and revive local industries and services. Some small businesses have already started forming internal groups dealing with drachma-based exchanges.

Another temporary alternative might be resorting to a two-tier exchange rate solution, i.e. using the euro exclusively for external trade and the devalued drachma to kindle local industry. This example was followed by China until 1994 to develop an export market, while supporting a local market with a lower exchange rate currency, the Renminbi (RMB); and the higher valued Yuan to be used more commonly for international trade.

The two-tier exchange rate system is against WTO (World Trade Organization) rules which were one of the reasons for China to introduce in 1994 a uniform exchange rate system, allowing her to become a WTO member. It would certainly also be in Greek's favor to exit WTO, at least temporarily, until Greece has rebuilt its economy to become largely self-sufficient – as she was before the euro entered the European horizon.

WTO is completely dominated by rich countries to the detriment of poorer countries, for example allowing highly subsidized US and EU agricultural goods to be exported to developing nations, thereby destroying their local agricultural production and markets. Greece can do without that; rebuilding her troika-destroyed economy by her own strength.

The third option might be the trickiest but also the slickest. The Bank of Greece (central bank) has every sovereign right to print its own currency – which is the EURO. There is no BCE rule against it. BCE has no constitution and was never really created with the characteristics of a true central bank to monitor and rescue countries in need at interbank rates. To the contrary, BCE lends at low interbank rates to private banks which then onlend the proceeds to member countries' central banks at exorbitant interest rates geared by US rating agencies, the usual villains, who are in bed with the TBTF bankster thieves.

There is legally nothing in the way of a sovereign country printing its own currency and then proceeding onlending the funds to its (temporarily) nationalized banks at favorable rates with the purpose of revamping the national economy. The Swedish example of the 1990s with later re-privatizing the nationalized banks at a profit for taxpayers, could serve as a reference.

Of course, under all three scenarios, Brussels would scream 'murder' and threaten with 'sanctions' – as they have learned from their Washington masters. So what? Greece would survive and grow instead of being asphyxiated under the weight of its debt – which to get rid of within the life time of a generation is virtually impossible.

It is likely that Greece's taking the nonconformist initiative to sidestep the abusive dollar-euro system would open a gate for other plagued EU countries to follow. The Eurozone – EU might collapse altogether. That would be a good thing. The European Union – the erstwhile beacon of economic and political cooperation in the world's largest economic block – has fully succumbed to the empire and can no longer be reformed. The EU has become a slave of the US, an economic colony of Washington, devoid of its own teeth and backbone, at the mercy of Washington's calling, be it for sanctions against Russia, or for war with Russia – or anything else Obama may see fit.

Here is the crux of the matter – the western (petro) dollar based currency scheme is rapidly decaying. The currency and oil price manipulation initiated by Washington against the Russian ruble is actually backfiring bad time. Russia and China have recently entered into a strategic alliance; a treaty that joins their financial and defense systems. By doing so, Vladimir Putin and Xi Jinping may have achieved a tectonic change in world geopolitics and economics. The two countries control about 27% of world GDP.

The new economic union has already brought about a new financial system, detached from the dollar. Russia has recently introduced an internal 'SWIFT' system to replace the US controlled casino exchange scheme. Once tested, the system could easily be expanded internationally for use of other countries who want to avoid the dollar scheme.

Both countries, Russia and China trade their hydrocarbons in their local currencies – i.e. no longer in the mandatory US dollar, which will undoubtedly reduce demand for the highly over-inflated petro dollar in the near future. Other countries – the SCO (Shanghai Cooperation Organization) members and those who aspire to become SCO members, like Iran, India, Pakistan, Mongolia, have already joined in trading with Russia and China in their local currencies.

The dollar is only keeping its value, because it is still used as the major reserve currency. Therefore, the FED still can and does print dollars at will. But as demand for the petro-dollar will fade, because hydrocarbons around the world are increasingly traded in other currencies than the dollar, the dollars privileged position around the globe will cease. Washington's attempts to defeat the Russia-Chinese economic behemoth will fail. The collapse of the petro dollar would have worldwide repercussions, affecting the closely associated and by now subordinated euro – as well as currencies of other countries whose economies are narrowly linked with that of the US.

This means for Greece, it's high time to leave a defunct monetary system. Greece may actually become the gateway for Europe to abandon the sinking ship and gradually work towards what Europe should have been from the beginning – an economic and political union of sovereign nations prospering in solidarity.

January 24, 2015

9

THE WAR ON VENEZUELA'S DEMOCRACY – A THWARTED COUP ATTEMPT

By Peter Koenig

This is a typical case of neoliberal Washington paid thugs and mercenaries false-flagging 'undesired' governments into chaos, for *'regime change'* - and then being taken over by the US, subjugating the population to US dictate and stealing the country's resources.

Being subjected to the constant stream of lies by the six Anglo-Saxon mega-media corporations controlling 90% of the western information - 'news' - system, it is easy to brainwash the western population into believing that the culprit is the Maduro government, exercising police repression.

We have seen it happen in Ukraine - where currently the Kiev Nazi government (sic) led civil war is killing thousands of citizens in the Donbas area of eastern Ukraine, putting millions of people into absolute misery in a cold winter depriving them of energy and food - a million and a half refugees fleeing to Russia--- and - who is the culprit, Mr. Putin, of course. Since the all dominant criminal lie and propaganda media machine is still to this day hiding the evidence, that the Maidan coup d'état in February 2014 was instigated and prepared during many years, and eventually directed and paid for by Washington and NATO.

A similar case is today's formal accusation of Cristina Fernandez de Kirchner of obstructing the investigation into the 1994 attack of the Jewish center AMIA that killed 85 people. This alleged car bomb attack follows a very similar attack demolishing the Israeli embassy in 1992. Last week the chief prosecutor of the case, Alberto Nisman, was found dead in his apartment, hours before publicly testifying about an alleged cover up by President Cristina Fernandez. She was allegedly covering up Iran's involvement in the devastation of the two buildings, again allegedly because of an oil for meat and food grain deal between Argentina and Iran may be at stake. All circumstantial evidence, even by anonymous witnesses, points to an agreement between Washington and Israel to blame Iran for the disaster, killing two birds with one stroke – incriminating the inconvenient Argentinian President with the objective of 'regime change', and demonizing once more Iran. Both of these deadly aggressions bear the hallmark of false flags, carried out or instigated by the CIA and Mosad.

Does it then come as a surprise that Washington is instigating, organizing and paying for civil unrest in Caracas and other major cities, stage by stage, leading eventually to a coup and control of the media, including *TeleSur*? – There is nothing new in this 'procedure'. It is actually old and full with ancient dirt, repeated umpteen times around the globe over the last century – and the western bought presstitute media, including of neutral Switzerland, trumpets around the world that President Maduro is a dictator and clamps down on protesters. What a shameful lie – misguidance of public opinion, brainwashing people into supporting more crime by the empire.

May public consciousness finally wake up!

February 14, 2015

10

"CIVILIZATION" OF THE NEOCONS

The West under neoliberal leadership (sic) has become a
horrifying merciless killing machine.

By Peter Koenig

*"We shall require a substantially new manner of
thinking if mankind is to survive."* ~*Albert Einstein*

Imagine – a bunch of French, CIA and Mossad special
forces, one of them or a combination of the three, attack a
racist, Moslem-insulting publisher in Paris and a kosher
supermarket at another end of town – killing altogether 17
people, notwithstanding the 'suicide' of the French police
chief in charge of investigating the atrocity.

A million and a half people in Paris take to the streets –
about 6 million throughout Europe – all screaming or
carrying posters with a maddening, inexplicable *"Je Suis
Charlie"* – depicting an utterly brainwashed mindset,

brainwashed for decades with Washington directed mind control.

They do not know, do not want to know, that the *Charlie* massacre was yet another staged event, another false flag that will eventually give their masters green light to intensify their 'wars on terror' around the globe. Terrorists are mostly Muslims; so is their dictum. Before the massacre, the powers that be identified three Muslims as the perpetrators of the crime to come. Soon after the Charlie attack, they sent killer squads to massacre them, before anybody could question them. The fight on terror – don't leave witnesses behind.

The millions of demonstrators' war cry is literally asking the western armies, led by NATO to turn- and speed up their brutal killing machine in the Middle East – to exterminate the Moslem population. The western public has been told and is constantly being told by the western powers dominated main stream media that Muslims are at the heart of all evil; when in fact quite the contrary is true. The West under neoliberal leadership (sic) has become a horrifying merciless killing machine.

That's *Paris Charlie* revisited and in a nutshell. – That's our neoliberal 'civilization' – with a purpose. *False flag* written all over the walls of Charlie Hebdo's blasphemous infrastructure. Waging even more savage war on the 1.6 billion Muslims. Killing 17 people by Empire and its stooges, will allow Empire and its stooges to kill more millions, perhaps tens of millions, to exterminate this 'evil' Muslim sect of 'terrorists'. A 'terrorist' is anybody who doesn't bend to the empire's boot. That doctrine has been impregnated in western minds ever since another *false flag* killed on 9/11 about 3,000 people in New York, allowing the beginning of the eternal war – wars, one succeeding the next – the criminal Bush-Blair legacy of the 21st Century.

The Afghanistan invasion of empire directed NATO forces was to control the TAPI pipeline project (Turkmenistan, Afghanistan, Pakistan, India), for which the Taliban were unwilling to negotiate with the Bush family, nor with a secret Congressional commission in 2001. The project is as of this day a bone of contention – and a good reason for Obama to leave a permanent 'residue' of troops in Afghanistan.

To keep a roving mindless populace tight – local *false flags*, à la Boston Marathon bombing are necessary to intensify repression, abrogate ever more civil liberties – and this even on demand from the very people affected by the repression. They want more security, more protection.

As with Charlie Hebdo, the bad guys were pre-identified,so that when the secret special forces launched their ugly plot, they were easy to trace and chase – and kill. One of the designated 'perpetrators' in the Boston case and all of them in Paris. Dead men don't talk.

The Bostonians literally invited armed police to take over their streets and invade their homes. In Paris the marchers of 1.5 million people were silently screaming, "Hollande go to war and free us from evil! " – What a depressing joke this is. It would be laughable if it weren't that serious. – It is one more step won by the neoliberal empire – a step towards full dominance and subjugation of the populace.

The Washington funded AlQaeda-turned-Taliban-turned-AlQaeda Osama BinLaden was made responsible for the Twin Tower's collapse – in no time. And in no time, two years to be exact, the wind shifted. Iraq's Saddam is the culprit. The power of the msm – in combination with the brainless masses works wonders.

Saddam, the newly designated culprit of the New York 9/11 monstrosity triggered the war on Iraq – the empire taking over the country's riches, her oil wells; at that time the world's cheapest oil to bring to the surface – and making sure that Saddam would not tell *who* helped and incited him to wage an eight-year war against his neighbor Iran, and *who* gave him the poison to gas in 1988 the Kurds in the North, and especially, that he would not convert his forced dollar denominated sales of hydrocarbons into euros, as he unwittingly announced – he had to be executed. He received a world stage hanging, propaganda for justice, for American justice – justice of the exceptional people, supported and road-mapped, as always, by the banking backed 'chosen people'.

The Bush-Blair led 'coalition of the willing' slaughtered more than a million and a half Iraqis, mostly civilians;women, children and elderly; creating other millions of refugees. Countless people murdered in Afghanistan. In parallel the NED-induced (National Endowment for Democracy) infamous machinery of 'regime change' produced the so-called Arab Spring which had nothing to do with spring, but everything with devastating one Middle Eastern and North African country after another. The obliteration of Libya and Syria through NATO bombing and NATO prompted civil wars, and more brutal and bloody conflicts all over Mother Earth.

Obama's personally directed drone war on Yemen, Pakistan, Sudan, Somalia, Syria, Turkey – and the list goes on – is further fomenting and funding local unrest, killing masses of defenseless people.

It is American judgment over nations by war. ISIS, a US-EU-NATO creation, generously funded by the empire and its European and Middle Eastern stooges, as a rebel force to fight Syrian troops and to take over Iraq, is torturing and slaughtering in the (concealed) name of the neocon empire, other thousands of people.

ISIS, supplied with cutting-edge weaponry by the US and NATO, is assailing Iraq, where George W. Bush notoriously declared in May 2003, two months after his shock and awe invasion, "Mission Accomplished".

Not to mention the horrifying eight more years of war Iraq and her people endured until Obama ceremoniously announced the end of war, pulling out US troops in 2011– not without leaving a core presence behind, though.

As Eduardo Galeano, the famous revolutionary Uruguayan writer and philosopher said – once US troops are in a country, they never leave. Hence, the more than thousand US military bases around the globe.

Wars must go on. The US neoliberal economy depends on them. The war machine and its ramifications contribute more than 50% to the US GDP.

Without wars, the country would collapse. All peace talks and negotiations initiated or feigned by Washington are fake, a deception, propaganda for the goodness of the naked emperor. Kudos for the exceptional nation.

World peace would mean a black hole for the United States, demise.

In both cases, Iraq and Syria, ISIS (Islamic State of Iraq and Syria) – the Sunni caliphate having merged in 2013 with Syria's al-Nusra Front – and whatever other names the 'rebels' may morph into –are paid to fight national armies unwilling to bend. In turn, they are justifying US interventions, bombing the same ISIS they created, though only a little bit, to make believe, lest ISIS might really be wiped out. Recent US helicopter food and ammunition drops behind ISIS Iraqi lines testify to the west's double standards and deceit.

In reality, when bombing ISIS, NATO is bombing Iraq and Syria for regime change, and as an added icing on the cake, to grease the US war machine, the ever hungry military industrial complex.

Estimates have it that US carried out and inspired wars and conflicts around the globe have killed over ten million people in the last decade and a half.

That's neoliberal 'civilization' – murdering 17 to kill millions – making billions by weapon manufacturing and selling, plus more billions by stealing hydrocarbon – the God of Energy of our ever growth-lusty western greed economy; and making even more billions by converting small-holder agriculture which still today feeds 80% of world population – into pesticide-implanted genetically modified food production, the Monsanto world.

As if this destruction, annihilation and misery of war and mass killing were not enough, there is reconstruction after war, another bonanza for the destroyer. The words of former World Bank president, Robert Zoellick, also known as the US neoliberal trade tsar, will not be forgotten, when he said in the midst of NATO devastating Libya in 2011 – "We hope that the World Bank will also be involved in the reconstruction of Libya." Well, this wish has not come through yet, but in other war-torn zones it has.

After destruction comes reconstruction with all the neoliberal strings attached, financial robbery of public goods, reduction of pensions, minimum wages, social services, privatization of education and health, expropriation and privatization of natural resources by foreign corporations –and the list goes on, all requisites of extreme austerity measures as conditions for the sacrosanct IMF, World Bank and ECBso-called rescue packages.

At times, countries whose existence remains somehow important for the empire, like those in Southern Europe, will be driven into misery without physical war, just by financial abuse and economic slavery. Greece, Spain, Portugal, Ireland and even Italy, were driven to the abyss of suffocation by the all-powerful, but appallingly criminal troika, the IMF, ECB and the European Commission.

After coercing or replacing their elected governments with neoliberal puppets, mostly former Wall Street execs, as is the President of the ECB, they – the troika and their masters – forced these countries into debt, after debt and more debt – debt that is virtually unrecoverable in a generation; debt that causes astronomical levels of unemployment, Greece, Spain and Portugal, hovering above 25% and 65% among the young people, slashing social services, health care, pensions, leaving a huge proportion of their population in absolute poverty and in physical and mental misery.

And who funds all these atrocities – wars and financial devastation? – Wall Street, the extended arm of the

Zionist-Anglo-Saxon controlled monetary system, and its puppets, the FED, IMF, World Bank, European Central Bank and their subordinate European mega-banks. Naturally.– Who else?

All of these neoliberal mayhems are guided by the invisible hand of the PNAC – the Plan of a New American Century, designed by Zionist Washington think tanks, the tail that wags the dog. The PNAC foresees the annihilation of the Middle East, the pocketing of Europe by implanting puppets – done! – and finally the encircling and eventual subjugation of Russia and China – the ascent of a Washington directed One World Order.

It shall not happen. There is hope in the solid alliance of Vladimir Putin and Xi Jinping, of Russia and China; a strategic economic and defense pact, the western media are silent about. The less the public knows of the truth, the more it will adore the 'exceptional nation', as its one and only master – so goes the theory of western self-adulation.

Neoliberalism wants it all, the supremacy of the 1% – addressing the lowest common denominator in human kind – greed, using the main stream media concocting lies and deceptions to nurture more greed which in turn is the engine that fuels the neoliberal doctrine of private property, of privatization of public goods, privatization – stealing – of other countries natural resources, the steady pursuit of instant profit, of police and military oppression of the few who refuse to comply. A Win-Win-Win situation – energy, food and money, as per Kissinger's infamous dogma– who controls energy controls continents, who controls food controls people, and who controls money controls the world.

Neoliberalism, the religion of the West, is the epitome of evil, of destruction of civilization itself.Neoliberalism – thanks to its unifying factor of greed, has ravaged the west like brushfire and taken over the world in less than 30 years, a feat grander than that achieved by mono-theistic Judo-Christianity in over 2000 years.

Citizens of Mother Earth – BEWARE ! – Wake up ! Open your eyes and ears ! – Become vanguards of a new world, new values – where the neocons and their globalization bite the dust, and where local production for local markets funded by local banks propels solidarity and harmony into new generations of mankind.

January 23, 2015

11

PARIS CHARLIE: THE "SHOCK DOCTRINE" PAR EXCELLENCE

By Peter Koenig

On 12 January the French Parliament approved with almost unanimity – with one abstention only – the budget for France's continuous and enlarged involvement in the new war on Iraq, a new war engagement led by Washington and supported by its vassals, UK, Canada, Australia and France. Aircraft carriers and troops were immediately mobilized, not even losing a day. Doesn't that conspicuously smell of an earlier preparation, just waiting for that crucial and appropriate event, prompting parliamentary approval?

At the same time France lawmakers agreed to display 10,000 troops throughout the country to protect 'vulnerable places'; spying on citizens, for their protection takes on new forms and formats. A direct reaction to the attack on Charlie Hebdo on January 7 and the assault on a kosher supermarket on January 9? – Killing 17 people in all? Is that it?

French Ministers of the Interior and of Defense have advanced their wish of substantially increased respective police and defense budgets, when the 2016-2017 allocations are being discussed later this year. No doubt they will get their way.

And – no doubt, this is the shock doctrine at its best. People are in awe and shock after the assault on the satirical and Moslem insulting Charlie Hebdo. A million and a half took to the streets in Paris this past weekend, the largest manifestation since the liberation of Paris after WWII in 1945. Some media report more than 6 million people marching throughout Europe. Almost all waving signs "I am Charlie" – Solidarity or stupidity? Hard to say. Most likely just sheer ignorance.

It's ignorance that kills our democracies, our human values; public ignorance allows leaders (sic) to wage wars, to aggress nations that refuse to submit, to fall to their knees. It's ignorance perpetuated daily by our mainstream media and swallowed without question, day-in-day-out like breakfast coffee.

Neocon leaders, all over Europe, the new patsies of Washington that we, the people, have voted into office, under shrewd but hardly perceptible Washington-funded propaganda, through NED (National Endowment for Democracy) and other well-endowed CIA sponsored so-called think-tanks, meddling in local politics, sowing subtle threats or acts of destabilization. Europe's new masters that a majority of the people doesn't really like, but who are in office anyway – these spineless stooges constitute Europe in Brussels, the EU itself having become a miserable colony of Washington.

So, with a populace under shock, politicians have it even easier to get away literally with murder, with whatever they want under the pretext of fighting the eternal enemy – the Moslem terrorist armies, Al Qaeda, ISIS and whatever other names they have morphed into or morphed out from in the course of the last couple of decades. Eternal war on eternal terrorists perpetuates evil and more terrorism and – war budgets yielding insane profits for the war industry throughout the western Washington-aligned world.

Under shock and awe, people will approve every aberrant and sick wish of aggression by politicians – if being told that it is for their good and protection. Yes, that's what the propaganda machine has done to the 'free-thinking' minds of the citizens of our ever so heralded democracies. Democracies, freedom of expression, freedom of press – mon oeil !

The Charlie atrocities reek all over of false flag. An attack so well and professionally carried out with cutting edge Kalashnikovs and get-away methodology, way beyond the capacities of the Kouachi brothers, who have no doubt criminal records, spent time with and were trained by the very AlQada and ISIS that were created and funded by Washington and by its European puppets – including the French, according to President (sic) Hollande's own admission.

Yes, the French were and are funding counter-terrorism in Iraq and Syria, the very counter-terrorism that provides them in turn with pretexts to bomb the two war-torn countries to even more rubble – just for regime change, with the added benefit of oil and gas, and a constant profit generating war machine – leaving millions of deaths behind, mostly civilians, women and children and elderly – and other untold millions as refugees, in miserable unsanitary camps, or fleeing across dangerous borders to unknown destinies, to disease, hunger and death – people the world forgets, the media stays away from – forgotten lives.

The Kouachi brother, as well as Amedy Coulibaly, the suspect in the hostage drama of the Hyper Cacher food market in eastern Paris, whose identities and past activities were well recorded in French police files, were most likely pre-identified as perpetrators of the probable pre-meditated murderous attacks that left 17 people dead within three days of horror in Paris; attacks so well organized and carried out that they could easily wear the stamp of French special forces, CIA, Mossad or all three of them – because, cui bono – who benefits? – Perhaps the Masters of all three of them?

The Kouachi brothers were identified only by a conveniently lost ID in the get-away car, reminiscent of the intact passport of one of the 9/11 'terrorists' found in the rubble of the twin towers. Are people really ignorant enough to believe such a farce? – All three were caught and killed almost immediately by police. Dead men don't talk.

And there is more – coincidentally, as reported by Michel Chossudovsky of Global Research, the Police Commissioner, Helric Fredou, Number Two Police Officer of the Regional Service of France's Judicial Police in Limoges, "committed suicide on the night of Wednesday to Thursday at the police station." Commissioner Helric Fredou had participated in the police investigation into the Charlie Hebdo terror attack.

The reason given for the 'suicide' is 'burn-out' and depression – depression when in charge of one of France's most prominent criminal investigations of the century? The incidence as of this day is hardly covered by the msm.

False flag written all over the walls of Charlie Hebdo's publishing house. – The publisher being controversial, having received frequent threats for its Moslem-offensive cartoons was normally under heavy police protection. Why was on 7 January only one police car with one police officer parked half a block away?

False flag – converted immediately into public shock, the perfect condition for ramming any police, military and surveillance legislation down the people's throats. Better, it doesn't even have to be 'rammed down', the population asks for it. They want to be protected and secured. They want their government going to war to wipe out Moslem terrorism, never mind how violent and how cruel they go about it, never mind the criminal acts these governments are committing in the name of protecting their citizenry.

Does anybody take to the streets in Europe, in the US with posters saying "I am.... blank" ... the million victims of Iraq, of Syria – of Libya, of Afghanistan, of Yemen, of Pakistan, of Sudan, of Somalia – and the list is almost endless. These millions of lives wiped out by Obama's drones and NATO count for nothing in the dulled minds of the western civilization (sic).

The war and killing machine that feeds the propaganda machine, driven by the six Zionist-Anglos-Saxon monster media that control 90% of the western information system, shy not from dishing out lie after lie after lie to indoctrinate the populace with believes that have zilch to do with reality – but they transform our western populace into hapless zombies.

What does it take to stop this vicious cycle and awaken consciousness?

January 16, 2015

12

EUROPE BEWARE! – WORLD WAR III COULD DESTROY EUROPE THIRD TIME IN A CENTURY

By Peter Koenig

Washington is determined to go to war with Russia. Its military industrial complex demands it. Its financial system – FED, Wall Street demand it. War is a debt machine. War brings insane amounts of profit. The European vassals go along with it. It is part of the PNAC (Plan for a New American Century) to take over the world.

After Russia, China would follow. That's the plan. China is being encircled as we speak. Already 50% of the US navy fleet is stationed in the Pacific, from Japan to the Philippines to Australia. By 2016, Obama has promised, the navy war contingent in the Pacific will increase to two thirds.

In mid-2014, China had surpassed the US in economic power. China must be annihilated in any way possible. Never mind that Russia and China have recently concluded a pact, a close financial and military alliance – which to defeat will be next to impossible.

Unless – and here is the crux of the matter – unless Washington, a dying beast, pouncing wildly its tentacles all around the globe, initiates an all-out nuclear war, destroying the planet, including itself – but foremost Europe. After all, the US of A is far away. Protected by two Oceans. Starting wars from foreign bases is much safer.

Of NATO's 28 member countries, 26 are in Europe, of which 12 – almost half – in Eastern Europe, countries that used to be part of or 'dependencies' of the former Soviet Union. And this happened despite Washington's promise at the time of the fall of the Berlin Wall, not to expand NATO eastward. A lie and sheer affront on Russia.

This provocation is exacerbated today by the Pentagon's further arming the NATO bases of Poland and Latvia, and by NATO's considering Ukraine's urgent call – or rather, the call of the Washington installed Kiev Nazi thugs – for NATO protection and to become a NATO member as soon as possible. Poroshenko declared that his government (sic) will do whatever it takes to implement the neoliberal NATO reform conditions, including give up the status of non-alignment (neutrality) under which it was created at the dissolution of the Soviet Union. "Neoliberal reforms" – akin to the IMF sledgehammer, meaning further privatizing and stealing Ukraine's social safety system – reduced salaries, pensions, health and education benefits. A disaster for the people; spiraling into outright misery.

Imagine, NATO at Moscow's doorstep. Would the Kremlin just bow and accept it? – Hardly. With NATO bases in 26 European countries – Guess – who would be the logical center of the next theatre of war?

Do the Obama stooges not realize this? – Do the vassals have no brains? Or would the coward leaders (sic) escape to Florida, while their people are smoldering to dust? – Wake up, Europe! Wake up! – People of Europe, take back your countries from the neoliberal puppets, from your spine and brainless coward leaders.

In fact, the West led by the naked emperor is waging war against Russia on several fronts: the bloody Ukraine coup and Maidan massacre in February 2014; arming and equipping the Kiev war criminals that has led to at least 5,000 savagely killed Donbass inhabitants most of whom civilians, women and children, and more than a million homeless refugees into Russia; relentless anti-Russia, anti-Putin propaganda, by the Zionist-Anglo-Saxon controlled MSM; CIA instigated false flag operations, like the downing by Kiev's air force of Malaysian Air MH17, killing 298 people; a salvo of countless economic sanctions which, albeit, hurt Europe more than Russia; and a currency war with an engineered fall of the ruble, combined with an 'engineered' drop of oil prices by conspiring with the Saudi clowns for hydrocarbon overproduction, a stab not only at Russia, but also at the economies of others who refuse to bend to Washington's dictum, like Iran and Venezuela.

In addition, there is the indirect attack front – the Middle East – creating and arming the IS caliphate to destabilize Syria; and in an act of make-believe attacking IS troops in disguise of bombing Syria – a close ally of Russia – for 'regime change', an objective that has been on the State Department's agenda for the last ten years. Iran, another ally of Russia and China, may be next. So it has been inscribed in the PNAC. The tail of the Zionist poodle that wags the empire (and largely authored the PNAC) knows no mercy.

Russia is taking it in with calm. Vladimir Putin is a chess player par excellence, out-maneuvering the west at every move. In addition to Russia's large foreign exchange reserves – estimated at close to half a trillion dollars equivalent – Ms. Elvira Nabiullina, President of Russia's Central Bank, entered into a currency swap agreement with China, pitting their combined economies, constituting about 27% of the world's GDP (US$85 trillion, 2014 est.) against the western economic aggressions.

A few days ago Russia's Central Bank started buying back cheap, down-graded rubles with its excess foreign reserves. The Russian currency gained 10% alone on 17 December, last day of trading before the weekend. With the fall of the ruble, foreign shareholders of Russian corporations, especially in Europe and the US, were afraid of losing out under a ruble collapse. They shed their shares – which Russia quickly bought and repatriated, thereby not only returning foreign holdings of Russian stock into Russian coffers, but also cashing in on the dividends of these stocks. According to some accounts (Spiegel Online), with this move alone Russia earned some 20 billion dollars.

It looks like the economic and propaganda war is progressively being won by Russia. On the political western front things are crumbling too. Hungary's government, a member of the EU and of NATO, has just declared an alliance with Russia against Washington. Turkey, once a contender to enter the EU, is disgusted with Europe and is instead aiming at membership in the SCO (Shanghai Cooperation Organization). Turkey is a strategic key NATO member. Will others follow suit, as more and more are seeing the emperor's nakedness and horrendous malignancy?

The veils are falling. Gradually. So-called allies of the empire are wary since long. Afraid of 'sanctions' or worse, of a possible take-over by the merciless killing machine, they have nodded and played along. So far. But, as they see the implosion of the beast, they increasingly dare jumping ship.

Europe – be aware! The center of the next war might again be Europe. A dying beast knows no mercy. It rather destroys the universe and itself than leaving survivors behind. – Unless its poisonous and killing tentacles can be paralyzed – terminally, by economic isolation; by destruction of its currency, the dollar; by making this worthless money irrelevant and obsolete. For good.

Europe – it's not too late! Your economic future is in your autonomy; in a coalition of European sovereign nations with the east – an alliance with the promising new economic Silk Road. Mr. Xi Jinping's offer to Madame Merkel this past spring is still open. Neoliberal thinking is short-term thinking. Instant profit for instant debt.

Europe, take the lead. Break loose from the corrupt debt-ridden dollar casino scheme. A new ruble-yuan based monetary system is in the making. The basket may soon expand by other BRICS currencies – and, who knows, maybe the Euro? – Our children, grandchildren and their children deserve a future of peace and harmony and wellbeing.

December 30, 2014

13

FREE FALL OF THE RUBBLE: WHO'S BEHIND IT? A PLOY OF RUSSIA'S ECONOMIC WIZARDS? WHOSE CHESS GAME?

By Peter Koenig

The world is still hell-bent for hydrocarbon-based energy. Russia is one of the world's largest producer of energy. Russia has recently announced that in the future she will no longer trade energy in US dollars, but in rubles and currencies of the trading partners. In fact, this rule will apply to all trading. Russia and China are detaching their economies from that of the western financial system. To confirm this decision, in July 2014 Russia's Gazprom concluded a 400 billion gas deal with China, and in November this year they signed an additional slightly smaller contract – all to be denominated in rubles and renminbi.

The remaining BRICS – Brazil, India and South Africa – plus the members of the Shanghai Cooperation Organization (SCO) – China, Russia, Kazakhstan, Tajikistan, Kirgizstan, Uzbekistan and considered for membership since September 2014 are also India, Pakistan, Afghanistan, Iran and Mongolia, with Turkey also waiting in the wings – will also trade in their local currencies, detached from the dollar-based western casino scheme. A host of other nations increasingly weary of the decay of the western financial system which they are locked into are just waiting for a new monetary scheme to emerge. So far their governments may have been afraid of the emperor's wrath – but gradually they are seeing the light. They are sensing the sham and weakness behind Obama's boisterous noise. They don't want to be sucked into the black hole, when the casino goes down the drain.

To punish Russia for Ukraine, Obama is about to sign into law major new sanctions against Russia, following Congress's unanimous passing of a recent motion to this effect. – That is what the MSM would like you to believe. It is amazing that ten months after the Washington instigated Maidan slaughter and coup where a Washington selected Nazi Government was put in place, the MSM still lies high about the origins of this government and the massacres it is committing in the eastern Ukraine Donbass area.

Congress's unanimity – what Congress and what unanimity? – Out of 425 lawmakers, only 3 were present for the vote. The others may have already taken off for their year-end recess, or simply were 'ashamed' or rather afraid to object to the bill. As a matter of fact, of the three who were present to vote, two at first objected. Only after a bit of arm-twisting and what not, they were willing to say yes. This is how the 'unanimous' vote came to be, as trumpeted by the MSM – unanimous by three votes! The public at large is duped again into believing what is not.

What new sanctions does this repeatedly propagated bill entail? – It addresses mostly Russian energy companies and the defense industry with regard to sales to Syria, as well more anti-Russia propaganda and 'democratization' programs in Ukraine – and Russia; all countries with the objective for regime change.

How do these sanctions affect Russia, especially since all Russian energy sales are no longer dollar denominated? – Sheer propaganda. The naked emperor once more is calling an unsubstantiated bluff. To show his western stooges who is in power. It's an ever weaker showoff.

Now – as a consequence of declining oil prices and of western 'sanctions' – of course, what else? – Russia's economy is suffering and the ruble is in free fall. Since the beginning of the year it lost about 60%; last week alone 20%. As a result and after serious consideration, says MSM, the Russian Central Bank decided a few days ago to increase the interest of reference from 10.5% to 17% to make the ruble more attractive for foreign investors. It worked only for a few hours. Raising the interbank interest was Putin's reply to Obama's bluff – feeding at the same time western illusion about Russia's decline.

The propaganda drums tell you Russia is helpless because the world has lost the last bit of confidence in President Putin – of course. Regime change is on the agenda. Mr. Putin must be blamed as the culprit, hoping to discredit him with his people. He is leading Russia into a deep recession; the worst since the collapse of the Soviet Union. The mainstream media show you interviews with average mainstreet Russians saying they have lost all their savings, their salaries and pensions are worth nothing anymore and they don't know how to survive this coming calamity.

In reality, at least 80% of the Russian population stands solidly behind Vladimir Putin. He has brought them universal education, health care and fixed infrastructure that was decaying after the fall of the Soviet Union. President Putin is literally revered as a hero by the vast majority of Russians – including the country's oligarchy.

In fact, nobody in the western economic system these days is dealing in rubles. In short-sighted connivance with Washington, the treasuries of the western vassals are releasing their ruble reserves – which Russia does not buy, thereby flooding the market. Russia not only has large dollar reserves, plus the ruble is backed by gold, a fact consistently omitted in the MSM. For now, Russia prefers to let the ruble plummet.

Under another 'arrangement' by bully Obama, Middle Eastern oil producing puppets like Saudi Arabia and the Gulf States are overproducing and flooding the market with petrol and gas, thereby driving the price down to the ostensible detriment of Russia and Venezuela, both countries where Washington vies for regime change. A double whammy thinks Washington, buying kudos with the stooges. The sheiks that control their energy output apparently have been promised enough goodies from Washington to bite the bullet and take their own losses.

Russia needs rubles. That's her currency. That is the currency Russia needs for future trading – detached from the western monetary system.

When Russia deems that her currency has reached rock-bottom, she will buy back cheap rubles in the market with massive amounts of dollars. Russia may then flood the western market – with dollars, euros and other western-allied currencies – and gold. Let's not forget, the ruble is backed by gold. By now we know what flooding a market with currencies may do to these currencies – and simultaneously buy back rubles from the West. A brilliant move to reestablish Russia's currency in a new emerging monetary system – which Europe would be welcome to join, but willingly, not by Washington style arm-twisting.

Surely, Russia is not interested to cause the sudden destruction of the dollar-linked financial world. She is not interested in a sudden death of the many countries that are potential new trading partners in a new monetary system. Instead, the fall of the western economy of deceit may be planned as a gradual slide, so that countries have time to switch – switch their reserves to rubles, yuans and other BRICS and SCO currencies. This move is on its way. Only ten years ago, dollar denominated securities constituted 90% of reserves worldwide. Today the rate is 60% and declining.

After all, perhaps as Plan B, there is also a pact of monetary alliance between Russia and China. China holds currently about 1.5 trillion dollars and in total more than 3 trillion dollar equivalent in western currencies – and undefined but huge gold reserves. Chinese, BRICS and SCO solidarity with Russia is a solid security for the ruble. Imagine – the first major action of the new BRICS Development Bank with a current capital base of 100 billion dollars would launch a massive ruble rescue operation. No worries, Russia's economy is on firm course.

The question begs – is this gigantic 'engineered' ruble devaluation scheme another precursor to war? A nuclear confrontation or Cold War II? – Precursor to another western, Washington-driven false flag attempting Moscow to fall into a lethal trap? – Not necessarily. Russia is playing a clever chess game, diplomacy at its best. Instead of sabre rattling – Russia is coin rattling. It might lead to a western financial fiasco early in 2015 for the dollar and euro denominated economies. And the winner is...?

December 19, 2014

14

THE EU TO BECOME A "U.S. COLONY"?

The Transatlantic Trade and Investment Partnership (TTIP) would Abolish Europe's Sovereignty

Is Madame Merkel Betraying the EU – Endangering the Lives of Future European Generations with her Push for the Nefarious TTIP?

By Peter Koenig

The proposed Free Trade Agreement (sic), the so called Transatlantic Trade and Investment Partnership – TTIP – between the US and Europe would be an infringement and final abolishment of Europe's sovereignty. It would expand the US corporate and financial empire which already today dominates

Washington's politics and that of much of the western world – to take over Europe. Europe's sovereignty would be jeopardized, meaning the sovereignty of the EU itself, as well as and especially the sovereignty of EU member countries.

At stake would be EU's and EU members' legal and regulatory system, environmental protection regulations – and Europe's economy. Europe's basic social infrastructure, what's left of it after the 2008 invasion of the infamous troika – IMF (FED, Wall Street), European Central Bank (ECB) and the European Commission (EC) – like education, health, as well as water supply and sanitation services would become easy prey for privatization by international (mostly US) transnationals.

This so-called 'Free Trade Agreement' (sic) between the US and Europe Obama is pushing on the European Commission and for which on behalf of Europe, Germany's Madame Merkel seems to be a forceful standard bearer, if signed, would be serving the interests of corporations rather than of the 600 million European citizens.

According to John Hilary, Professor of Politics and International Relations at the University of Nottingham, and expert on trade and investment, the TTIP is a Charter for Deregulation, an Attack on Jobs, and End to Democracy.

"[The] TTIP is therefore correctly understood not as a negotiation between two competing trading partners, but as an attempt by transnational corporations to praise open and deregulate markets on both sides of the Atlantic." http://rosalux.gr/sites/default/files/publications/ttip_web.pdf).

In his State of the Union address of February 2013, Obama first announced the TTIP, for which the first round of – secret – negotiations started with a specially designed clandestine and restricted EU committee already July 2013. The objective is to complete talks fast and outside of the public domain, so that the peoples of Europe and the

US will not find out the true magnitude of the agreement with all its threats before the treaty has been signed. Negotiation documents are to be kept under vaults for 30 years. Outside this EU special committee, EU and member countries parliamentarians have no access to the details of the contract.

Why is that, if the TTIP is to bring benefits to the peoples of both sides of the Atlantic? – Because this assumption is an illusion. In fact, officials of both sides of the Atlantic unofficially admit "the main goal of TTIP is to remove regulatory 'barriers' which restrict the potential profits to be made by transnational corporations." These 'hindrances' include labor rights, food safety rules (including limitations on GMOs), environmental and health restrictions, such as the use of toxic chemicals, as well as regulations on digital privacy and – the newly introduced banking safeguards.

The TTIP's most blatant transgressions into Europe's sovereignty, environmental and social regulations include:

- Opening of flood gates for privatization of public services such as water supply and sanitation, health services and education – for profit;
- Jeopardy of public health – as practices which are legal in the US would also be legalized in Europe, such as genetically modified food production, and hormone treatments of livestock and poultry;
- Endangering small-scale agriculture, as it would favor large agro-corporations over family farming;
- Making fracking legal in Europe;
- The universal right of foreign corporations to sue countries for compensation in secret arbitrary courts for foregone profits in case governments pass laws that could reduce profits – case in point: the Swedish energy

company Vattenfall is seeking $6 billion in compensation for Germany's nuclear phase-out – and chances are that Vattenfall may win its case;

- Opening ways for increased internet monitoring and surveillance; and
- Opening of flood gates for privatization of public services such as water supply and sanitation, health services and education – for profit;
- Jeopardy of public health – as practices which are legal in the US would also be legalized in Europe, such as genetically modified food production, and hormone treatments of livestock and poultry;
- Endangering small-scale agriculture, as it would favor large agro-corporations over family farming;
- Making fracking legal in Europe;
- The universal right of foreign corporations to sue countries for compensation in secret arbitrary courts for foregone profits in case governments pass laws that could reduce profits – case in point: the Swedish energy company Vattenfall is seeking $6 billion in compensation for Germany's nuclear phase-out – and chances are that Vattenfall may win its case;
- Opening ways for increased internet monitoring and surveillance; and
- Excessive copyright regulations (pharmaceuticals and other monopoly prone industries), restricting free access to culture, education, and science.

The excessive copyright regulations (pharmaceuticals and other monopoly prone industries), restricting free access to culture, education, and science.

The TTIP is practically irreversible. Once agreed and signed by Brussels and Washington, the treaty would be enforced in all EU members and could only be amended or revoked by agreement of all 28 EU members and the US. This would almost be impossible. An individual (no longer) 'sovereign' EU member government could no longer decide to drop out of the agreement if and when it realizes that the TTIP works against its public interest, since it is not the individual country that signs the TTIP, but the EU.

The only way out would be exiting or dissolving the EU.

It is not a coincidence that the so-called negotiations are rushed and carried on in secret. If ratified and signed by the EC, the TTIP would be a monumental disaster for Europe's future generations. It would further curtail the peoples of Europe's constitutional rights and make them mere serfs of industrial and financial corporations and their elite.

Why is Madame Merkel so adamant to defend the interests of Washington rather than those of her own country, let alone those of the EU as a block? – It is clearly also a blow on Russia, since the TTIP would almost certainly mean a definite cut between Europe and Russia – and most likely between Europe and Asia.

The question may be asked – did the NSA find out something mortifying when they were eavesdropping on Merkel's cell phone? – When she found out about the White House tapping her phone, she appeared extremely furious about Obama. Many politicians, including in Europe, hoped this would suggest a break from Washington – which would have allowed other European puppets to follow their ascribed European leader. Then suddenly she made a U-turn. It is difficult to believe that she is so naïve. Whatever they may have on her -putting the future lives of more than 600 million Europeans at stake is a crime.

As a curious coincidence, at the 8-10 November APEC

Meeting in Beijing, Obama also proposed a Trans-Pacific Partnership (TPP) – a 'free trade agreement' that would include Australia, Brunei, Canada, Chile, Japan, Mexico, New Zealand, Peru, Singapore, the US and Vietnam. Its implementation, like the enactment of the TTIP is one of the primary goals of Obama's trade agenda.

Strangely, China is not included in the proposed partnership countries. The Western mainstream media says that Obama wants to sideline China – a 'sanction' for not falling in step with Washington's agenda for a One World Order.

However – what if it is the other way around – China sees the fraud in these so-called free trade agreements and opted not to part take in them?

If the proposed TTIP combined with the proposed TTP would be ratified and signed, it would be like a corporate empire taking over the world, especially Europe and Asia – less China and Russia. The Unite States is already in the claws of transnationals.

Let's keep in mind, these are secret negotiations, taking place behind closed doors, with little to no access to politicians and parliamentarians of the countries concerned. The talks are to be rushed through as fast as possible, so as to put the people at large before a fait accompli.

Only We, the People, can stop this crime – a new layer of US propelled world hegemony – by launching and supporting anti TTIP referenda on internet and in the streets.

December 2, 2014

15

ARGENTINA AND WALL STREET'S VULTURE FUNDS: "ECONOMIC TERRORISM" AND THE WESTERN FINANCIAL SYSTEM

By Peter Koenig

Today you pretend making a coalition against the Islamic State of Iraq and the Levant (ISIL), but in fact you're their allies," Those are the frank words by Cristina Fernandez Kirchner, the Argentinian President, spoken in a calm and secure voice at the UN General Assembly last Friday, 3 October 2014.

Similarly, she referred to the western financial system as economic terrorism, as in vultures – the vulture funds that thanks to New York judge Griesa have put Argentina – a solvent country, willing and capable of paying their debt, in default. He ruled that the vulture funds, Griesa's clients and paymasters, needed to be paid in full, i.e. 100%, equal to US$ 1.5 billion, when close to 93% of all creditors agreed on a restructured reimbursement rate of about 20%.

Without any international right to interfere in the affairs of a sovereign country, Griesa would allow the vultures reaping in a profit margin well in excess of 1,000%. – Paul Singer, king of the 'vulture capitalists', knows no merci. He is in bed with Wall Street and Griesa – and with whomever other financial hooligans who share his greedy endeavors. Greed is their prayer. It's knocked around the world. Exploits poor nations, makes them poorer, and keeps them dependent on the powers of money, being well aware that the poor are too weak to defend themselves.

Except for Argentina. Her able President Cristina Fernandez, speaks not only for her country, when she talks about victims of economic and financial terrorism, but for all those African, Latin American and Asian countries which are oppressed by the killing boots of Wall Street and the IMF. It cannot be said often enough – the IMF is a mere extended arm of the US Treasury and the FED.

Vulture capitalism exerted by these usual villains and the European Central Bank, a mere puppet of Wall Street and led by a former Wall Street banker, are responsible for the economic collapse of the western economy. They have driven countries like Greece, Portugal, Ireland, Spain – and lately also Ukraine – into misery.

They have stolen their social safety nets, pensions, employment, housing, education, health care, water supply and other public infrastructure – by privatizing public capital for their private benefits. They could do so thanks to the connivance of corrupt leaders they first put in place with sham elections – or no elections at all.

Case in point is Greece, where the Parliament decided

to dismiss the socialist Prime Minister George Papandreou, who attempted to launch a referendum in December 2011, asking the people whether they wanted the troika's (IMF, ECB, European Commission) imposed second 'rescue' package of € 130 billion (after a first one on € 110 billion) that would drastically increase Greece's sovereign debt and force literally a killer austerity program upon its people. At the onset of the manufactured crisis, in May 2008, Greece's debt to GDP ratio was a manageable 105%. In 2014 the ratio is 175%.

Under the structural adjustment program social health care was basically abolished. Many cancer and other chronically ill patients were deprived of their free medical attendance, unemployed and destitute could not afford to pay full price for their medication and treatment – and quietly died.

Under extreme pressure from Germany and France – the infamous tandem Sarkozy / Merkel called Papandreou to meeting in Nice at the beginning of November 2011, literally ordering him to withdraw the referendum – or else. Papandreou went home, canceled the referendum on 3 November and resigned. He was promptly replaced by Parliament – without a public vote – by the neoliberal Lucas Papademos, former deputy head of the ECB and – a former Goldman Sachs executive, who allowed the dance of debt and destruction to continue.

Argentina would not allow such financial terrorism on its shores – not since they dared to counter the economically suffocating peso-dollar parity in 2001, allowing the country to start breathing and growing again; a highly distributive GDP growth allowing to cut poverty from above 60% in 2001to below 10% today.

The same escape from the western kleptomania was – and still is – open to Greece and all those southern European countries in the fangs of greed capitalism. But their leaders and finance ministers are goose stepping to the financial marching orders of Washington's money masters, Wall Street, FED and IMF.

Ms. Fernandez did not mince her words. She also talked openly about western military terrorism, "You killed many innocent people in Iraq and Afghanistan under the name of war against terrorism," or as the new refrain goes – "Making war for Peace". She referred to the West in general and to Washington in particular, for whom war and conflicts, weapons sales, is a means of economic survival, as the US economy depends to more than 50% on the military / security industrial complex and related industries and services.

Shamefully, many western leaders and representatives left the assembly hall when Ms. Fernandez spoke, of fear they may be associated with her views if they listened to her calling a spade a spade. Perhaps they feared the ridiculous western sanctions, if they don't behave. It is sad to see spineless world leaders; so-called leaders (sic), who bend over backwards to please the powers that utterly exploit them, stealing their natural resources, putting their people and the environment in peril.

A terrorist is whoever does not conform to the western doctrine, whoever insists on national sovereignty – whoever defends their national interests over the voracious interference of Washington and its European puppets – and their killing bulldozer, NATO.

The UN should make it an obligation and expression of mutual respect that every country leader and representative attending the UN General Assembly must listen to all the speeches. Each country has a message to give – a message that in one way or another concerns all of us, as we are all connected as humans in a solidary union, regardless of political alliances.

The latest economic terrorism inflicted on Russia by the US supported Wall Street et al financial cabal is the down manipulation of the ruble vs the US dollar and other 'western' currencies. The ruble has lost 22% of its value since the beginning of 2014 and 15% in the last quarter alone. Call it 'sanctions' – if you will – for not bending to the political demands of Washington on Ukraine. The western MSM would like you to believe it has to do with the chaos and continuous murderous atrocities in Ukraine's Donbass area, for which – of course – Russia is made the culprit, not Kiev's gang of thugs, a Nazi government, created and funded by Obama and his western puppets.

Russia is now forced to buy dollars and Euros – what they least want and need – to stabilize her currency, the ruble. Buying dollars – playing even more into the sledgehammer of the empire – is certainly the last thing Russia wants to do. Currency manipulation is only possible due to the predatory US dollar system, where all international transactions have to be channeled through Wall Street and cleared through the privately owned BIS – Bank for International Settlements, whose owners are a similar lot of financial shenanigans as are those owning the FED. The expected outcome is a devalued ruble, shunned by investors.Little do they know that this usual western shortsightedness is but accelerating the process of Russia and China issuing a new combined currency, delinked form the dollar-euro fiat money and its SWIFT exchange system. In fact, it has already begun. The Central Bank of China has recently offered a hand to the EU, inviting the Euro as one of several currencies that will no longer need the western clearing system for transactions with China.President Fernandez puts the finger right on the wound when she refers to the entire western monetary system as vulture economics. She knows that such an economy is bound to falter and be replaced – gradually as may be – by one that is based on fairness, integrity and that respects nations' sovereignty.

October 10, 2014

ABOUT THE AUTHORS

ANDRE VLTCHEK

Philosopher, novelist, filmmaker, investigative journalist, poet, playwright, and photographer, Andre Vltchek is a revolutionary, internationalist and globetrotter. In all his work, he confronts Western imperialism and the Western regime imposed on the world.

He covered dozens of war zones and conflicts from Iraq and Peru to Sri Lanka, Bosnia, Rwanda, Syria, DR Congo and Timor-Leste.

His latest books are *Exposing Lies of the Empire*, *Fighting Against Western Imperialism* and *On Western Terrorism* with Noam Chomsky.

Point of No Return is his major work of fiction, written in English. *Nalezeny*, is his novel written in Czech. Other works include a book of political non-fiction *Western Terror: From Potosi to Baghdad* and *Indonesia: Archipelago of Fear, Exile* (with Pramoedya Ananta Toer, and Rossie Indira) and *Oceania – Neocolonialism, Nukes & Bones*.

His plays are *'Ghosts of Valparaiso'* and

'Conversations with James'.

He is a member of Advisory Committee of the BRussells Tribunal.

Investigative work of Andre Vltchek appears in countless publications worldwide.

Andre Vltchek has produced and directed several documentary films for the left-wing South American television network teleSUR. They deal with diverse topics, from Turkey/Syria to Okinawa, Kenya, Egypt and Indonesia, but all of them expose the effects of Western imperialism on the Planet. His feature documentary film *'Rwanda Gambit'* has been broadcasted by Press TV, and aims at reversing official narrative on the 1994 genocide, as well as exposing the Rwandan and Ugandan plunder of DR Congo on behalf of Western imperialism. He produced the feature length documentary film about the Indonesian massacres of 1965 in *'Terlena – Breaking of The Nation'*, as well as in his film about the brutal Somali refugee camp, Dadaab, in Kenya: *'One Flew Over Dadaab'*. His Japanese crew filmed his lengthy discussion with Noam Chomsky on the state of the world, which is presently being made into a film.

He frequently speaks at revolutionary meetings, as well as at the principal universities worldwide.

He presently lives in Asia and the Middle East.

His website is: http://andrevltchek.weebly.com/

And his Twitter is: @AndreVltchek

CHRISTOPHER BLACK

Christopher Black is an international criminal lawyer based in Toronto, Canada.

He has been a trial lawyer for 37 years, first for Canadian National Railways and Air Canada, then with TransCanada Pipelines concerning regulatory tribunal proceedings in Canada and the United States. In 1987, following years of social justice activities since his university days, including involvement in several strikes, and social justice and peace movements, he decided to dedicate his career to helping the working class in a criminal setting and became a criminal defence lawyer doing legal aid work in Toronto and other cities in Ontario. In that role he was involved in a number of high profile murder cases.

In 2000 he became lead defence counsel at the Rwanda War Crimes Tribunal where he defended General Augustin Ndindiliyimana, Chief of Staff of the Rwanda Gendarmerie and won his acquittal on all charges of genocide and crimes against humanity in 2014. During the same period he was a Vice-Chair of the International Committee For the Defence of Slobodan Milosevic and Chair of the Legal Committee.

He has written numerous essays, articles and papers on international law and other issues. He has had some of his poetry published in both Canada and Russia and has completed his first novel, Beneath The Clouds, a novel about resisting the secret police state, and is working on a book about the trial of General Ndindiliyimana.

PETER KOENIG

Peter Koenig is an economist and geopolitical analyst. He is also a former World Bank staff.

He worked extensively around the world – Latin America, Africa, East- and South Asia, as well as the Middle East and North Africa – in the fields of environment and water resources. Increasingly his focus has become water as a human right, the theft of water through privatization by transnationals and too-big-to-fail banks, and the annihilation of water resources, bio-diversity, social fabric and community health by reckless and outrageous mining – by ever increasing exploitation of unrenewable resources to satisfy the steadily growing appetite of the western war and killing machine.

He writes regularly for Global Research, ICH, TeleSur, RT, Sputnik News, and other non-mainstream media.

He is the author of *Implosion – An Economic Thriller about War, Environmental Destruction and Corporate Greed* – fiction based on facts and on 30 years of World Bank experience around the globe.

Peter lives in Europe and Latin America.

Printed in Great Britain
by Amazon